THINKING OF ANSWERS

A. C. GRAYLING is Professor of Philosophy at Birkbeck College, University of London, and a multi-talented author. He believes that philosophy should take an active, useful role in society. He has been a regular contributor to *The Times*, *Financial Times*, *Observer*, *Independent on Sunday*, *Economist*, *Literary Review*, *New Statesman* and *Prospect*, and is a frequent and popular contributor to radio and television programmes, including *Newsnight*, *Today*, *In Our Time*, *Start the Week* and *CNN News*. He is a Fellow of the World Economic Forum at Davos, and advises on many committees ranging from Drug Testing at Work to human rights groups.

The Long March to the Fourth of June (with Xu You Yu)
China: A Literary Companion (with S. Whitfield)
The Quarrel of the Age: The Life and Times of William Hazlitt
What Is Good?

The Meaning of Things
The Reason of Things
The Mystery of Things
The Heart of Things
The Form of Things

*Among the Dead Cities: Was the Allied Bombing
of Civilians in WWII a Necessity or a Crime?*
Descartes
Truth, Meaning and Realism: Essays in the Philosophy of Thought
*Towards the Light: The Story of the Struggles for Liberty
and the Rights that Made the Modern West*
Against All Gods: Six Polemics on Religion and an Essay on Kindness
*The Choice of Hercules: Duty, Pleasure and
The Good Life in the 21st Century*
Ideas That Matter
*Liberty in the Age of Terror: A Defence of Civil Liberties
and Enlightenment Values*
To Set Prometheus Free: Reason, Religion and Humanity

THINKING
of ANSWERS

Questions in the Philosophy
of Everyday Life

A. C. Grayling

für Alla

Warm wishes —
fashion is Art!

Anthony Grayling

B L O O M S B U R Y

LONDON · NEW DELHI · NEW YORK · SYDNEY

RA
Oct/8

Bloomsbury Publishing Plc
50 Bedford Square
London WC1B 3DP

www.bloomsbury.com

Bloomsbury Publishing, London, New Delhi, New York and Sydney
A CIP catalogue record for this book is available from the British Library

ISBN 978 1 4088 0953 2

10 9

Typeset by Hewer Text UK Ltd, Edinburgh
Printed and bound in Great Britain by CPI Group (UK) Ltd, Croydon CR0 4YY

www.bloomsbury.com/acgrayling

CONTENTS

Dimissis nunc praeceptoribus nostris incipimus
per nos moveri et a confessis transimus ad dubia.

– Seneca, *Naturales Quaestiones* II.21

For Madeleine and all questioners

Introduction

We bark our shins against the stones of life with sufficient frequency, whoever we are and wherever we live – even in peaceful and prosperous parts of the world – to find ourselves obliged to seek answers to the philosophical questions that such bruising prompts. We might not call them philosophical questions, or think of ourselves as engaged in anything so profound (to some, so pretentious) as philosophical reflection; but the truth is, that is exactly what such questions as these are: 'What matters? What is the right way to live? What do I owe to myself, to others and to society? What kinds of lives are good and meaningful?' Moreover, these are only the most obvious and frequently asked among philosophical questions, for reflective people are also likely to wonder about such further matters as the nature of the universe, whether mind is separate from body, the nature and extent of human rights, the best political organisation for society, and much more.

The pages that follow address some of these questions, not to answer them so much as to provide material – suggestions, considerations, arguments – that might be useful in seeking answers. There are indeed books that offer definitive answers to questions like these; dogmatic books, books of persuasion or exhortation selling one or another party line on the great questions. This book is not one such. Its premise is different: it starts from the fact that philosophy is, among other things, the enterprise *par excellence* of thinking things through, and engaging in the conversation of mankind about these great

1

questions – and about the myriad lesser questions that are part of the fabric of life too. Ultimately philosophy is about thinking for oneself, and making choices, and seeking to live according to them, with the aim of achieving something good. It is opposed to one-size-fits-all nostrums, to authorities ancient or modern who claim to have all the answers and who instruct everyone else not to think, but just to believe and obey.

It is also, indeed, about the realisation that not all questions have definitive answers; some have no answers, and others have a variety of answers dependent on other things.

But it is also about the realisation that sometimes, when there are no answers, exploring the questions can by itself bring a great gain in understanding and insight.

In some of these discussions I state my own view, sometimes emphatically. That invites response, comment, agreement or disagreement; the important thing is that it is an invitation to a conversation, not the dogmatic termination of one. Some of the questions will not look at all philosophical, but instead practical, historical, literary or something else; but there was a reason why they were asked of someone who is expected to reflect on the philosophical dimensions of possible answers, and they show that everything has such dimensions, however unobvious that might seem at first.

Almost everything that follows in these pages has its ancestor in essays I wrote in response to questions. In two cases this was explicitly so: in a column in *Prospect* magazine called 'Grayling's Question' (a title chosen by the magazine's editor) I responded to philosophical conundrums sent in by readers, and in a column in *The Times* I commented on questions prevalent in the atmosphere of public concern each week. In other places, such as the *New Scientist*, the *Dubliner* magazine, the *Guardian* comment section, and elsewhere, the questions to which I responded were implicit: but there too the task was to think of what might contribute to answering them, or at least to understanding better what was being asked.

Hence my title, *Thinking of Answers*. The questions and the answers have a range and diversity that are reflective of the multiple and miscellaneous character of the interests, problems, dilemmas and concerns that arise when people think and talk; it has been an education in itself to be invited to respond to them in this way. I am grateful to the editors of the various journals and newspapers where the ancestors of these essays first appeared, for the opportunities from which this volume arises.

As the word 'ancestors' in that last sentence suggests, I have revised and extended almost all of the essays, but I have also kept most of them fairly short because the purpose in hand – offering suggestions and ideas about answers, not dictating what the answers should be – invites brevity. Given that these essays are intended as a stimulus for thought, and not as the final word on what to think, it is worth repeating this point for emphasis: offering stimuli for thinking is the opposite of offering extensive treatises in search of definitiveness. This is a starting point; the rest of the endeavour is for the reader.

Happiness and the Good

Does being happy make us good?
And does being good make us happy?

Bertrand Russell was emphatically of the opinion that being happy makes us good, and equally emphatic that certain ideas about what is good make people unhappy. It is tempting to agree with both points, even if they need qualification; for assuredly, being happy is far more likely to make us good than if we are unhappy, and puritanism of all forms has certainly made plenty of people unhappy.

But there are, of course, no guarantees in either direction. The feckless ruffian might be happy but not good, the rigidly orthodox practitioner of a narrow and self-denying morality might suffer in order to obey its strictures, yet take pleasure in thus suffering; human nature is various and not infrequently weird.

On the face of it the questions here might seem to be empirical rather than philosophical. One can imagine a votary of the new school of 'experimental philosophy' – consisting of philosophers who hand out questionnaires to find out what people think about morality, knowledge, the self, truth, rationality, free will and other great staples of philosophical enquiry – seeing this as an opportunity to exercise ingenuity. Critics of this approach point out that work of this kind is better done by empirical social science, and anyway only results in descriptions of what people think – not always a secure guide to what people *should* think.

But in fact there is a deep philosophical point behind the idea of a relationship between goodness and happiness. More carefully phrased, the two questions concern the quality of lives perceived by those living them as being flourishing and satisfying, with valuable relationships at their core, and directed at the attainment of aims worth pursuing. Suppose one had a conception of such a life, and could make a sound case for its value: it would be hard to disentangle the fact of its being a well-doing and positive life (in which, therefore, the person living it is a 'good' person) from that person's sense of 'eudaimonia' – Aristotle's idea of flourishing and satisfaction, now usually and rather feebly translated as 'happiness'. On this view of the matter, happiness and goodness turn out to be the reverse and obverse of the same coin, making their relationship a peculiarly intimate and mutually reinforcing one.

But given the thoughts mentioned above – that there might be some happy but bad folk and some good (by some lights) but unhappy folk – the connection cannot be a necessary one. They only become reciprocal in the optimal way suggested when the notions of goodness and happiness at stake are appropriately defined. And that is an obvious enough point: Cyril Joad would have produced his standard *Brains Trust* remark – 'It depends what you mean by . . .' – on being asked either question, for one can only get so far with generalisations. In this case that means one cannot give a fully satisfactory answer until a clear and detailed account has been given of what each of the vague feel-good words 'good' and 'happy' means: which is a large part of the task of ethics as a whole. The following discussions between them seek to contribute towards a clarification of both, sometimes by direct and sometimes by indirect means. With such large, amorphous and important concepts, the task of exploring them has to involve a variety of approaches, one of which – to quote Wittgenstein – is to 'assemble reminders' of things we otherwise know.

Morality and Empathy

Does the basis of morality lie in the brain's 'mirror neurons', and if so, does that refute moral relativism?

It is a familiar fact that the technological applications of science can create serious ethical dilemmas. This applies at both ends of the moral scale of our efforts to destroy one another and to save one another. We have sophisticated weapons that kill people without damaging buildings; we have sophisticated medical technology which is so expensive that its use has to be rationed, forcing us to choose who shall live.

These are just two of many examples. They are not the work of science itself, but of political and social decisions about the use we make of science. When science – usually, social science – addresses itself directly to morality, it does not do so to solve moral problems, but to investigate the nature and sources of moral sentiments and attitudes. This is an empirical proceeding, aimed at discovering and describing facts, not a 'normative' proceeding, aimed at telling us what we should think and do.

But empirical enquiry can have a major impact on normative considerations. Current research in neurology appears to be doing just this in connection with one of the most vexing problems in moral philosophy: the problem of relativism. In fact, what neurology reveals about brain function might already have refuted relativism and established the ground for saying that the basis of morality is shared by all humans. If so, this is a truly major result.

Moral relativism is the view that there are no universal truths about what is right and wrong, but rather that what counts as such in each different society is determined by that society's own traditions, beliefs and experience. Since these can differ markedly among societies, it follows that different societies can have quite opposite views about what is right. And, says the relativist, there is no objective ground for deciding between them.

This view seems compelling when we consider such contrasts as different societies' views about, say, polygamy and homosexuality. The motive for relativism is the worthy one of avoiding the arrogance of cultural imperialism as practised by dominant societies in the past, as they colonised other peoples and imposed moralities upon them. Relativists wished to assert the equal dignity and validity of different societies and their moral outlooks, even when they clash with one's own.

One of the aspects of neurological research that challenges moral relativism concerns the function of 'mirror neurons' in the brain. Located in the motor cortex, these neurons activate in sympathy with what their possessor perceives in the activity and experience of others. When others act in any way, including smiling, yawning, weeping and grimacing, the neurons associated with these actions in one's own motor cortex fire in response. Their activation provides a model within oneself of what others are experiencing, giving a form of direct insight into their states of mind.

And this therefore strongly suggests that the ability to understand others, read their intentions, interpret their emotional states, predict their behaviour, and respond appropriately – the very basis of social capacity itself, and thus of morality – is linked to the involuntary modelling of others that mirror-neuron activity makes possible.

Some researchers hypothesise that malfunction in the activity of these neurons might be a significant factor in autism, one of whose major symptoms is the inability to engage socially with others. There are also strong links between mirror neurons and language capacity, the chief human social tool. The essential point is that mirror neurons underwrite the ability to recognise what pleases or distresses others, what they suffer and enjoy, what they need, what is in their interests, what helps and what harms them; and this means that the ultimate basis for moral judgement is hard-wired – and therefore universal. So even when customs differ, fundamental morality does not; and if it does, one of the differing moralities must just be plain wrong.

These thoughts are controversial because in pulling the rug from under relativism's feet it appears to reintroduce a form of moral imperialism: for whichever culture of morality can be claimed to be the closest to the neurological basis of fellow feeling and empathy will have an entitlement to be regarded as the 'right' one. It also exacerbates the problem of how to explain the appearance, at least, of moral disagreement within a culture, let alone moral differences between cultures.

This last is an interesting as well as important matter, because if differences over questions of morality are indeed only apparent, and actually rest on underlying but unobvious agreement, that fact would be a significant help in resolving some of the tensions in the world. For an example of how an apparently great difference can in fact only be a difference of how a moral imperative is manifested, compare these two societies: in one, people eat their aged parents, while in the other they buy them a bungalow at the seaside. Both behaviours are equally rooted in a desire to express respect and duty towards the parents in question, in the first kind of society by giving the ageing parents continued existence in their offspring's bodies, and thus a kind of immortality as generation after generation incorporates (literally) the previous generation in themselves. (The example I use is of the South Fore people of Papua New Guinea, whose practice of 'transumption' – the mortuary practice of consuming the dead – was identified as the primary vector for kuru, a brain disease.) It is an act of filial respect and kindness, just as, in a developed Western society, is the practice of buying a pleasant retirement home for one's ageing kin.

Could all differences of moral practice and attitude be explained in this way? An ingenious empirical study might show that at least many can. The basic requirement would be to further show that what we know about mirror neurons and other relevant features of brain function have an explanatory connection with those behaviours.

This will not satisfy critics of the reductionism they see in this, because the rich and complex variety of social and moral phenomena seems far too great for a brain-only attempt to explain them. Such critics pose a challenge to those who think, or hope, that – to encapsulate the matter in a slogan – neurology will one day make sociology redundant. The debate is a lively example of how advances in neuroscience open prospects and raise problems of a new and significant kind.

Friendship

Is friendship, as Aristotle says, the highest form of human relationship?

However desirable it is to have neat definitions of important ideas, the fact is that most of them are too internally complex to be caught in a formula. 'Friendship' is one such. There are many kinds of friendship, achieved by many different routes, and the most they have in common is that – somewhere in the ideal version of them – loyalty, sympathy and affection standardly figure.

Aristotle indeed says that friendship is the summit of human relationship, but not everyone agrees. Literature and the movies conspire to give this place to romantic love, while another convention yields the distinction to parent–child relationships, and especially to the tender and devoted passion of mothers for their babies. But each of these is successful only if it matures into friendship at last, which is why Aristotle – and he is not alone among sages, some of quite different traditions – extols friendship as the best, the most central, the most necessary link in the social web. Given that humans are essentially social beings, friendship thus turns out to be a defining component of life worth living.

It is an interesting coincidence, and perhaps more, that both Aristotle and his Chinese contemporary Mencius described a friend as 'another self'. If one cares fully about another person, they argued, his well-being and flourishing matter as much to oneself as one's own: so a pair of true friends are 'one mind in two bodies'.

Most will justifiably think that this overstates the case, except in those rare iconic instances glorified in literature – David and Jonathan, Nisus and Euryalus – which are anyway examples (in the latter case expressly so) of love more romantic than companionate. But it reflects the way that friendship embodies not just camaraderie and enjoyment, but a mutual tie which at its best, and during its best period, is supportive, forgiving and durable. Among other things this means that a friend is one who knows when to help you by telling the truth, and when to help you by lying. As Oscar Wilde put it, 'a friend is one who stabs you in the front'.

Nothing can count as friendship which lacks time and a few real tests behind it. Too many acquaintanceships are dignified by the name without having earned it. But friendships do not fail to count as such because they end; sometimes people who were friends in the fullest and richest sense cease to be so after a time, for any number of reasons, usually bad ones. This was the case with Samuel Taylor Coleridge and William Wordsworth, whose dozen years of intimacy changed English poetry, and who fell out at last because of misunderstandings and hurt feelings rather than any tectonic shift in their philosophies.

While their friendship lasted they understood one another's genius, and felt the highest mutual respect for each other as well as real affection. Even when Coleridge's gifts were obviously running into the sands of opium and alcohol, Wordsworth and his family continued to house him and encourage him, and Wordsworth himself continued to hope for Coleridge's help in the grand project they had together envisioned, which was the writing of a monumental philosophical poem.

But Coleridge was an unselfdisciplined monologist addict who left a few brilliant poems and poetic fragments behind him, along with a blather of sometimes suggestive but mainly inane lucubrations, while Wordsworth was an increasingly prickly and self-important lone male in a household of admiring women (with consequences that Coleridge had foreseen and warned against), so between them a falling-out was inevitable. Later a thin and faltering acquaintanceship rose from the ashes of their friendship, but not its intimacy and collaboration.

Equally productive during the time it lasted was the brilliant friendship (for this it was, even more than a love-affair) between

Voltaire and the remarkable Émilie, Marquise du Châtelet, one of the most unfairly neglected (because a woman, and an aristocrat at that) contributors to the growth of modern science. Émilie translated Newton's *Principia* into French with a commentary in which she made original contributions, for example deriving from it the principle of the conservation of energy. She did other important theoretical work in physics besides, notably on the nature of light and the energy of moving bodies, anticipating the discovery of infrared light and showing that the energy of a moving body is proportional not to its velocity, as Newton and others had thought, but to the square of its velocity.

The relationship between this highly gifted woman and the equally highly if differently gifted Voltaire was full of fun and storms, the balance between the two shifting from a preponderance of the former to the latter as time passed. It was an erotic comradeship, especially in its first years, and it was political, not least in the sense that Émilie protected Voltaire as best she could from the injudiciousness of some of his writings. But above all it was intellectual, and they encouraged each other, directly and by example, to some of their best work.

There is much to relish in the escapades that enlivened their relationship – not least the occasions on which Voltaire had to flee arrest in the middle of the night, and on which Émilie had to pay debts by fiddling the lottery and dreaming up tax-farming schemes. There is always much to enjoy in stories of sharp wits and high achievement, especially in uncertain times of the kind these two free spirits inhabited: their friendship makes an enlivening tale.

Some might say that these two examples of friendship cannot be regarded as standard because the parties to them were such extraordinary people. But my guess is that when any two people like each other, enjoy each other's company, come to rely on and need each other's companionship, feel comfortable in each other's presence, laugh together, share experiences and thereby come to share memories, these things – the core of what binds them – are the same whoever they are. And these things constitute friendship.

The Moral and the Ethical

Is the use of 'moral' and 'ethical' in the same phrase merely a rhetorical flourish or is there a real difference between them?

In the mouths of politicians and pundits the phrase 'moral and ethical' is a pleonasm – a redundancy – and a particularly sloppy one, because if asked whether they use both words in the same phrase because they recognise a difference in meaning, and wish to denote either the union or the intersection (but then they should specify) of those meanings, such folk might be hard pressed to explain the difference. And indeed, they almost certainly think the words are synonyms, even if they know that they are etymologically of Latin and Greek derivation respectively – itself increasingly unlikely in these increasingly unclassical days.

And yet there are arguably several significant differences between the term 'ethics' on the one hand, and 'morals' or 'morality' on the other hand, and the adjectives formed from them. Depending on context, 'ethics' is either the organised philosophical study of the concepts and principles involved in systems of morality, or it is the set of principles, attitudes, aims and standards adopted by individuals or organisations by which they live and act.

In the first sense, 'ethics' is a second-order enquiry into the first-order principles and practices constituting a normative moral outlook ('normative' meaning 'guiding' or 'prescribing'). In the second sense, 'ethics' is itself normative, but it is much broader in scope than 'morality', because it concerns practices and aims that are not distinctively moral ones. For example, a corporate ethics might include prudential guidance about good practice in customer relations and product quality. Such guidance can typically be framed as a 'hypothetical imperative': 'If you wish to maximise profits, ensure that . . .'

Morality, by contrast with these sorts of considerations, is 'categorical' as opposed to hypothetical; it is about intrinsic questions of right and wrong, the good and the bad, obligation and duty, consequences and intentions, as these apply in our conduct and relationships, where the right and the good are under consideration in themselves and not merely as instrumental to some non-moral goal such as profit, corporate image, or the like.

But ethics includes morality; it is broader in scope than morality, but morality is an integral part of it. Ethics is about ethos, about what sort of person one is, or what sort of organisation one belongs to. Morals is about right or good action and intention. Obviously, the latter flows from, or partly determines, or both, the former, and is inseparable from it.

The following example illustrates the difference precisely: considered as a matter of what sort of person one is, and what sort of life one leads, it is an ethical but not a moral matter what colour you paint your front door. If the colour really upsets the neighbours, it is a moral matter.

Politicians and pundits, accordingly, need ever only say 'ethical', unless they particularly and more restrictively mean 'moral'.

The Entitlement to Moralise

Can you express ethical concern about a given matter only if you yourself are perfect in your behaviour in relation to that matter?

When well-known figures take a stand on global warming or the effect of fast foods on childhood obesity, they thereby issue a standing invitation to the press to challenge them on their personal credentials to speak out. There have been two egregious examples of this in recent times. After winning an Oscar for his film on global warming, *An Inconvenient Truth*, Al Gore was met with newspaper headlines claiming that his home in Nashville, Tennessee, uses twenty times more energy than the average American household.

Likewise Prince Charles's critical reference to Big Mac hamburgers, made while visiting a health centre in the Arabian Gulf, prompted newspapers to reveal that his own Duchy Originals Cornish Pasties contain more fat, salt and calories than a Big Mac.

The implication is that because Al Gore and Prince Charles do not do as they tell everyone else to do, at best they undermine their own message, and at worst they deserve the name of hypocrite.

The Prince's Cornish Pasties indeed have marginally more fat and salt than Big Macs, though neither is especially bad on a one-off basis. Al Gore, however, gets his energy from renewable sources through his local Tennessee electricity company, so even though his life of public commitment doubtless leads him to burn far more energy in the use of communications and computing equipment than does the average household, he can legitimately claim to be green nevertheless.

The tension here is that both Gore and the Prince are obviously well-meaning, and their campaigns for environmentally sensitive alternatives to consumerist depredations on the planet are important and timely. If they failed to be as greener-than-thou in their practice as in their message, does that fact impugn their message? To think so is to commit the *ad hominem* fallacy, in which the truth of what someone says is taken to be undermined by the fact that he does not act accordingly. But clearly, although saying one thing and doing another makes a person inconsistent or, when the aim is to cheat in some respect, dishonest, it does not falsify what he says if what he says is true.

There is a point of philosophical importance here for the endeavour of trying to live an ethically good life. It is that there is such a thing as 'doing one's moral best', which may and usually does fall short of what counsels of perfection require, but nevertheless constitutes a serious gesture in the right direction. Take the example of a person who is vegetarian on the grounds that he thinks it morally undesirable to kill and eat other sentient creatures, but who owns leather shoes and belts. This latter is certainly inconsistent with vegetarianism, but the person might reason that being an habitual meat-eater makes a vastly greater slaughter footprint (to coin a phrase) than owning a pair of leather shoes, and moreover the effort involved in being completely strict in his practice demands a degree of time and effort – given that he has other calls on both – not justified by the effect he thus achieves. So he takes a stand short of the logical limit of his commitment, and trusts that it will make some degree of difference towards the good nevertheless.

Clearly enough, the idea of 'doing one's moral best', where this is understood to be less than the true best that might be possible in the case, is wide open to abuse and readily serves as a fig-leaf for hypocrisy. Quite possibly it does this more often than it succeeds in being a sincere effort to balance practicalities with a desire to be oriented in the right ethical direction. Yet this kind of sincerity really is possible, and it is what is at work in the thought that if everyone did at least something (about recycling, say, or in offsetting carbon emissions caused by their air travel), the cumulative effect would be worthwhile. And obviously it is better that people do something towards the good rather than nothing.

The 'something' is of course sure to be far less than individuals could do if they really devoted all-out effort to the right thing – for example, to making their homes and lifestyles maximally green. So there would remain large room for improvement across the board. But that is acceptable, because the point is that for most people the all-out effort is unsustainable, so the pragmatic alternative is for them to seek a reasonable balance between their concern and what they can do about it without interfering too far with other legitimate, and doubtless personally significant, commitments and avocations.

The alternative is to say that unless a person achieves the utmost, let him do nothing; which is the same as letting him be careless and indifferent. Obviously we do not want this;

obviously we would rather he made some degree of effort, as much as he could without turning what he does into a penance or a serious interruption to other concerns. In thinking this way we are admitting that 'doing one's moral best' is a legitimate and worthy compromise.

And in admitting this, we thereby admit that Al Gore and Prince Charles can be applauded for standing up for the right causes, even if we find out that they are not much different from the rest of us in the progress they have made towards living conformably with them. That does not mean we cannot expect them thereafter to smarten up their performance in the relevant respects, given that taking a stand is naturally allied to giving a lead. But if we are going to point the finger at them for not doing as they say we should do, does that not imply that we accept they are right, and that this obliges us to act appropriately ourselves? The editors of the first newspapers that published facts about Al Gore's energy consumption and Prince Charles's pasties should themselves be audited on their energy footprints and their dietary habits, so that the rest of us can measure the height of the moral ground on which they stand in the case.

What the idea of 'doing one's moral best' comes down to, when it is sincere and genuine, is something close to Aristotle's idea that, in effect, one lives an ethically good life by trying to do so. The trying is itself the succeeding; otherwise the only good people would be perfect people, and all those striving to do their moral best would not be good people. The notion that it is the trying that is the succeeding is not paradoxical, but realistic – realism and truth to life are two of the great virtues of Aristotle's ethics. He talks of forming 'habits' of virtue, where 'virtues' are character traits that achieve a middle course between opposing vices; thus courage is the middle way between cowardice and rashness, and generosity is the middle way between meanness and profligacy. By always trying to recognise the middle course between opposite failings, said Aristotle, using their practical intelligence and experience in the process, people form the desired moral habits; and it is these that together make a person, and his life, good.

The Greeks had an interestingly different view of moral failure from the later and more widespread Christian view. According to the latter, to do wrong is to sin, and a sin is a stain on one's immortal soul, requiring redemption, cleansing, expiation, forgiveness. (Literally 'sin' means disobedience to divine command.) The Greeks, by contrast, gave to moral failing a name that literally means 'a bad shot', as when one fires at a target and misses. The remedy is to try again, and do better next time. This robust and healthy view is forward-looking, constructive and positive. Ideas of sin and the damnation it invites if unexpurgated have a very different cast, and give a very different colour to the idea of moral endeavour.

Much of the traditional idea of sin persists in our contemporary attitudes to moral failure. In accordance with it we somehow export the idea of a stain, an enduring flaw of character, to the case of people who do not live up to ideals, especially those they themselves proclaim. This is where a hostile media can inflict a body-blow not just on the likes of Al Gore and Prince Charles themselves, but on what they are trying to do, because in a sin culture even the suspicion of hypocrisy in the messenger is enough to harm the message. The tacit idea is that if the source of the claim is polluted, the claim itself must be questionable. In the Greek view the value of what is said and the character and actions of the person who says it are separable things, and can be independently evaluated on their merits.

None of this is intended for a moment to excuse or minimise hypocrisy or deliberate inconsistency. The very idea of someone 'doing his moral best' rules out the availability of anyone claiming to do his moral best as a mere excuse; here people can legitimately be caught out. The important contrast is with people trying to do as much of the right thing as is feasible for them without claiming or even aspiring to be paragons. Consider a city dweller recycling household rubbish, using public transport as much as possible, subscribing to Greenpeace, and the like; once again, the point is surely that even if it is true that greater such commitment would be better, and indeed needed, this degree of it is nevertheless desirable on its own terms.

One question that increasingly presses, and seems hard to counter even on these grounds, concerns cheap air flights. While the world waits for less polluting aviation fuels, the best solution is reliable carbon offsetting (non-scam versions), and less travel. There are many reasons why less travel is undesirable – the world is not exactly in need of fewer opportunities for people to get to know others, and other places and ways – but limiting travel has to be a serious option, and is one of the chief ways that 'doing one's moral best' really bites.

Throughout history earnest moralisers have stood in the way of the good by accepting nothing less than the utmost. Human beings are a mixed alloy, familiarly enough; the very same person is capable of being good and terribly bad at different times or in different respects, and that inescapable fact makes the greatest moral philosophers – these being novelists and dramatists – almost at one in insisting that we should resist the mistake of thinking that anyone is wholly one or the other, even at their best or worst moments respectively.

I would rather have an energy-wasting Al Gore fighting to save the planet than an energy-wasting Al Gore not caring about the planet. People like Gore and Prince Charles have a platform, and the worst thing they could do is fail to use the platform in support of worthwhile causes, whether or not they are personally no better than the rest of us in doing their individual bit.

Ethics and Darwin

Can ethics be derived from evolution by natural selection?

Given that human beings have evolved by natural selection (with genetic drift and some other factors perhaps assisting), and are ethical creatures, it follows *ab esse ad posse* – whatever is, is possible – that ethics can be derived from evolution by natural selection.

That, though, might not be to answer the purport of the question, which asks: would natural selection be sufficient to produce creatures with a consciousness of ethical principles and a tendency to wish to observe them and see them observed?

The idea might be that whereas other social animals have evolved behaviours that subserve the interests of their sociality – dominance orderings, co-operation in hunting and in keeping a look-out for predators – this does not amount to ethics, the idea of which at least premises an awareness of the demands and responsibilities ethics involves, and the possibility of their non-observance, not least deliberately. Among other animals the evolved social behaviours are largely invariant and automatic; a putative 'ethics' that is choicelessly a result of hard-wiring could not be ethics.

Immediately one says this, one has begged what is possibly the hardest question known to metaphysics and moral philosophy: the obdurate and seemingly impossible question of free will. Almost every indication from the kind of evidence adduced in sociobiology, evolutionary psychology and neurophilosophy supports the deterministic side of the argument, entailing that our sense of being choice-makers, deliberators, option-possessors, who could have done otherwise in most of our actions, is an illusion. On the evidence flooding in from neuroscience, we are as other social animals, only worse off in that we operate under an enormous error theory about our own nature, falsely thinking that we have free will and that we are therefore genuinely ethical creatures. It was from this error, if error it is, that Spinoza sought to free us by arguing in Books IV and V of his *Ethics*, respectively 'Of Human Bondage' and 'Of Human Freedom', that once we recognise that we live by necessity, we cease to repine, and thus are liberated from the unhappiness caused by futile struggle against inevitability.

But does not this mean that the idea of ethics as we normally understand it is an illusion, as the 'error theory' says? For the very idea of ethics has traditionally premised freedom of the will. There is no logic in praising or blaming individuals for what they do unless they could have done otherwise, any more than one would praise a pebble for rolling downhill upon being dislodged by rain. So the question becomes, by these selective pressures:

could natural selection, resulting in the adaptations otherwise distinctive of human descent, have produced free will?

To answer that requires a clearer conception of 'free will'. Its chief identifier is the 'genuinely could have done otherwise' requirement: but not only does that itself require unpacking, but we also need to look for the functional Magnetic Resonance Imaging (fMRI) traces that suggest which structures in the brain import novelty into the world's causal chains, making their possessor a true agent, and not merely a patient – a sufferer – of the universe's history. So the question evolves yet again: could finding such a thing – an fMRI trace of agency, of causal novelty – even be a possibility?

There is an alternative tack: which is to retain the idea of ethics but to deny that it necessarily requires free will. All the evidence showing that we favour kin over strangers, that we are prepared to save the lives of five people by sacrificing the life of one person if this one person is far enough away, but not if we actually have to push him off a bridge or shoot him (these are findings from work in 'experimental philosophy', which is amateur social science done by philosophers who have forgotten that describing how things are does not reliably tell us how they should be), strongly suggests that our 'ethical intuitions' have evolved just as our upright posture and opposable thumbs have evolved, and are therefore the same as the evolved behaviours and reactions of other social animals. If we call these behaviours and reactions 'ethics', then all social animals have ethics. On this view it only *seems* odd to say that ants and chaffinches are ethical creatures. After all, we can train some social animals to suppress certain instincts and emphasise certain others – that is what the domestication of dogs and cats amounts to – so we might think that debate about ethical matters, adjurations to behave one way rather than another, promotion of self-discipline, punishment of ethical failure, and the like, are just our more complicated human way of trying to train each other and ourselves.

If this last thought rings true, then ethics evolves by natural selection in a perfectly straightforward way. If it seems to miss something – the notions of freedom and responsibility that give the idea of ethics its real bite and significance – then we are invited to think that ethics evolves by natural selection via a more complex route, namely, one that necessarily involves free will and reflection.

But either way, ethics evolves by natural selection.

Human Rights and Politics

Are human rights political?

Aristotle ended his lectures on ethics by turning attention to the state and its laws – thus preparing the way for the following lectures that we now know as his book *The Politics* – on the ground that questions about the good for individuals are inseparable from the constitution and laws of the community to which they belong; ethics and politics, he said, are seamlessly connected.

There are other ways of making the point, but Aristotle's embedding of ethics within politics is attractive for a number of reasons, one of which is that it illuminates the practical implications for any society that takes ideas of human rights seriously. Talk of human rights is talk of what is required for individuals to have a chance of making lives for themselves that by their own and any reasonable standards are good and flourishing. This is centrally an ethical enterprise, where ethics is understood as a more inclusive matter than morals. Ethics is about the character and quality of one's life as a whole, and how one lives it; in short, it is about what sort of person one is – from which the nature of one's specifically moral agency generally follows.

But to recognise, protect and enhance the rights intended to have the effect of giving individuals the chance to make good and flourishing lives, a state has to erect a fabric of laws and institutions fitted to the task. The project of devising those laws and institutions requires the familiar political processes of debate, negotiation, consent, and through them the building of the fabric in question. So, human rights are political: they are an important part of what the state exists for, and an important focus of activity and concern within it.

Independently of the explicit regimes of human rights that in recent times have been adopted internationally and nationally, states have always existed to protect the interests, often enough regarded as rights, of at least some section of their citizenries. That protection was aimed at both external and internal threats to those interests, and took the form of laws, sanctions and institutions. All this is through and through political, so its extension to the idea that all individuals have interests likewise meriting protection by law and institutions – interests in life, security, privacy, the getting and imparting of information, and so on for the other familiar matters variously constituted as rights in all codes – is in the same way political.

Human rights are also political in the sense that they are the subject of occurrent politics, involving arguments over the form and strength of the instruments embodying them. Governments enact human-rights provisions in good times, and find them inconvenient in bad times when they are most acutely needed by everyone else: that is the current experience in the Western world, enacting liberty-restricting measures in the hope of promoting security against terrorism and crime, thereby proving beyond doubt the politicality of human rights and civil liberties.

Poverty

Is Peter Singer right to argue that we can halve world poverty by treating strangers with the same moral regard as those close to us?

You naturally value your own life more than the life of a stranger in another country. Could you say how many times more valuable you think your own life is? Peter Singer tells the story of one Zell Kravinsky who, not content with giving away most of the fortune he made in real estate, not content even with devoting all his time to charitable work, felt he should donate one of his kidneys too. Moreover he did so to a hospital serving low-income African-Americans. Kidney donation carries a 1 in 4,000 chance of complications; Kravinsky's argument was that if you withhold a kidney from someone otherwise sure to die, you value your life as 4,000 times more important than his; which, he says, is 'obscene'.

Is it? Singer does not directly answer this question in the affirmative, but he uses this and other somewhat less saintly stories to drive home the point that very few people do enough to help reduce world poverty and the ills that accompany it. His book, *The Life You Can Save* (2009), and the accompanying website have a thoroughly practical purpose: to persuade people that it is wrong not to give charitably – wrong, note: we all know that it is good to give, but his point is that it is positively wrong not to – and to show by a snowstorm of facts and figures how much we should give if we are to take this obligation seriously.

Singer begins with the familiar point that if any of us saw a child drowning, we would plunge in to save him, not minding such incidentals as, for example, whether we were wearing new clothes. Now consider the fact that a thousand children die every hour because of poverty – and that the principle behind saving a drowning child one can see with one's own eyes, and saving an unknown child on the other side of the world is the same.

Singer sets out this point systematically thus: suffering caused by deprivation is bad; if it is in one's power to prevent bad things happening, without sacrificing anything important to oneself, one should do so; charitable giving can help prevent bad things; therefore it is wrong not to give charitably.

This argument is both valid and sound. It is logically compelling. It is the key to Singer's case, which is unanswerable: we do wrong not to give some of our income to reduce world poverty. The questions are: why do people not give, or not give enough? And, how much should one give?

The answers to the first question are familiar. People might wonder how much of what they give will go on administrative costs instead of helping the poor. They are only moved by suffering they can directly see. They are concerned about those near them, not people far away. They feel that what little they can do makes too little difference in the face of a gigantic problem. They feel that everyone else, or governments, should be shouldering the burden too, and if not, then why should they do it alone?

A little reflection shows that these are mainly rationalisations in favour of doing nothing or little. The truth is that most people in the richer countries of the world – all those who have at least the standard of living of the Portuguese – can easily afford to give 5 per cent of their gross income (and if significantly richer, then more: billionaires can give as much as 30 per cent without even noticing the difference), and that doing so would at least halve world poverty within the next half-dozen years. Singer's aim is to make us see the logically unanswerable moral case not only for doing our share in this, but more – because there will be some who will not do their share.

'Logically unanswerable': it really is so. The irritation some people feel when confronted with the fact that they give too little too infrequently is proof that they realise it. Some of the tales of selflessness that Singer tells, and his concluding remarks about the warm glow one gets from giving, are not likely to soothe the annoyance of those who think, 'I worked for this money, I turned my own time, my own life, into this money, so I am jolly well going to spend it on myself.' But Singer points out that we can spend on ourselves because we live in places where making money is possible; millions work exceedingly hard, harder than we do, to scrape a pittance for themselves and their families, and sometimes fail, because of how things are in their parts of the world, with drought and unforgiving soil, with civil wars, disease, lack of education and health-care, short life expectancy, high infant mortality, absence of clean water, social and religious inhibitions, corruption, and more. Once one realises this, self-regarding justifications fall flat.

One cannot expect everyone to become a saint, but as Singer argues, we can all certainly give more. He is right; it is that simple.

Is Beauty Subjective?

If beauty existed only in the eye of the beholder,
would that make it an unimportant quality?

Some of the principal Enlightenment thinkers who regarded beauty as subjective – that is, as what the preferences and tastes of individuals project onto the world – took this very fact to be a reason for applauding the human mind, on the ground that it is praiseworthy and admirable that the human mind should impute beauty to things. Hume held such a view, and it was central to Francis Hutcheson's aesthetic theory. They thus made taste a key concept in aesthetics, and incidentally found themselves agreeing with St Thomas Aquinas, another subjectivist, who identified beauty as a form of pleasure.

A quarrel of saints lies in the offing here: St Augustine had long before argued that beauty is the cause of pleasure, not identical with it; he and Aquinas therefore mark out between them the traditional space of the quarrel between objectivists and subjectivists, the former holding that beauty is a property of (some) things in the world, a property existing independently of our human choices and tastes.

Augustine had august antecedents for his objectivist stance.

There had been a degree of consensus among the ancients that beauty consists in harmony, which the Pythagoreans attributed to underlying mathematical relations, as found – for a chief example – in the Golden Section, observed in a line segment apportioned into two unequal lengths such that the ratio of the shorter to the longer length is equal to the ratio of the longer to the whole. A near-contemporary of Hume and Hutcheson, the great Leibniz, took the same view, with the added tweak that he thought most observers are unconscious of the proportions that underlie beauty. Recent psychoneurological studies of the effect of baroque music on the human mind seem to bear out his view.

But suppose that these objectivists are wrong. First, one has to note a prejudice in the view that what exists independently of thought or emotional response somehow has greater existential importance than what is 'only' or 'merely' in the mind. Pain and suffering are 'only' in the mind too, yet they are highly significant (and very real), both to those experiencing them and to others whose sympathies are invited by the fact of them.

If judgements of beauty are in effect projections from subjective states of pleasure and admiration, why should that be less important (to whom? or in what scale of things?) than if intrinsic and independent features of an object existed and coerced all observers into an identical aesthetic response? For surely Hume and others are right to say that the human capacity for finding things beautiful does honour to humanity, not least in cases when someone finds (say) someone else beautiful whom no objectivist about beauty could ever agree is so.

The irenic suggestion of Kant to the effect that the experience of beauty consists in disinterested non-conceptual pleasure that one is convinced everyone else would share if similarly placed, was meant to bridge the fruitless division between earlier views. But he might as well have said that some things are indeed objectively beautiful, perhaps because of their harmony and proportion, while other judgements of beauty are indeed subjective, because they have other (and sometimes themselves beautiful) motivations. Such is the view I favour. But either way, beauty is never an unimportant quality.

Proving a Negative

Is it impossible to prove a negative, or just difficult?

The claim that negatives cannot be proved is beloved of theists who resist the assaults of sceptics by asserting that the non-existence of God cannot be proved. By this they hope to persuade themselves and others that at least the possibility remains open that a supernatural agency exists; and this is enough for them; from there they make the inflationary move from alleged mere possibility to not eating meat on Fridays or covering their womenfolk in black from head to toe.

They are however wrong both about not being able to prove a negative, and about not being able to prove that supernatural agencies exist and are active in the universe. Seeing why requires a brief refresher on the nature of proof.

Proof in a formal deductive system consists in deriving a conclusion from premises by rules. Formal derivations are literally explications, in the sense that all the information that constitutes the conclusion is already in the premises, so a derivation is in fact merely a rearrangement. 'All men are mortal, Socrates is a man, therefore Socrates is mortal' is a valid and sound deduction, and there is no information in the conclusion that was not already in the premises; the conclusion is a rearrangement of the premises' informational content. Thus there is no logical novelty in the conclusion, though there might be and often is psychological novelty, in the sense that the conclusion can seem unobvious or even surprising because the information constituting it was so dispersed among the premises. This is shown by the story of the Duke and the Priest; while giving a house party the Duke went downstairs to fetch more wine, leaving the Priest to entertain the guests. The Priest did so by saying that the first person to whom he ever gave confession was a murderer of an especially horrible kind. His fellow guests shuddered accordingly. On returning, the Duke clapped the Priest on the shoulder affectionately and said, 'We've known one another for ages; I was the first ever person whose confession he heard.' The guests all promptly left; for here was psychological novelty aplenty.

Demonstrative proof, as just explained, is watertight and conclusive. It is a mechanical matter; computers do it best. Change the rules or axioms of a formal system, and you change the results. Such proof is only to be found in mathematics and logic.

Proof in all other spheres of reasoning consists in adducing evidence of the kind and in the quantity that makes it irrational, absurd, irresponsible or even lunatic to reject the conclusion thus being supported. This is proof in the scientific and common-sense meaning. The definitive illustration of what this means, especially for the use that theists would like to make of the myth that you cannot prove a negative, is Carl Sagan's dragon-in-the-garage story, which is surely too well known to require rehearsing, and if not then it should be; read it at: http://www.users.qwest.net/~jcosta3/article_dragon.html.

No self-respecting theist would go so far as to claim that 'you cannot prove the non-existence of a god' entails 'a god exists'. As mentioned, their aim is merely to leave open the possibility that such a being might exist. But Sagan's dragon dashes even this hope. For one can show that it is absurd, irrational, intellectually irresponsible or even lunatic to believe that fairies, goblins, the Norse gods, the Hindu gods, the gods of early Judaism (yes, there were several), and so endlessly on, 'might exist'. It would compound the felony a million-fold to grant this and yet insist that one's own (Christian or Muslim, say) deity 'nevertheless' exists or might exist.

For a simple case of proving a negative, by the way, consider how you prove the absence of pennies in a piggy-bank. You break it open and look inside: it is empty. On what grounds would you assert nevertheless that there might possibly still be pennies in there, only you cannot see or hear or feel or spend them?

Body and Soul

Why would anyone wish to believe that he or she is a combination of a body and a disembodied mind or soul?

One should never underestimate human ingenuity in search of support for implausible views. The idea that human beings (not, usually, dogs or newts) consist of a body and a mind or soul is older than history; but the reasons for the belief are not empirical ones. Dualists – those who hold the view that we are composites of two different substances, one physical and one mental or spiritual – remain in the majority in today's world, if only because almost all religions involve belief in an afterlife.

There are even a few philosophers who are dualists too, protecting the reputation of their profession to provide representatives of every opinion, mad or sane, invented by mankind.

A genealogy (in Nietzsche's sense) of dualism would bring together such thoughts as these: that the phenomena of consciousness seem so amazing that one simply cannot believe they must end with bodily death; one cannot believe that the people one loved or feared have vanished with death – they seem asleep when they die, and must be in a dreamland somewhere, but still watching us; one hopes, wishes or needs to believe that one will re-encounter the dead whom one loved; ignorance, timidity and the superstitions they jointly prompt give rise to confused legends and beliefs about continued existence in other forms; religions promote belief in an afterlife variously to keep control of people with the prospect of posthumous reward and punishment, simultaneously solving the problem of religion's inefficacies in this life (petitioning the gods so rarely works; the bad seem to flourish; promising that all will come right in an afterlife pre-empts disaffection); and so variously on.

Somewhat more reflective motives for accepting dualism turn on considerations about the essentially different nature of material and mental phenomena. Typical physical objects have spatial locations, weights, heights, colours and odours, whereas thoughts and memories, hopes and desires do not. A more modest form of dualism recognises that there are two kinds of things one can say about brains – that they are inside skulls and weigh such-and-such, and that they are involved in the production of thoughts and desires. But this *property dualism* is not the *metaphysical dualism* of, for example, René Descartes, for whom mind and matter are two essentially different substances; and this latter is what is needed for afterlife beliefs and their ilk.

What has rightly been called 'the hard problem' of consciousness – namely, how it arises from brain activity – has yet to be solved, but the shortest answer anyone can give to a dualist who hopes that this means that brain science leaves wriggle room for minds or souls is this: hit someone hard enough on the head, and a mental function regularly correlated with the resultantly damaged part of the brain will be lost or compromised. This covariance is enough to render profoundly unpersuasive any of the reasons, wishful and otherwise, offered in support of dualism.

Knowledge of Harm

*Is it possible for one to suffer a misfortune or a
harm of which one is completely unaware?*

There are many different kinds of misfortunes and harms, some physical, some psychological, some incident upon career, possessions, relationships or other like things. Depending on type, some kinds of harm can only exist if they are felt, whereas other kinds might occur without the victim ever knowing it. The clearest examples of the first category include being subjected to physical or psychological pain, while clear examples of the second include being the unwitting target of mistakes in medical or security records, and malicious gossip.

The first category is simply dealt with. It is not possible to be in pain without feeling pain; think of the absurdity of saying to someone, 'You only think you have a headache, but in fact you don't.' Likewise it is only true that someone has been harmed by someone else deliberately attempting to embarrass him if he actually feels embarrassed. If he does not respond by feeling embarrassed, he is not harmed by the effort to embarrass him.

More interesting is the kind of case in which mistakes on, say, a person's security file result in his never being invited to interview for a job, or selected for promotion, or included in an advantageous arrangement of some kind, unbeknownst to him both at the time and ever thereafter. This probably happened all the time in Iron Curtain countries, where files were kept on most people and contained all sorts of unreliable bits of gossip. It doubtless also happens in our putatively squeaky-clean and responsible democracies.

A mistaken entry on a medical record might constitute a harm – and certainly a misfortune – without the victim's knowledge, or indeed anyone's knowledge, in the particular sense that it is the inaccurate record that is or does the harm, even though a consequent harm in the form of a mistaken diagnosis based on that record, or an adverse drug reaction, is recognised as such by the victim.

It might be thought that – to adapt Wittgenstein – whereof one is ignorant, thereby one is unharmed. This last example shows that is not so. This is because of the already-mentioned variety of respects in which one can suffer loss and misfortune, which apply not only to the focal cases of one's felt experience, but in one's estate and situation, the latter including what a suitably placed observer would recognise as positive possibilities for one's life, but which are prevented from actualisation by something that the same observer would recognise as constituting a harm in the circumstances.

To substantiate this claim one can point to the desirability of allowing citizens access to files kept on them by employers or the authorities. Why? Precisely because misinformation of any kind can do harm without the victim knowing it. If harm could only occur if it is known to occur, secret files would be, by definition, harmless.

Justice as Inspiration

If both sides in a conflict can passionately believe that theirs is a just cause, does this mean that the idea of justice is empty? If so, how can it have been such an inspiration for so many reform movements?

It is difficult to resist the temptation to quote the remark, attributed to Thucydides, that history is philosophy teaching by example; so I never do. In the case of opponents in a conflict each claiming justice for his side, the lesson of history is twofold. One possibility is that one of them is wrong, or that both are. The other possibility is that both are right. The latter case is typical of the hardest moral dilemmas, and is precisely what makes them dilemmas. History further shows that cases in which both disputants have some claim to be right are not all that rare. And the debate about justice from Plato to Rawls gains some of its poignancy from this fact.

The key point in the question is the motivating power of demands for justice. It underlies movements for liberty, rights and entitlements, political participation, equitable treatment, a fair share, proper remuneration – these notions overlap, and in one familiar way show that the concept of justice is at least intimately connected with that of equity or fairness. From infancy most people insist on fairness, as if the sense of it were instinctive; and its absence is a ready source of resentment. It is easy to understand why injustices are a spur to demands for remedy: injustice is felt as injury.

Correlatively, justice is both felt and recognised as conclusive when it is done. A compromise between disputants which gives both as much as or more than they claimed, will definitively end their dispute. That is an interesting fact; the closure, settlement, finality of justice when it is recognised as having been done suggests that whereas arriving at justice is a matter for rationality, accepting that it has been done is a matter in significant part for emotion. Part of the reason why justice is a concept with content, and deeply motivating content, surely lies here.

History also teaches that most economic and political arrangements are unjust, because the processes that led to them involved inequalities of power. That is one reason why conflicts about justice are endemic. Liberal democracies institutionalise the means for managing such conflicts, and sometimes even try to reduce their causes. But since inequalities also arise from differences in talent, intelligence, hard work and luck, and since these are not always accepted as justifications for inequity, the negotiations for justice are as endemic as the conflicts themselves.

It is little comfort to victims of injustice to hear from Friedrich von Schiller that history is the supreme court of justice. Nor is his dictum wholly true; the myriad petty injustices that are the pixels of the human condition have no chance against time's indifference. But it is true enough for big things: historians will pick them over, and judge, and few will escape posthumous whipping who deserve it. That is a motivation to labour for justice even against the steepest odds, so long as one is sure of one's ground: that an injustice exists, and that one's proposed remedy will right it.

Apology and History

In what sense, if any, does the past entitle us to one or more of apologies, reparations, restitution and recognition in the present?

It is easy to suppose that history gives us our entitlements just as it tells us who we are. The land our forefathers occupied, the apologies due to us now for the harm done to them then, the works of art they made that are now in other people's museums – all the sentiments involved here, and many more like them, are bequeathments of history, and the source of lingering resentments that can easily flare into conflict, of claims and counter-claims, of romantic yearnings and loyalties.

Consider: today's Serbs did not want to relinquish Kosovo because of the Battle of Kosovo near Pristina in 1389, where defeat by the Ottomans became a tribal memory that in the nineteenth century fuelled nationalistic longing for independence. Likewise the Jews and Israel, the Greeks and the Elgin Marbles, Islamists and the Caliphate, today's African-Americans and the history of transatlantic slavery, Scottish separatists, the Flems and Walloons of Belgium, are all examples, different in scope and scale, of the past's influence – some might say, stranglehold – on the present.

Does the past sanction the claims we make in the present: for land, art works, reparations, independence? The answer is a paradigm of philosophy: it is Yes and No, for it genuinely depends on cases, and there is no general rule. This is mainly because some past-based claims, such as those about 'national identity', are a load of nonsense, and others, such as claims by post-Second World War German Jewish survivors to the property expropriated from them by the Nazis, are manifestly just.

Consider the question of apologies and reparations to the descendants of Africans taken into New World slavery between the sixteenth and eighteenth centuries, some twelve million of them by most estimates. This was a horrible crime. Direct descendants claim a special relation to this history, which some regard as entitling them to reparations now – say, from the cities of Bristol and Liverpool, which profited from the trade in human flesh and suffering. A hidden premise is that direct descendants have more claim to be appalled by the history of slavery than others. That is very questionable; but if one grants that it is true, it then becomes relevant to point out that every single one of us is descended from slaves – slavery was ubiquitous in human history, and demographic arithmetic relates all of us to them. It also relates all of us – and, with us, the descendants of the transatlantic slave trade – to slave-owners sometime in the past too: a not-so-comfortable meditation for today's claimants.

These thoughts, like the one that points out how mongrel nations are, and how almost all national borders are drawn in the blood of past conflicts, should make us pause in claiming that history is on our side when it would be advantageous to think so, for it just as often teaches us – if we are prepared to listen – to think very differently.

Social Evils

Are there greater social evils in today's society than in the past?

In 1908 the philanthropist Joseph Rowntree said that the greatest threats to society's moral fabric were poverty, drunkenness, the opium trade, 'impurity' (meaning prostitution and sexual licence), gambling, war and slavery. He set up the Joseph Rowntree Foundation (JRF) to 'search out the underlying causes of weakness or evil in the community' as a contribution to addressing those problems.

In 2008, a century on, the JRF posed the question again, conducting an extensive consultation to identify what members of the general public thought were their own day's greatest social evils. Decline of the family, the involvement in crime of youths either as perpetrators or victims, crime and violence generally, drug and alcohol abuse, poverty and inequality, and immigration, were salient among the responses.

The Foundation's report on the consultation distilled these concerns under four heads: decline of community, individualism, consumerism and greed, and an overall decline in shared values. If one reflects on this list for a moment one sees that the four headings really all say the same thing: the rise of individualism and its concomitant solo pursuit of advantage is *ipso facto* the fragmentation of community and its values.

Reflection on Joseph Rowntree's original list of evils suggests a division into those that were characteristically Victorian obsessions (drink, drugs, sex) and the serious evils of poverty, war and slavery. It is interesting to note that today's list not only overlaps with it in the specifics of drugs and poverty, but in its general tenor, reflecting unease about the personal morality – or lack of it – relating to excess and licence generally.

I am one of those whom the JRF invited to comment on the findings of its consultation. It struck me as important to contextualise them immediately by saying that every age sees itself as beset by 'decline', whereas by almost all measurable standards the opposite is now true: life in today's wealthier countries is vastly better for vastly more people than in Joseph Rowntree's day.

London then teemed with child prostitutes, the indigent died in its streets, and its streets were too dangerous to walk at night. What poverty meant then and what it means now are very different things. Then it was the hopeless who abused drink and drugs, as their only means of escape. Now the minorities who do so are not without resource.

This is not to deny that there are serious problems of poverty, crime and community fragmentation in contemporary society, for indeed there are. But it is to say that in any large pluralistic society such problems are endemic, and need to be placed in perspective so that social problems are not inflated into social panic. This is the real debate any society needs to conduct with itself, and it has to start not just from surveys of contemporary attitudes and from statistics, important as both are, but also from an exploration of the conceptual scheme in the light of which attitudes and facts are interpreted.

For example: the reality of life for the majority of people in Victorian England was harsh, and the way drink and sex (the two great preoccupations of middle-class Victorian moralisers) entered into it was a far cry from the prim self-denial that the epithet 'Victorian' standardly suggests. In fact 'Victorian' as a term denoting an historical reality should mean drunkenness, widespread prostitution, bastardy, violence and brutality, crime, disease, squalid slums, ignorance and illiteracy – all of these things a consequence of the deeply unfair and divided society that almost exclusively served the interests of its wealthy upper strata. Such alleviations as existed for these appalling conditions were the work of individual philanthropists and reformers, whose limited resources and patchwork application of them could make only a limited dent in the problem. It was not until the labour movement gained political traction in the following century that change began to occur in the disposition of society, towards one that now, as described above, is vastly better for the vast majority than it was then.

Historical breadth of vision puts today's problems, though very real, into better perspective. It might even suggest some ways of dealing with them – for a start, by helping to adjust one's assumptions. If Victorian moralisers had stopped their misguided fretting over drink and sex, and had seen that the real immorality was poverty, ignorance, squalor and hopelessness, the adjective 'Victorian' might have deserved its actually undeserved high tone after all.

Fear of Illness and Death

What is the difference between
valetudinarianism and hypochondria?

There is an important difference between valetudinarianism and hypochondria, and a significant difference between the latter and hypochondriasis. Before explaining these differences, it is as well to explain why all three have such long names. The reason is that in the past, before the practice of medicine became genuinely effective – a very recent event – physicians coined polysyllabic terms from the ancient tongues not only to mask ignorance and impotence, of both of which they had plenty, but to make more effective the only tool in their kitbag: authority. To offer patients comfort and confidence, the physicians gave the appearance of knowing what was going on by stroking their beards learnedly and uttering enormous and incomprehensible words. The placebo effect of this was not inconsiderable; it still works to this day, though the patchily effective project of involving patients in their own medical care ('empowering' patients) undermines it.

Some dictionaries treat 'valetudinarian' and 'hypochondriac' as synonyms. This is wrong. The former is a person who takes good, indeed excessive, care to protect his health. He sits with a rug over his knees at the first sign of a breeze; he refuses rich foods, consumes quantities of health supplements, and becomes querulous at suggestions that he do anything that interrupts his careful and protective habits of life.

A good example of a valetudinarian is Mr Woodhouse in Jane Austen's *Emma*. He is not only concerned to safeguard his own health, but that of others; he does not like them to suffer the stress of change (such as getting married) or, when they do, to expose themselves to the hazard of eating rich food (such as wedding cake). He is quite a nice old valetudinarian; most of his kind are not nice – they are whining, passive-aggressive, obdurate, silly and tiresome.

Hypochondriacs are afraid of illness, are frequently convinced they are dying, and make a frightful nuisance of themselves at their GPs' surgeries. They look up their symptoms in medical dictionaries or on the Internet, and find that they have several simultaneous conditions, all independently fatal. This they report to their GPs, who are obliged (by the Hippocratic oath and fear of litigation) to take them seriously. Tests follow, invariably showing all to be normal, reassuring the hypochondriac until the next niggle or twinge sets him off again.

A good example of a hypochondriac is 'J', the narrator of Jerome K. Jerome's *Three Men in a Boat*. Feeling a little peaky, he goes to the Reading Room of the British Library to consult a medical dictionary, and by its end finds that he has all the diseases in it except Housemaid's Knee, which by then he is quite indignant that he lacks. He visits his doctor to tell him the bad news, whereupon the doctor advises him to adopt a routine of eating a quantity of steak and walking five miles every day.

Hypochondriasis is the advanced form of hypochondria in which anxiety actually produces the symptoms of disease without any underlying physical reason for them, such as paralysis, swellings, breathlessness, palpitations and the like. It is a 'somatoform' disorder, a mental illness that causes bodily distress despite the person not having an underlying physical pathology to produce it.

Most think that hypochondria is prompted by fear of death. I think it is prompted by fear of failure. It is a concomitant of ambition, and it is generally a youthful complaint. As people grow older, they graduate to being valetudinarians instead. This, if whining and nuisance are avoided, is preferable for all concerned.

Still, though hypochondria and hypochondriasis might be regarded as 'only psychological', even dubbed by the French *les malades imaginaires*, there is nothing imaginary about the suffering involved. The anxiety is real, as are the palpitations, sweats, hyperventilation, dizziness, and other products of panic attacks that the anxiety can provoke. When hypochondriasis results in pain and swelling, breathlessness and weakness, even paralysis and unconsciousness, there is nothing imaginary about the dangers that can impend. The lesson is obvious enough: that the 'only' in 'only psychological' is misplaced.

Celebrity

Is it possible to say who among contemporary celebrities will be remembered decades or generations after their own time?

Death confers dignity and importance on well-known people, at least for a time. A year or two later their reputations begin to dip, and stay that way for decades. Then time repeats what death did, if there is a reason for it: it reconfers dignity and importance. Some of the deceased are rediscovered, and a more realistic assessment of their legacies can be given.

The reason for the dip is twofold. First, those who were sceptical about a deceased celebrity's merits keep quiet during the first months. His family mourns, so do his fans, almost everyone feels that death, in general, deserves a respectful reticence, in which mention of the good and silence about the bad aspects of the departed's life and character are appropriate. It is regarded as bad taste to launch too early the kind of attack that the deceased often enough suffered in his lifetime.

But when a sufficient interval has passed, the sceptics can begin to take aim. 'Facts' start 'coming out', which change the deceased's image. Family and acquaintances speak more freely. The hallowing effect of recent death wears off, and a more complicated and less glowing picture emerges.

Secondly, the recent past always seems tawdry and passé in comparison to the more distant past, and this applies to the people who were celebrities in it. Look at images of people and fashions in the 1980s, and compare them to images from the 1950s; the latter seem far more interesting because more remote and magical. The 1980s just seem old hat. While the past moves through its old-hat to its magical stage, the personalities in it have to suffer the same fate.

These are the reasons why it is difficult to assess a famous person's legacy until sufficient time has passed. Most fame is of its moment; most of the stars, the politicians, the cynosures of fashion and public interest whom the paparazzi once pursued, sink into oblivion under history's weight. Those whose memory survives either were truly outstanding in their generation, or did something that had real effects on what came after them.

This has always been so. In the world of classical Greece and Rome, and in ancient China, immortality was a matter of reputation. The greater your contribution, the more people you would be remembered by, and for longer. To have a noble posthumous reputation, marked by a statue or immortalisation in an ode, was the highest ambition of the ambitious.

Matters are no different now. There are not many people one can confidently say will be remembered and applauded in twenty years' time, other than by a coterie of devotees. We forget this fact when a celebrity dies; and then we forget the celebrity himself.

Health and Appearance

Are changing fashions in health and appearance arbitrary, or do they represent a better understanding of what is good for us?

There is an oblique way into this topic, through what you might call the modern form of sun-worship. By this is not meant a successor to the ancient Egyptian worship of Ra, the sun, a god as real and potent to the Nile dwellers as the mighty river itself, and as essential to life; but rather, the widespread phenomenon of sunbathing.

Just as archaeologists are fascinated by the contents of ancient mankind's rubbish bins, as more revealing than jewellery and weapons, so students of human nature are fascinated by the fashions that grip whole populations. After the First World War the suntan, formerly a mark of low caste, became a mark of health and vigour, and its becoming so was given its imprimatur by an iconic individual: Coco Chanel.

A suntan was once the badge of the labourer, exposed to the elements through base toil. No lady would be without her parasol even on a cloudy day, to protect the whiteness of her skin against the sun's excoriating rays. But in the 1920s the young and dashing discovered that the French Riviera, popular with northern Europeans in the winter months, was empty and cheap in the summer.

Coincidentally one of the health fads of the day was 'heliotherapy' for acne and other skin conditions. Scott Fitzgerald and the Roaring Twenties generation flocked to the beaches; elegant resorts that had once been popular as summer retreats among Switzerland's lakes and mountains were emptied of the young. When Coco Chanel returned to Paris at one summer's end, glowingly and spectacularly bronzed, the seal was set on the new fashion. In their lemming-like way, the entire white population of the earth thereafter tore off its clothes and spread itself in the sun as soon as it appeared, devoting hours to the cultivation of the kind of skin damage that gives the desired wholemeal appearance.

Well: we know the result. Australia has the highest rate of the most dangerous form of skin cancer, melanoma, and the wizened, leathered, dried skin of older people who were among the more assiduous sun-worshippers in their youth tells its own tale. So now the manufacturers of spray-on tans are doing well; they have an advantage over the sun in that they can service legs and arms even in winter. The brown hunger remains, an indirect obeisance to desire for the sun's realm and its works. And not all have stopped worshipping, even yet.

The penchant for skins browned by the sun – though not by inheritance: racism survives too – is of a piece with other shifts from white to brown as the colour of health and desirability. In the nineteenth century white bread, white flour, white sugar, 'refined' foodstuffs from which the peasant fare of the husk or whole grain had been milled away, was extolled as pure, classy, good. Now brown bread, brown rice and brown sugar demonstrate the extent to which brown has become the colour of health: even food has caught a tan.

Are these mere fashions? Sunbathing certainly is; and its harmful effects are now established and common knowledge. The consumption of brown – brown because whole – grains is not a fashion. If anything, the refined white grains that became widely available in the nineteenth century were a fashion, and as harmful a one in their own way as sunbathing. For all of history beforehand people ate the whole grain, and their return to doing so is simply a return of common sense.

Abstinence and Fasting

What is the difference between abstinence and fasting?

Food, eating, not eating, feasting, fasting, abstaining: the focus on food in almost all religions is a mark of the life-and-death importance of eating. It is certain that one of the main wellsprings of religious belief and practice in history and prehistory was the desperate attempt to influence the forces of nature – rain, the growth of crops, the danger of locusts or flood, drought or fire, disease in the herds – so that there might be food to eat.

The focus on food and eating remains in residual ways in the rich and overfed West. Who now knows about, for example, Egg

Saturday? It is a day in the Christian season of Shrovetide, the preamble to Lent. Shrovetide is named after 'shriving', which is the absolution that follows confession, and traditionally it is a season of feasting and jollification, the tail-end of the long Bacchanalia that traditionally started at Christmas. In many places the celebrations still culminate in Mardi Gras, Fat Tuesday, there and elsewhere often called Pancake Day. The immediately following day is the first day of the sharply contrasting period of Lenten austerity and abstinence which leads to Easter.

The religious meaning of these events is still remembered, but their true meaning has long been lost. This is that winter was once the season of plenty and ease, with the previous autumn's harvest in store, meats preserved, and little to do outdoors. This is when people sat round the hearth, mending clothes and telling stories. Spring and early summer were the leanest times, when stores were depleted and some of the hardest work of the agricultural year awaited.

So what is now Lent was the beginning of hungry times, when winter fat and unfitness were combated. Making a tradition out of necessity, the Church adapted this experience to its calendar, just as it borrowed the ancient pagan festival of lights and feasting that cheered winter's darkest days, and called it Christmas.

Lenten abstinence is, strictly speaking, not fasting but avoidance of meat, all other foods being permitted. Fasting, technically, means eating just one meal a day, though the Roman Catholic Church permits 'collations' morning and evening as well as dinner, denoting a meal of no more than eight ounces of any foodstuff. Before Henry VIII's time abstinence also applied to sex: he was the appropriate monarch to abolish that aspect of Lent, in England at least.

There is another reason for abstinence, or at least continence, in all traditions: the health benefits, and the moral lesson of experiencing what the poor feel all year round. An old saying has it that 'the poor man must walk to get meat for his stomach, but the rich man must walk to get stomach for his meat', and this captures not only the world's injustice, but the truism that a main cause of ill health is excess. Since abstinence is easier than moderation, a season of abstinence is as good for the body as the soul.

These last two reasons – health, and the salutary lesson of what life feels like to the billion or so of our fellows who live on a dollar a day – are compelling ones for practising abstinence. But the best kind of abstinence is abstaining from meddling in other people's lives by trying to impose one's moral views on them: that would be the best of all things to give up for Lent.

Recent research in biology suggests that calorie restriction promotes longevity. Underfed mice can live up to half as long again as their normal span; obesity in humans is known to be a life-shortener. It is not an especially comforting thought that if one wishes to live beyond the normal life allotment one has to do so on short commons, but the practice is probably less onerous than it sounds, given how soon one would become used to it and even therefore prefer it. The question really is: how much does quantity of life add to its quality? If the quality of lived experience is what should really interest us, we might look askance at efforts to increase quantity of life at the expense of other goods. If one could have quantity and quality of life together, that is obviously good; when there is conflict between them, quality would seem the right alternative.

Adornment

*Do moralists have a case when they criticise
and sometimes condemn adornment?*

Moralists in all periods of history have directed fire at the human practice of adorning faces, bodies, dress, homes and lives with whatever makes them seem better, more beautiful, colourful or cheerful. What troubles the moralists is the great difference there can be between appearance and reality, and the fact that adornment is so often about changing or masking reality.

Truth, say the moralists, is its own adornment and needs nothing further to beautify it, any more than a child's skin needs rouge, or the lily needs gilding. Falsehood, on the other hand, needs decoration to cloak it, just as a bad odour has to be hidden under a spray of perfume. The moralists are therefore in favour of what they call simplicity: the unadorned, unvarnished, naked originality of things.

Adornment can be disguise, but obviously it is not always so. Having flowers around one's home is adornment, but not concealment. I once knew a woman who would spend the last portion of every overdraft on filling her flat with flowers. Her instinct was right even if her action was unwise: she adorned her surroundings not to hide anything, but to make a spirited gesture of defiance, and to lift her spirits.

We think of adornment mainly in connection with personal appearance: cosmetics, hair, dress, jewellery and accessories. This has never been the province of women alone. Here the moralists have a field day, and easy targets: they can easily apostrophise the rouged crone, the enamelling of hidden corruption. They even dislike the innocuous fact that most faces look better when carefully made up, and most bodies likewise if well clothed, all meaning, in the moralists' view, that what one sees is not a real but an artificial – therefore a deceptive – thing.

And of course adornment, if skilfully employed, improves; that is what it is for. The question is whether the moralists are right to imply that such improvement in personal appearance is invariably dishonest. The answer, surely, is No. On the contrary, it can be argued that improving things – our educations, our gardens, our incomes, lives, marriages; and therefore why not our looks, and thereby our confidence? – is a good thing, even indeed a duty.

There is another point. It is a plain fact that first impressions count, that we say much about ourselves by how we present ourselves to the world, that most people judge things by how they appear, and that good looks succeed. In the face of this, and whether or not we deplore these facts, it would be irrational not to make the best of ourselves; and that is going to involve adornment, if only in the form of what we wear.

On this view, the conclusion is secure enough: adornment is justified, and the moralists are, as so often, wrong. It is a bonus that adornment can makes things more attractive than they might otherwise be.

Note that this leaves the child, the lily and the truth where they quite properly belong: in the realm of things not only in no need of adornment, but which lose by adornment. It is a typical manoeuvre of the censorious to say 'the lily and the truth need no adornment, therefore neither should you', but obviously enough such reasoning is fallacious. Hamlet was right to say that no matter how thickly his mother Gertrude painted her face, she would end as Yorick had done, a bare skull; but even that fact is not to the point, unless you believed – which was the assumption behind Hamlet's view – that painting your face stains your soul. We are beyond such thoughts now, and take the view that painting your face (if well done) can cheer your soul, secularly understood.

Drugs and Laws

Which is more harmful, drug use or the criminalisation of drug use?

There are two little-known but important facts about drugs. One is that almost all human beings use them – aspirin, alcohol and nicotine included – and have always done so throughout history. The second is that drugs became illegal less than a century ago, initially for soldiers in the First World War who used them to combat the horrors of the trenches, and then as part of the 'prohibition' lunacy that saw, in the triumph of Temperance moralism, the banning not just of drugs but of alcohol in the United States.

As Prohibition proved, outlawing things is a godsend to criminals, who are energetic entrepreneurs and who will provide what people want at great profit to themselves and great cost to society – think gang warfare, murders, police time, marginalised users. And since the dawn of history people have wanted to ingest substances that alter their states of consciousness for pleasure, relief, recreation, spiritual experience and wonders. Religion got a boost from the visions induced by ergot poisoning or accidentally fermented foodstuffs; lots of substances cause intoxication (the word means 'poisoning'), which gives the experience of flying, seeing gods, travelling to distant worlds: think of Aldous Huxley and peyote.

Much milder, though also mind- and mood-changers, are chewed coca leaves, betel nuts, tea, coffee and chocolate. If moralisers were logicians these would be outlawed too. At the very least alcohol – as dangerous if not more so than some of the other commonly used drugs – would be banned.

Or more sensibly, every other drug would be unbanned, but controlled as alcohol is: at a stroke liberating the police, the public purse and the populace, who would not become any more drug-crazed than they were before 1914.

The teenaged son of an acquaintance of mine decided, with a friend, to try heroin. They managed to buy some, but knowing nothing about it they did not realise that they had secured an especially pure form, and they did not know how much to take. They both died as a result of their one experiment with it. If heroin were sold in pharmacies, it would be of a uniform strength and the instructions on the box would indicate the amount to be taken. If it were legal to buy heroin at a pharmacist's shop it would be less alluring to youths seeking to cock a snook at parents, school and society. There would still be a significant minority who would use and abuse it – they are there today, only they are at present criminals and their practice is underground, making everything about it worse – just as there are those who abuse alcohol. One will never get rid of those who have to rely on chemicals to get their kicks: a pretty despicable resource, when one looks at the world itself, and the prospect of knowing something about it, which is a richness of possibility beyond the dreams of anyone so feeble that he must inject oblivion into his veins instead. But to criminalise him and his doings is to make everything about drugs and the problems they cause worse.

Laughter

Is laughter the best medicine?

There are two things everyone knows about laughter: that only humans do it, and that it is medicinal, even if it is not quite the best medicine for everything – it does not, for example, cure influenza unaided. When other animals draw back their lips to show their teeth it means they are about to attack. Hyenas and the Pacific laughing gull naturally produce ha-ha noises, the latter in an especially hilarious way; but it is humans alone for whom bared teeth and convulsive gasps express pleasure.

Of course there can be a dark side to laughter. There is an ocean of difference between laughing-at and laughing-with. There can be cruel and mocking laughter, humiliating, contemptuous and nasty laughter. A laugh can cut more sharply than a whip, destroy confidence, wound and disable. Just think of the harm done to a laughed-at child.

And you would expect one of philosophy's gloomiest exponents, Friedrich Nietzsche, to have a wet sponge to throw at the subject: only humans laugh, he said, because only they suffer enough to need laughter as an antidote. He might, alas, be right.

But generally to think of laughter is to think of jollity and delight. It is a cathartic activity; it emotionally cleanses, and keeps us from going insane in face of the world's absurdities. Laughter cuts through most tangles, it punctures pomposity, and often constitutes a more effective counter to one's opponents than all the massed tropes of logic. The comedian-pianist Victor Borge once said that laughter is the shortest distance between two people; when people are laughing together they are not fighting each other, for it is hard to dislike anyone with whom one shares a joke. It is even said that no woman can love a man who does not make her laugh.

A sense of humour is a mark of intelligence. There is a big difference between telling jokes and being witty, the latter constituting the true expression of intelligence, though seeing the point of a joke requires grey matter too. One can even be witty about jokes: 'An Englishman, Irishman and Scotsman go into a bar. The barman says, "Is this a joke?" '

Freud wrote screeds about jokes, concluding that they have just two purposes: either to express unconscious hostility, or sexual feelings. Here, one feels, is a man who probably laughed little.

For laughter is about far more than jokes. People can laugh for no other reason than that they are happy. They can laugh at past sorrows and unlucky turns; they can laugh with delight at unexpectedly meeting a friend. That all these things prompt laughter is a happy fact about human beings, and a hopeful one, given how much cause they otherwise have to weep. The witticisms prompted by tough times and bleak circumstances are a testament to the realism and courage human beings often display. They are also a testament to the absurdity of the world, and the amazing folly its human occupants equally often display. As we say when presented with the caprices, lunacies and incredibilities of the human condition, you have to laugh.

Praise

Are praises a greater reward than prizes?

Twice every year, with much international fanfare, there are announcements of prizes for outstanding achievement. Spring is the season of reward and recognition in the entertainment industry, chief among them the Oscars. Some of the winners will not only get prizes but will merit praise – note the difference – for although everything said as the awards are given consists of praise, a longer view would doubtless be more selective.

Autumn every year is the season for a weightier set of prizes: the Nobel Prizes. Noting the seasons in this connection is not just a reflection of the contrast between the ebullience expected of spring and the sobriety expected of autumn; there is a genuine difference of kind. The Nobel Prize, unlike an Oscar, is almost always a statement of praise genuinely merited because long proved. Oscars are hit-and-miss in this respect.

In both the Oscar and Nobel cases there are financial rewards, but what matters far more in both is the appreciation shown. In this lies the clue to why praise, especially when merited, means so much to its recipients.

Praise is an expression of recognition and a conferment of status. No matter how well paid someone is, if his efforts are never acknowledged the cash will not be quite enough to compensate. By the same token, someone who feels recognised and appreciated will cheerfully put up with other inconveniences, including a less-than-desirable income.

The most valuable kind of praise has no flattery in it, but amounts to recognition that its recipient knows, with equal modesty and satisfaction, to be appropriate. Nietzsche remarked that we are more troubled by undeserved praise than by undeserved blame, which is a mark of the importance we attach to others' opinions of us. Generally, if we find ourselves having to do our own praising, this is also a mark – and soon enough a guarantee – of other people's quite different opinion of us.

There should be no praise for anyone's doing what he ought to do. Praise belongs to what the philosophers call 'supererogation' – that is, going above and beyond the proper expectations that others and society have of us. In today's world we make the mistake of praising people for the most ordinary things, as if getting out of bed merited a mini-Oscar. We do well to remember that it is praiseworthy to praise only if praise is genuinely due.

It is reported of Augustus Hare, the finicky Victorian author who wrote superior travel guides to European cities, that he insisted on reading the morning service to his house servants and guests every day, but that what he read out always sounded odd. One of his guests one day peered into Hare's prayer book and found that considerable portions of the text had been inked out. Asked why, Hare replied, 'I've crossed out all the passages in glorification of God. God is certainly a gentleman, and no gentleman cares to be praised to his face. It is tactless, impertinent and vulgar. I think all that fulsome adulation must be highly offensive to him.' In this Hare seems to be mistaken, for it is hard to see why else, if there were a deity, it would create human beings, other than to offer it endless worship, dependency, fear and adulation: for what possible use could they be to an omnipotent being otherwise?

There is precious little evidence from any of the great religions that if there are any deities they are gentlemen, or that they are averse to praise. But Hare's point applies well enough to the famous and celebrated among mortals, few of whom enjoy slavish and hyperbolic praise once they have got over the first taste of it. One reason why the famous tend to consort mainly with the famous is so that they can have reasonably normal exchanges with them, ordinary conversation rather than breathless one-sided expressions of admiration. A corrective to excessive admiration might be to visualise the object of praise seated on the lavatory: reminders of shared humanity always have a sobering effect.

One thing few people realise when they watch the annual awards ceremony of the Academy of Motion Picture Arts and Sciences in Hollywood is how heavy the Oscar statuette is. It weighs 8½ pounds. It is made of gold-plated metal, and would inflict a painful dent on any toe it was dropped upon, if an emotionally overwhelmed actress lost her grip.

In fact few people know anything about the Oscar statuette itself, other than that it is the best-known award trophy in the world. It is a 13½-inch-tall representation of a naked knight whose arms rest on the hilt of a crusader's sword, and who stands on a five-spoked film reel. The number of spokes stands for the main departments of film craft: acting, directing, producing, writing, and technical matters.

The first Oscar was awarded in 1929 to a now-forgotten actor called Emil Jannings for his part in the now-forgotten films *The Last Command* and *The Way of All Flesh*. The fact that hardly anyone can remember which actors and films were awarded Oscars, even from a few years ago, is significant. Most films are temporary presences in public consciousness, and not all films that stick in the memory have won Oscars. Richard Burton and Peter O'Toole never won an Oscar despite each being nominated seven times; that is a more memorable fact than that most Oscar awards in recent years have gone to films, and the actors in them, that cost huge sums of money to make – such as *Titanic*, whose $250 million outlay earned it eleven out of the possible total of seventeen Oscars (and more to the point, a worldwide box-office gross of $1.8 billion – the most ever made by a film).

It might be said that the Oscars are more important to film-industry insiders than to the general public, and for good reason: they are the experts' form of applause, surely more gratifying to their colleagues than the less-informed plaudits of the public. Of course the fact that a film won one or more Oscars is useful for publicity purposes, and attracts additional audiences because of it. But the award comes after the film's general release, by which time its commercial success or lack of it is already a fact. The crop of Oscars won by *Titanic* was in part a response to its popularity and earnings, not a cause of them.

The chief point about the Oscars and their universal recognisability as an award is that film is the great popular art form of the twentieth century, and almost remains so at the beginning of the twenty-first century. As a result everything to do with it is amplified in the public mind: actors, directors, even (in the past) such studio heads as Louis B. Mayer, play an Olympian part in the popular mind: these are the gods and goddesses of a larger-than-life world, the films are the greater reality against which mundane existence hardly matches up; the Oscars are the marks of approval and quality for these amplified, glamorous, expensive, imagination-capturing, dream-inducing, amazing people and productions.

Accordingly Oscars are the quintessences of the hyper-real celluloid world, standing for everything associated with the process that pours meanings into the lives of millions who sit with enraptured upturned faces in the reflected light of the cinema screen, mouths open, tears streaming, hearts beating, box of half-eaten popcorn dangling from their nerveless hands, as the mighty ship on the screen sinks with the brave hero still aboard, and the heroine in the lifeboat looking helplessly on.

Does film have a future, at least on the big screen? That is the question asked when television first made inroads into the cinema industry in the mid-twentieth century, when cinema houses closed by the score, only for the industry to revive after a while and once again become a giant. But the new question is what form the film industry will take in this age of portable electronic devices that are everything from telephones to television and cinema screens all in one, enabling people to phone for a film and watch it while on a bus journey. In an age when film has to compete on the miniature screen, not just with television programmes but with everything else that can appear there, most notably the Internet, the singular importance of film will diminish, and with it the meaning of the Oscars.

An interesting fact about the contrast between the Oscars and the Nobel Prizes is how sharp it is. Oscars are for the most universal, demotic and popular form of entertainment, Nobel Prizes are for the most recondite achievements in scholarship and enquiry. The latter are not subject to changes in fashion, commercial demands, the need to please multitudes, the transient and fluctuating pressures of popularity and personality. The Oscars reward success in the same frantic scramble to do what the Roman circus did in the days of Nero: to distract and appease the masses, who shouted for spectacle, excitement, blood, thunder, passion and death. Nobel Prizes come long after the achievements that earned them, when they have proved their worth definitively. It would be interesting if the Oscars were awarded for films made twenty years ago: interesting, but useless to all concerned.

God

What does the word 'god' mean to you?

What religious people mean by 'god' means nothing to me beyond an incoherent cluster of concepts from which religious apologists choose the most convenient subset, different subsets for different apologists and different purposes.

But the word brings to mind the man-made phenomenon of religions, whose net effect on humanity now as throughout history has been, by a considerable margin, negative. It would be so just because of the falsity of belief; and the consequent distortions of behaviour premised on the idea that there exist supernatural agencies who made this very imperfect world, and who have an interest in us that extends to our sex lives and what we should and should not eat on certain days, or wear, and so on.

But it is worse than false: it is far too often oppressive and distorting as regards human nature, and divisive as regards human communities.

It is a frequent source of conflict and cruelty. Crimes have been committed in its name that could not have been committed for any other reason: murder of those who 'blaspheme' or are 'heretics' (that is, disagree with those currently in charge), who 'profane' objects and texts regarded as 'sacred' (at the time of writing a number of Christian Pakistanis have just been murdered for allegedly mistreating a copy of the Koran) – and so distressingly on.

And more often than not religion has stood in the way of efforts at human liberation and progress, not least scientific progress: examples are legion.

Apologists for religion point to the Sistine Chapel and Bach's Mass in B minor as some sort of justification for it. I answer: first, the Church had the money to commission these things, and artists have stomachs like other men; second, lots of wonderful art is about naked women and bowls of fruit, and requires no belief in deities to prompt its production; and third, the existence of religious art does not excuse burning people at the stake for disagreeing with one or another doctrine or piety.

Apologists point to charitable works as some sort of justification for religion also. I answer: non-believers perform such works, too, out of simple fellow feeling, not requiring the idea of pleasing a deity or getting into heaven to prompt them to it.

Apologists point to Stalinism and Nazism as murderous ideologies, as if their existence made Torquemada and the Taliban somehow acceptable. I answer: all monolithic ideologies, claiming to possess the One Great Truth and demanding that everyone submit to it on pain of penalty, with their prophets and pieties and shibboleths and sacred cows, come to the same thing when allowed to go to their all-too-natural extremes – which is precisely the objection to religion. This does not stop anyone having the same objection to Stalinism and Nazism, which I very much do.

The basic doctrines of the major religions have their roots in the superstitions and fancies of illiterate peasants living several thousand years ago. It is astonishing that these superstitions, in the partial guise of sophistical successor versions, retain any credibility. The reason they do is proselytisation of the very young, the institutionalisation of religious sects, and certain psychological factors.

I would wish people to live without superstition, to govern their lives with reason, and to conduct their relationships on reflective principles about what we owe one another as fellow voyagers through the human predicament – with kindness and generosity wherever possible, and justice always. None of this requires religion or the empty name of 'god'. Indeed, once this detritus of our ignorant past has been cleared away, we might see more clearly the nature of the good, and pursue it aright at last.

Mortification

What explains, and what could justify, such religious practices as self-flagellation?

Along the borders between modern secular society and the religious traditions it has (or at least by now should have) evolved beyond, there are periodic flashes of conflict. Examples are legion; just two recent cases are frictions over religious objections to stem-cell research, and the demand by Catholic adoption agencies for exemption from discrimination laws because they do not wish to serve homosexuals.

Another area of conflict is the practice of self-harm or mortification in religious ritual. In a Manchester courtroom not long ago a Shiite Muslim was found guilty of child cruelty because he made two teenage boys participate in a self-flagellation ritual using a whip made of knife blades. The defence offered by the convicted man was that this is a traditional ceremony commemorating the death of Hussein, Mohammed's grandson, at the massacre of Karbala in 680 CE. On the day of Ashura some devotees whip their own backs with bunched knives known as *zanjirs*; others beat their chests rhythmically with their hands.

Sunni Muslims and even some Shiites are opposed to the Ashura ritual, condemning it as barbaric. But it would be a mistake to think it is exceptional in religion generally. Both Christianity and Hinduism have examples to offer that make *zanjir* self-flagellation look like a haircut.

In the Hindu festival of Thaipusam a ritual known as *Kavadi* is performed. It ranges from carrying heavy weights uphill, to piercing the body, face and tongue with long skewers, or dangling from meat-hooks passed through the flesh of the back and legs. 'The greater the pain,' says one text on *Kavadi*, 'the greater the god-earned merit.'

In the festival for the goddess Draupathi, believers walk on red-hot smouldering coals as an act either of devotion or penance. Descriptions of the proceedings claim that the devotees feel nothing, having entered a trance-like state; which would seem somewhat to reduce both the devotional and penitential value.

The idea of 'mortification of the flesh' – literally: putting the flesh to death – has been an aspect of Christianity from the beginning. Christianity's first scriptures are the letters of St Paul, which are the source for its ascetic tradition. Romans 8:13 says, 'If ye live after the flesh, ye shall die; but if ye live through the Spirit to mortify the deeds of the body, ye shall live.' Even more explicitly Colossians 3:5 registers the fears about sex (and less importantly, food) for which death-bound 'flesh' is a euphemism: 'Put to death, therefore, whatever belongs to your earthly nature: sexual immorality, impurity, lust, evil desires and greed, which is idolatry.'

As a result Christianity has a permanent tradition of mortifications ranging from self-denial, wearing hair-shirts and chains, fasting and self-flagellation, all the way to self-castration. The 'Desert Fathers' lived eremitic lives, anticipating the self-denying existences of monks and nuns, who with their vows of celibacy and poverty abnegate their normal humanity in hopes of pleasures to come, not only greater but everlasting.

The only 'Religion of the Book' which does not contain ritual traditions of self-inflicted suffering – except perhaps psychologically in the mothering relationship, as some Jewish folk might themselves quip – is Judaism, though it absolutely requires male genital mutilation in the form of circumcision. Sackcloth, ashes and fasting are the norm for penitents; punishments, which are biblically plentiful and savage, are mostly inflicted by the deity.

Studies of self-inflicted suffering in religious observance suggest that it has two main purposes. One is the hope of rooting out sexual desire or some other physical appetite, thereby achieving purity and self-mastery, and thus merit. The other, much the majority purpose, is to induce an ecstatic or transcendent state, often interpreted by believers themselves as contact with the divine. In this respect self-harming practices are allied to ritual drug-taking as in peyote cactus consumption in Mexico; and to dancing as with the Whirling Dervish Sufis of Islam.

The connection with drugs and dance takes the subject of inducing transcendent states of mind beyond the borders of religion and into human practice at large. Drugs and dancing are a commonplace of the clubbing scene every night of the week – though the divine encounters sought there are not noticeably religious. Elective suffering is the staple of sadomasochistic sexuality. The mission statement of the 'alternative' movement 'Only Flesh', based in Columbus, Ohio, reads: 'Only Flesh is a group of piercers and tattoo artists that formed a group dedicated to combining body modification (flesh pulls, brandings, cuttings, object suspension, piercing) flesh suspension and performance art to shock, arouse and entertain.'

There is even a Church of Body Modification in the United States which practises everything from tattooing to hanging from meat-hooks 'to promote growth in body, mind and soul' on an 'interfaith' basis.

The existence of organisations like these, and the phenomenon of sadomasochistic sexuality generally, raises two questions. The first concerns the limits of society's right to interfere with what people consent to do to or with their own bodies in their own private lives. British society in the form of its courts of law has reaffirmed the idea that those limits are generous ones: adults can go quite far in their private lives in the direction of what most would regard as unusual or exotic behaviour involving pain and harm.

But that raises the second question. We do not like the idea of children being involved in activities of elective suffering such as sadomasochism or Shiite rituals, among the many reasons being that we do not think they are in a position to give properly free and informed consent. But this in turn raises the further question of what else children should be protected from, especially in the way of religious practice, or even doctrine: for psychological effects and harms are every bit as real as physical ones. One might think that teaching, say, six-year-olds the Calvinistic dread of eternal torment in hellfire is as harmful as flagellation (the youths mentioned in the Manchester court case had begun their self-flagellation in Pakistan at that age). But what about teaching children false or weird beliefs as fact? What about the children of so-called witches, or voodoo worshippers, or astrologers, or Satanists, or Scientologists, or Jehovah's Witnesses, or any Christians or Hindus or Muslims? Where does one draw the line? There is no difference in the evidential basis or quality of the belief systems constituting any of these outlooks: should we not protect children from the harm they can all do?

Once one begins to ponder where these lines should be drawn, one has begun to ponder again that border between a modern secular society and religion. In my view, leaving adults to do what they like in private – providing it does not harm the unconsenting – is the right course: but that includes acquiring religion too. Leave the children out of it; that is, out of both the believing and flagellating, until they can make a free and informed choice for themselves.

Remorse

What is remorse, and how does one tell whether it is genuine?

In the third act of Samuel Taylor Coleridge's play *Remorse*, which was a great success on the London stage in 1813, the crime for which one of the characters feels remorse is revealed by a then-stunning theatrical device: a tremendous flash of light produced by a phosphorous explosion onstage, which reveals – when the audience's retinas have recovered and the stage smoke has cleared – a painting depicting a murder.

The flash of light which, in the year of grace 2008, first exposed the turpitude of bankers and financiers in the City of London and on New York's Wall Street was the onset of the 'credit crunch' that plunged the world into recession and lost so many people their jobs and homes. One of the vignettes that followed was of some of Britain's leading bankers seated in a row before a parliamentary committee, like the 'see no evil' monkeys, expressing their remorse for what they had done. The sight of them suggested an interesting question: what is remorse, and how do you tell if it is genuine?

In fact the way to show what remorse is, is the same as showing when it is genuine, as follows. The remorseful individual must show that he really understands what he has done by giving a full account of it and an explanation of why it is an offence, and he must acknowledge his responsibility for it; then he must show that he knows how he has damaged others, by giving a detailed description of the effects on them; then he must express his regret, and put forward proposals for how he can make amends to the fullest extent possible in his post-offence circumstances. Anything less than this is an effort to wriggle out of the consequences, and shows that what he really regrets is not having committed the offence, but having been caught.

It became apparent immediately after the world's leading banks gambled and speculated the world into crisis that the bankers themselves still expected to get their obscenely inflated bonuses. Etymological dictionaries explain that 'bonus' is 'Stock Exchange Latin' meaning 'good' – thus, a reward for doing well. If you lose billions, get bailed out by the taxpayer and still demand a bonus, you plainly do not feel one jot of remorse for anything other than being caught.

Greedy bankers are a relatively anonymous example of those who should, but do not, display remorse for actions that in their effects are no different from crimes. What of those charged and found guilty by tribunals at the Hague for crimes against humanity and genocide? In recent years a small army of indictees, including Slobodan Milosevic of Serbia and Charles Taylor of Liberia, have sat in the dock before the tribunals, and horrendous crimes attributed to them have been described by witnesses and victims, one after the other, harrowing the observers assembled there. These are the Nuremberg Trials of our day, tragically illustrating the fact that the crimes of the type committed by the Nazis continue yet. Milosevic and Taylor denied responsibility for the crimes for which they were indicted: that is the way with those who feel no remorse, no sense of guilt, no need to shrive themselves and to help palliate the wounds they have caused by providing the one thing that victims need above all else: recognition.

It was found in studies of armies in the First World War and afterwards that only about 20 per cent of conscript soldiers are effective in the heat of battle, and that these are usually men who feel no remorse afterwards at the thought of having killed enemy soldiers. Their psychological profile resembles that of recidivists in prisons; among these too there are few regrets and little sense of remorse for what got them into prison. The other 80 per cent of military conscripts tended to delope or not fire at all when confronted by enemy combatants, and to be emotionally affected by the experience of combat. All this points in the direction of a psychological typology marked by the presence and absence of a capacity for remorse respectively.

Where, one wonders, does this put bankers? The following tale might help.

Animal Farm Revisited: at the Anaplasmic Institute at Valles Marineris, an interesting experiment is being conducted into the appetite-passion cycle associated with the feeding habits of *Sus scrofa peculata*, this being the zoological name of an otherwise familiar large semi-domestic mammal, the 'banker' pin-striped hog. When released into a feeding pound, a square formed by full feeding troughs, the hogs struggle, fight and squirm to get at the troughs, and eat as fast and as much as they can, typically submerging their whole faces into the swill and both swallowing and inhaling it in large quantities. Because of the speed with which they eat they almost as often regurgitate the swill as quickly as they ingest it, so that the volume of swill plus regurgitate stays almost constant for a time, though it recognisably diminishes in quality and, after a while, in volume (some of it begins to find its way out of the other end of the hogs; but because many of them are in the troughs with all four feet this does not decrease the volume in the trough as much as it might otherwise do).

Because the nature of the contents of the trough are changing as they come to consist more and more of regurgitate and defecate, the capacity of the hogs' digestive system to cope with what they ingest begins to change. There are some warning signs: a few of the hogs begin to look a little green, and only then do their neighbours at the trough start to edge away, subconsciously aware perhaps that the gastric secretions and enzymes mixed into the regurgitations of the greener pigs are adding greater degrees of toxicity to the regurgitate. But at a certain point the level of toxicity in the swill-cum-regurgitate as a whole reaches a level at which the entire herd of hogs flips into a sudden panic mode: now aware that they cannot continue to eat very fast and in large quantities without doing themselves injury, they all immediately stop eating, and begin to run around the feeding pound emitting loud fear-and-warning noises – and at the same time emitting noisome efflations resulting from the degree of toxicity of the swill overindulged in, which has caused them tremendous bloating. It is a truly pitiable spectacle to see so many frightened flatulent 'banker' hogs dashing fruitlessly about, begging for the keepers to come and clean out their feeding troughs and to administer medications to solve their digestive crisis.

Researchers at the Valles Marineris Institute point out that the noise and efflations of frightened squealing hogs have a serious effect on other animals in the farmyard, peaceably trying to go about their business. Although there is relatively little wrong with the rest of the farmyard, the disruptions caused by the furore in the hogs' feeding pound is seriously disruptive, and without swift firm action the whole farm can be harmed by the hogs' panic-attack.

The researchers further say that their original assumption had been that the hogs were intelligent creatures, able to self-regulate their feeding habits; they somewhat abashedly say they had thought that the gobbling and elbowing that went on at the troughs in normal times were simply bad manners, not something systemic and dysfunctional, and not in need of keepers with sharp sticks to stop the hogs going too far. Fat hogs, they say, were thought to be good for the farmyard's income because of the revenue they generate, earning more than eggs and pick-your-own strawberry promotions. They now say that their studies of appetite and emotion in hogs have revealed that hogs have only one appetite – greed – and one emotion – fear – and that these govern all the hogs' behaviour in the feeding pound. In fact, they have concluded with surprise that the hogs' brains consist almost entirely of an amygdala, the organ responsible for arousal, autonomic responses associated with fear, emotion generally, and hormonal secretions. The hogs appear to be functionally bereft of higher cortical layers of the brain which in other animals are associated with rationality and intelligence; which makes them a much more dangerous farmyard animal than they had hitherto been believed to be.

Asked what solutions the researchers propose, the answer is: more keepers with sharp sticks, and encouragement to the public to eat more roast pork.

Ethics in Business

Is business amoral?

Until three-quarters of the way through the twentieth century it was widely assumed that business is, in the neutral sense of this term, an amoral affair. So long as a company kept within the law it was not otherwise obliged to distract itself from its purpose, which is to make profits.

It was an assumption that was often enough challenged, but by lone voices mainly. In the early phase of the Industrial Revolution the poet William Blake decried the effect of 'dark Satanic mills' on the environment, implying a responsibility on the part of business to consider the effects of its operations beyond the bottom line of its balance sheet. In the course of the nineteenth century, reformers such as Lord Shaftesbury and the nascent trade unions incrementally obliged government to legislate for the reduction of working hours to twelve and then ten a day, to limit the use of child labour in mines and factories, and to improve health and safety, thus further implying the responsibility of business to consider the human rights and interests of employees, even though it meant an addition to costs.

It was relatively late in the day that legal requirements were imposed on companies not to mislead clients (the Trades Descriptions Act, for example, was passed in 1968), though common law on contract and tort already enshrined the assumption that companies had a range of cognate responsibilities whose failure was actionable. So by the time 'business ethics' became a buzz-phrase after the 1960s, a partial framework governing the relationships between companies and their clients, staff, suppliers, partners, competitors, governments and the wider community – thus, not just to shareholders but to wider circles of 'stakeholders' as the fashionable term has it – already existed.

But the law is famously a blunt instrument, only capable in the main of drawing large thick lines through problems, leaving an enormous amount to the discretion of leaders of companies about how they and their businesses behave. And on this front a new and demanding sensibility had come into existence following post-Second World War and especially post-1960s changes in society and its attitudes. The essential feature of this change is a refusal to accept that the profit motive by itself can serve as an explanation, still less an excuse, for businesses and those running them to act in ways that, despite being within the law, neglect or harm the interests of stakeholders other than shareholders. This arena, between the law and demands of the new sensibility, is the arena of business ethics.

What is ethics? In the parlance of academic philosophy, 'ethics' is the name of a field of study, specifically the study of moral concepts such as 'good' and 'right', of moral reasoning such as 'it is wrong to do so-and-so because . . .', and of moral codes and systems. This is a restricted use of the term. In its more general sense it denotes not just moral codes or systems themselves, but how these relate to the more inclusive question of one's overall character, attitudes, choices and behaviour. Ethics is thus about ethos, about what sort of person one is and what sort of life one chooses to live. One's morality is part but not all of this.

As applied to business, ethics is thus about how a company chooses to behave and concomitantly how it regards itself and others. It includes the moral standards of the company itself, and individually of all who work in it, such standards typically requiring more scrupulous standards even than those required by law; for the demand goes beyond mere matters of compliance into the heart of company ethos, deep into attitudes and company sentiment.

And this, as one should never fail to point out to companies when talking to them about ethics, handsomely pays off on the bottom line too: ethics is profitable in every way. Only think: which companies tend to keep their clients and attract others in a downturn? Which companies benefit from seeing their chairmen or CEOs facing the press over embarrassing revelations, or answering criticisms about company behaviour?

Among the examples of ethical win-win are some of the major extraction companies which learned lessons from the barrage of criticism they faced in the past over environmental degradation and treatment of workers in developing countries. One could name the shining example of a mining company which, when negotiating with host governments, voluntarily contracts to build infrastructure, housing, schools and clinics for staff, to invest in jobs for them when the extraction is over, to undertake environmental restitution and relandscaping once the resource is exhausted – and fulfils the contract not to minimum specifications, but handsomely. Such a company is welcome wherever it goes, sets standards thereby, and flourishes as a result.

Business ethics is a wide subject. It covers all the obvious things: questions of good corporate governance and leadership, and all aspects of behaviour on either side of the legality line relating to creative accounting, transparency, compliance, insider trading, fraud and bribery (when is a 'facilitation payment' – in a developing country, say – a bribe?). It covers probity in sales and marketing, pricing and price-fixing, honesty in advertising and the propriety of advertising to children, and involvement in black and grey markets. It covers executive pay and perks, employee relations including questions of diversity and discrimination, affirmative action, surveillance and privacy in working hours, trade-union relations, fairness in contracts, and the nature of arrangements over health, safety, leave and training. It covers questions about the impact of new technologies, genetic modification of foods, animal experimentation in research, marketing of dangerous or unhealthy products (such as cigarettes and alcohol), responsibility for pollution and environmental damage, and degree of product liability. It covers responsibility over intellectual property, including patent and copyright infringement and misuse, employee raiding, and commercial intelligence and espionage. It involves exporting standards and practices adopted in demanding ethical environments to less demanding environments where temptations are greater and ethical behaviour is looser – especially when competitors are cutting corners, a universal problem in the globalised economy.

Obvious as these areas of consideration are, they jointly make a comprehensive and complex fabric, maintaining the good order of which challenges reflective and aware business people to ask themselves the right questions about overall ethos. And when they have decided on their answers, it then asks that they behave with consistency, determination and courage, to be good citizens of the business community. To repeat: although the value of doing this surely speaks for itself, it is highly relevant that the return for this invisible investment is very real on the bottom line, so even self-interest can be invoked to justify it.

The least effective way of making a company ethical is for senior management to send a Code of Conduct round to employees by email. Top-down nostrums have a habit of failing to stick. Companies have to engage all staff in discussing and thinking about ethics in a bottom-up programme, so that uptake of principles and resulting behaviours really works, with everyone seeing the point because they have had an input into deciding what is right. This procedure is effective because people know that what is wrong for individuals is wrong for institutions, and if each member of the family is actively involved in identifying the good, they are far more likely to embrace it and live by it in the corporate setting.

Recent major scandals in the business community – Enron and Arthur Andersen have become the typically cited examples

– are proof of the fact that values have changed, putting ethical concerns at the top of the agenda. A generation ago Enron would not have been much of a news story; now the world and attitudes – and in consequence regulatory standards – are different. Enron's conductors committed the crime of fraud, but the fraud arose from dishonest attitudes and culpable disregard of the interests of a variety of stakeholders. Such ethical failings are thus sometimes not merely unethical, but serve as natural precursors to criminal behaviour. It is obvious that the latter is unacceptable, but the ethical point is that it is no longer just crime that is so.

This is the age when recognition of the great importance of business in the life of good societies has come into its own, and that is why questions of ethics now take centre stage along with the other great economic questions in the global economy. Businesses that take ethics seriously are doing well, as proved by levels of return on ethical investment. 'Good business' is therefore a good pun; and it nicely sums up the point of business ethics.

Profit

Is there any guarantee that the profit motive, so destructive in causing the financial collapse of 2007–9, can be restrained in the interests of all?

Pythagoras said that there are three kinds of people, who can be classified by analogy with those who attend the Games: the competitors, the spectators, and those who come to buy and sell under the stands. He likened philosophers (a term which for him denoted mathematicians and scientists also) to the spectators, and he meant by this to impute a certain superiority to them, especially when compared to those who barter and haggle.

The global financial meltdown of 2008, caused by the greed and fecklessness of people in the finance industry of Wall Street and the City of London and elsewhere, made it easy to feel like one of Pythagoras's spectators if one were not directly affected by it. Greedy speculators and bankers, wild fear-driven fluctuations on stock markets, the consequence of insufficient regulation, added up to a dismaying mess which had all-too-real consequences for ordinary folk deprived of their homes and jobs.

The meltdown started because financial organisations made unsafe loans, and packaged them into securities for sale to other organisations, which bought them because of the high rates of return they promised – at least to begin with. Several years ago financiers saw that there was a problem with these debts and began trying to shed them. When the honeymoon period of many of those debts ended – mortgage rates rising from 'teaser' levels, and repossessions dramatically increasing as a result: in the US by 79 per cent in 2007 over 2006 – the extent of the infection throughout the money markets became apparent.

And then financial institutions lost faith in each other, and began to refuse to lend to each other. Banks depend on loans to service their daily workings. Without credit they can fail. The 'credit crunch' was centrally a freeze on interbank loans, gumming the entire financial system and threatening its collapse. That is a prospect so hideous that governments could do nothing other than intervene to prop things up.

The Latin root of the word 'credit' is *credo*, 'I believe'. The banks and other institutions had lost mutual belief for the good reason that they knew they were not themselves trustworthy.

Neuroscience has shown that oxytocin is the substance that influences behaviours associated with – among other things – bonding, trust, and suppression of anxiety. Rather apt work has been done by researchers in neuroeconomics on subjects participating in a game called 'Investor'; nasally administered oxytocin was shown to double levels of trust among players in comparison to controls. This prompts the thought that instead of pumping billions into the money markets, governments might more cheaply have sprayed oxytocin into the noses of bankers and speculators instead.

The serious point here concerns the fact that the financial meltdown is a classic display of non-rational behaviour. Greed prompted dangerously high risk-taking, and was followed by panic that made stock markets veer about wildly, causing a number of blue-chip companies to collapse or be nationalised. Yet unless serious steps are taken to avoid a repetition, as soon as everything stabilises the sequence will restart: the profit motive, which appears to trump all other motives and by any legal or near-legal means it can, will reassert itself and eventually get out of hand again.

It is important to note this because there is another arena where the profit motive wreaks even worse havoc and is poised to wreak more: the natural environment. As the ice caps melt, increasing the accessibility to a host of desirable natural resources, not least oil and gas, and promising new and quicker sea routes, there will be a rapid increase in exploitation of the polar regions unless international agreements to prevent it are reached.

If there is one thing the global financial meltdown, and the melting of the polar caps, should both emphatically teach, it is that the world cannot afford unbridled greed for profits. In itself there is nothing wrong with profit; energy, inventiveness, useful service, the production and sale of good things, all merit their reward. There is nothing wrong with people becoming rich as a result – unless their doing so is at a cost to, not to the benefit of, others. Making profits by endangering the well-being and prospects of others is immoral and should be criminal. That is what the bankers and financiers did, and that is what the extraction companies will do if the ice caps expose rich veins of natural resources. It cannot be beyond the intelligence of mankind to devise ways of allowing the profit motive to drive innovation and excellence without licensing those thus driven to trample on other people's lives in the process.

Science and Religion

Is Darwinism compatible with religious belief?

In giving a negative answer to the question 'Is Darwinism compatible with religious belief?' I shall take 'Darwinism' to be a general synonym for evolutionary theory in biology, taking it that biological evolution is a fact, though detailed questions about its mechanisms continue to be explored. The term has, familiarly, been used for a number of variants and offshoots associated with Darwin's discoveries, although his concept of natural selection remains at the core of the modern evolutionary synthesis, which among other things has added to his original insights discoveries about genes, population genetics, and a deeper understanding of how speciation occurs. I use 'Darwinism' to connote this synthesis.

By 'religious belief' I mean any belief in the existence and activity of supernatural agencies, or one such agent (a 'god'), either in the universe or outside it ('outside it' because allegedly outside space and time) but somehow operative in or on it. There are many historical, anthropological and psychological reasons for the many different forms of religious belief which, now as throughout recorded history, have variously been held by different groups of people, but it is certain that one common feature of early religion was that it served as a form of proto-science and proto-technology, in the sense that it offered explanations of natural phenomena (for example: thunder is a god walking on the clouds) and a means of influencing them (for example: sacrifice to that god to encourage him to cause or withhold rain).

This feature of early belief systems persists today mainly in the view that the origin of the universe and life within it was a purposive act by an agency suitably empowered to perform it. Literal biblical creationists ('young Earth' creationists) and intelligent design creationists regard evolutionary biology as directly controverting their views, which is why they devote so much time and money to attempts to rebut it. They have an uphill struggle, not just because of the strength of evidence in geological and biological science, but because intelligent appraisal of what observation and reason jointly reveal about the world has always been at odds with religious stories about origins.

A large part of the philosophy of classical antiquity – the point at which enquiry of a recognisably scientific stamp enters the record with Thales, Anaximander, Parmenides, the atomists Democritus and Leucippus, and others – consisted in the search for non-supernaturalistic and non-fabulist accounts of the nature of things. The Greek thinkers premised their views on the recognition that creationist accounts are projections from the human experience of agency, and that their plausibility rested on the absence, at that time, of any better explanation. This anthropomorphic projection seemed all the more plausible to those who also believed that the planet we inhabit is the chief feature of the universe, lying at its centre with all the heavenly bodies orbiting it, and that mankind is its chief ornament. For such folk, the belief that the world and we in it are the work of a deity who takes a close interest in us seems entirely appropriate.

It appears not to have occurred to them that attributing the origins of the universe and life to a conscious agency merely defers the explanatory task. If nothing can exist without actively being created, then the supposed creator requires a creator, and so on for each creator in turn. Efforts to block this regress typically involve such claims as that there is only one creator but it is 'self-creating', or exists 'eternally' and therefore requires no creation. These are arbitrary and obviously ad hoc moves; theology seeks to protect them from charges of meaninglessness by describing them as 'mysteries' lying beyond human comprehension. They accord with the natural psychological need of humans for everything to be explicable in narrative form, with beginnings (and future endings: religion offers detailed accounts of these too) to provide neatness and closure for thought.

Modern science, after a long intermission in which people could invite death if they dared think differently from what religious authorities imposed as dogma, resumed the tradition begun by the Greek philosophers of examining questions about the world on the basis of observation and reason, without recourse to religious explanations. Still, until the nineteenth century's advances in geology and biology, the question of the development of life on earth was an open one, even though many (from classical antiquity onwards) had hypothesised – on good observational grounds – forms of evolution, and had noticed the similarities between different species. Because it was social suicide to profess atheism until the later nineteenth century, most people who expressed views about matters on which religion claimed knowledge were content to call themselves 'deists', deism being the minimalist view that an agency created the world and then ceased either to exist or to be interested, therefore playing no further part. This is the residuum of the explanatory need to have something to say about beginnings. It is unlikely that many intelligent folk really believed this idea; one mark of intelligence is an ability to live with as-yet-unanswered questions.

Darwinism demonstrates the redundancy of the idea of a creator-designer agent in biology. More, it shows that such an idea is inconsistent with the observable facts of nature in general, as clearly as the geological evidence shows that 'young Earth' creationism is not merely false but absurd. This is the key point: for if Darwinism is not compatible with religious belief as such then it is not compatible with any particular version of religious belief such as Christianity. Let us look at some of the reasons why. I ignore the claims of literalist six day creationists as too much even for most religious folk, and concentrate on the kinds of views taken by 'intelligent design' proponents and believers in general.

Take first the religious apologists who accept that biological evolution occurs over great periods of time, yet say that a deity is involved in designing and sponsoring those processes. Consider a parallel. Suppose it was once believed that flowers are coloured because fairies paint them while we sleep. Once we understand the natural processes by which flowers come to be coloured, it would not merely be redundant but contradictory to claim that *in addition* to the biological process that causes floral coloration, it is also part of the explanation that they are painted (in the very same colours) by fairies. For if the biological account is correct, the fairy-tale account is false (and vice versa): one cannot hold both to be true together.

However, most religious apologists who accept that biological evolution occurs just as the Darwinian synthesis states do not claim that it is a dual process, happening by natural and simultaneously by supernatural means. Instead their claim is that a deity planned and initiated the evolutionary processes in question, and then let it take its course; and that for this reason religion and Darwinism are compatible.

But these apologists are in the same situation as a fairy-believer would be who claimed that although floral coloration is indeed the outcome of wholly biological processes, these latter occur *because fairies want them to occur* (evolution happens by wholly natural means *because a deity willed that it should*). Each of the following objections is fatal: the claim adds nothing to the biological account, requires very considerable independent motivation, and – even more fatally, if that is possible – *any arbitrary superfluity whatever* of this kind is 'consistent' with the biological account. Thus, to claim that fairies designed the world to look and behave

as if it was not designed by fairies is consistent with science –
because of its meaninglessness.

As a last resort, some defenders of religion might concede
that Darwinism removes the need to invoke a purposeful agency
to design living things or govern the changes and variations
among them, but they still argue that the concept of a deity
is needed for other explanatory purposes – say, to explain why
we must be moral, by arguing that the deity exists to enforce
morality with promises of reward and threats of punishment.
The fallacy here is quickly pointed out: some atheists can be
highly moral; they do not need the concept of a rewarding and
punishing deity, nor should morality be premised on promises
and threats.

Again consider a parallel. Suppose that fairy-believers at last
accept that floral coloration happens naturally, and begin to
invoke other arguments instead to support their belief that
fairies exist. Suppose they say that the concept of fairies is
still required to explain why (say) people find the colours of
flowers pretty – perhaps by putting fairy-spells on them. What
is notable in this effort to find work for fairies to do, now
that flower colouring is denied them, is the fact that the chief
raison d'être for hypothesising their existence in the first place
has gone. Thus it is with the religious who concede that the
world and life do not require a creator, but find alternative
employment for the concept of an agency whose original *raison
d'être* was to create the world and life.

Another tack that can be taken to show the incompatibility
of Darwinism and religion concerns the concepts of 'design'
and 'purposive design'. Traditional revealed religion assigns
omnipotence, omniscience and benevolence to deity. The
presence of 'natural evil' in the world – the suffering it contains as

a result of predation, disease and such occurrences as droughts, floods, earthquakes and volcanism – prompts even theologians, or some of them, to regard the alleged characteristics of omnipotence and benevolence as incompatible: one of the two has to give. But what most emphatically rebuts the attempt by some religious apologists to accord deity a hand in evolution – and this especially applies to outright creationists and so-called intelligent design theorists – is the obvious fact that if organisms were purposively designed, the designer would have to have been mighty incompetent, wasteful and cruel. The biological realm universally manifests evidence of emergent naturally occurring design, the result of the mechanisms by which descent with modification works – including many imperfections, redundant organs, dead-end lines of development, new problems caused by genetic adaptations to 'solve' old problems, and the like.

A further inconsistency, therefore, obtains between religious beliefs about the existence and development of life, and the observable facts of biology: biological 'design' is manifestly not the outcome of previous planning and execution by an intelligent purposive agency, unless that agency is markedly incompetent (for example, the optic nerve making a blind spot at the centre of the retina) or markedly malevolent (for example, the prevalence of agonising diseases).

It has to be taken seriously that Darwin himself saw, in the light of his observations and discoveries, all credibility vanish from religious beliefs. He was baptised an Anglican, but his early religious observance was Unitarian, a rational and liberal outlook, which however he abandoned for more traditional Christianity while at Cambridge, where he was immensely impressed by William Paley's *Evidences of Christianity* and *Natural Theology*. Having given up the study of medicine while at Edinburgh University, he contemplated becoming a clergyman. First, though, he joined the *Beagle* as gentleman companion to the ship's captain, Robert Fitzroy, a biblical literalist who required everyone aboard to attend daily worship conducted by himself. It is interesting that Darwin collected the evidence for his great discoveries, profoundly influenced by the geology he observed and which screamed aloud the vast age of the planet, while he was in the constant company of a fundamentalist who regarded every word of the Bible as literally true, down to its account of the six days of Genesis and the creation of fixed species in the Garden of Eden.

Darwin began the voyage a practising Christian, and by its end five years later was full of doubt. He had read Charles Lyell's *Principles of Geology* while afloat, and later remarked that it was the basis of 'everything which I have done in science'. In the late 1830s he wrote 'that the Old Testament was no more to be trusted than the sacred books of the Hindoos or the beliefs of any barbarian'; not long afterwards he wrote of the New Testament that 'the more we know of the fixed laws of nature, the more incredible do miracles become . . . the men of that time were ignorant and credulous to a degree almost incomprehensible to us'. Even then he hung on to a residual Christian commitment until – by his own account – 1849: he wrote, 'I never gave up Christianity until I was forty years of age.'

'Christianity' meant 'religious faith' in general; when, at a dinner party in Darwin's company, the Duke of Argyll said that he saw the operation of purposive mind in nature, Darwin shook his head. The traditional pre-scientific beliefs of religion simply could not survive scientific insight into nature, and Darwin experienced that truth at first hand.

Democracy

Is genuine democracy possible?

Democracy of a sort probably existed among the small tribes of early mankind, but the word and the political theory of democracy come, as does so much else in Western civilisation, from ancient Greece, and particularly from Athens of the classical period between the late sixth and early fourth centuries BCE. Historians even put a date on when Athens became a democracy and called itself such: 508 BCE, the year in which Cleisthenes put the government of the city into the hands of its citizens. Or rather, into the hands of adult male citizens, where 'adult' meant over the age of thirty, and 'citizen' meant a free-born Athenian. So women, slaves and immigrants – the majority – were no part of the democracy.

Still, the new system was striking in that it required all adult males to take their part in the government of their country, and it was a matter of moral as well as political duty – these were the same thing for the Greeks – to fulfil this responsibility. Those who did not do so were called *idiotai*, because their lack of participation was disruptive.

The nature of Athenian democracy had much to do with the fact that Athens was relatively small, as were all the city-states of ancient Greece. Aristotle said that the criterion for the ideal state is that all its citizens should know each other. In his book *The Politics* he wrote, 'It is necessary for the citizens to be of such a number that they know each other's personal qualities and thus can elect their officials and judge their fellows in a court of law sensibly.' And this was indeed practicable in Athens, where boys were educated together, and served alongside each other in the army, and when they grew up they elected each other to office, debated with each other in the agora, and – if the occasion arose – as jurors decided on each other's fate.

The historian Thucydides recorded (perhaps with some paraphrase) a famous speech by the great Pericles of Athens, describing democracy as the system in which government acts for the many and not the few, gives equal justice to all, and regards merit as the sole criterion for office. These values lie at the centre of democracy today, and even in false democracies – those Third World regimes where elections are rigged and fraudulent – the fact that they pretend to be democracies pays lip-service to these ideals.

Contemporary democracies, even small ones, have populations so large in comparison to classical Athens that nothing like the Aristotelian ideal of mutual social acquaintanceship is possible. Moreover, for the entire span of history between the Greek city-states and the nineteenth century, it was Plato's hostile view of democracy that prevailed: which was that democracy is no better than ochlocracy – that is, mob rule. Giving government to the ignorant and self-interested mob, said Plato, is what ruined Athens and is anyway irrational, for the state should be run by the most intelligent and able – which meant aristocracy, 'rule by the best'. Aristocracy has since come to mean inherited privilege, and there are no guarantees that a person whose ancestors once achieved something worthwhile is now, generations later, among the best: rather the opposite, if too much indulgence, wealth and idleness have characterised the family history since.

The developed democracies of the Western world have rather cleverly achieved a seeming contradiction: of giving the people ultimate control over government through systems of democratic elections, while avoiding ochlocratic outcomes. These latter would result if government were conducted by referenda, which a moment's reflection shows would be highly undesirable: rule by referenda would too often consist in an at best partially informed majority often reacting emotionally to immediate events and therefore passing unjust and inappropriate laws in response. For example, capital punishment is favoured by the majority of people in most countries, although most advanced countries have now abolished it in the interest of civilised values. This illustrates how 'representative' democracies work. Those elected are not delegates who do as instructed by their electors, but are representatives who think and act on behalf of their electors. If they do it badly their electors can get rid of them at the next election. Representation thus gets rid of the ochlocratic risk, while retaining the periodic sanction of popular control.

Democracy is far from a perfect system, but it is by quite a long way the least imperfect system. It has the best chance of delivering social justice, and of being responsive to the plurality of needs and interests characteristic of modern advanced societies. It gives every adult a role, imposes restraints on what governments do, and allows for peaceful change in the political process. But it requires two powerful adjuncts to work: a free press, and the rule of law administered by an independent judicial system. In the ideal it would further require an educated and reflective electorate – but this has so far proved one requirement too far.

One of the chief imperfections of democratic systems is that, as economist Mancur Olson argued in his *The Rise and Decline of Nations*, they inadvertently encourage the growth within them of powerful and well-organised special-interest minority groups, which come into existence because their promoters, knowing that they lack the numbers to get their way through democratic means, seek to do so by influence, pressure, and the judicious use of money and expertise in focused campaigns. Their commitment to their causes not infrequently gives them an advantage, because the majority is not organised in opposition to them, or well enough informed about what is at issue. So special-interest groups get their way, not infrequently at the expense of the majority's interests. All the mature democracies are beset by such interest groups, whose lack of accountability to the people as a whole is what can make them disruptive presences.

History

History cannot do without eyewitness reports;
but how do we guard against the bias and error
that doubtless infect many of them?

If we pride ourselves on learning from experience, then the experience of humankind is a required source of instruction. For although what happens in the world rarely imitates its antecedents exactly, the present's resemblances to the past tend to be uncanny. We know that the price of not knowing history is to repeat its worst mistakes; the benefit of knowing history is that we can have some understanding, at least, of the mistakes currently being made – and we might occasionally even be able to avoid them. Reading history should be a standard part of everyone's week.

The word 'history' has two senses: what happened in the past, and what we say in the present about what happened in the past. In the first sense, history as past events is envisaged as a country stretched out 'behind' us which we could visit if only we had a time-travel machine. History as the surmises, interpretations and narratives constructed today is based on what those past events bequeathed to us – it survives in the form of documents, letters, diaries, ruins unearthed by the archaeologist, artefacts known or judged to be old. These are the detritus and residue of what has otherwise gone; historians study and arrange them, like pieces of an incomplete jigsaw puzzle, in order to fashion a coherent story. History, in the sense of past time, is accessible only through history in the sense of today's incomplete jigsaw puzzle; we can get at it in no other way.

Among the indispensable resources of the historian are contemporary accounts of past events written by witnesses. Of course these accounts have to be approached with scepticism; the historian must remember the human propensity to embellish, dramatise, enlarge a share or minimise a responsibility, write with bias, distort the facts whether deliberately or unconsciously, 'spin' the events or tell outright lies. Even so, first-hand reports are valuable and important. Without diaries and reports, memoirs, newspapers and other contemporary records, historians would have a very hard if not impossible time. This was what Thomas Carlyle had in mind when he defined history in his *Heroes and Hero Worship* (1859) as 'a kind of distilled newspapers', though of course he thereby ignores the task of checking and interpretation that the historian uses to turn those records into an organised whole. Moreover a great deal of the raw material used by historians consists of other more mundane factual records, such as bills of lading, ledger entries, lists of names, account books, legal documents, and the like; a far cry from, say, diary entries and personal letters, reportage and memoir.

It is these latter accounts, though, that give the freshest and most vivid impression of the past, however much spin and bias they contain. 'Take from the altars of the past the fire, not the ashes,' said Jean Jaurès, the French political philosopher, in an article published in 1911. The documentary raw material of history has the immediacy of presence, the directness that characterises communication from someone who was there and felt and saw the things reported. Any policeman will tell you that four witnesses at the scene of an accident will give four different stories of what happened; so we must accept that every contemporary account is one person's account, filtered through subjectivity and the often treacherous channel of memory. Nevertheless it is impossible not to be gripped, absorbed and often moved by letters, diaries, dispatches and court records. It is a quite different experience from reading novelised versions of the events, and even historical accounts of them. The consciousness that the writer was there makes a big difference. If, as you read, you recall the cynical view of Santayana that 'history is a pack of lies about events that never happened told by people who weren't there', you might not be able to resist a smile. He meant today's historians writing about the past; but the same applies to the creators of their resources. Some letters and diaries might indeed be a pack of lies, and their authors might not really have been where they claimed to have been – but it is reasonable to suppose that most are the authors' version of the truth. And the fact that they were written close to the described events makes them compelling.

So, reading eyewitness accounts from the past is a kind of intermediary exercise, between doing the coal-face archival and archaeological work of the professional explorer of the past, and the interpretative accounts they accordingly write. One becomes one's own professional, so to speak, consulting the past's documents and testimonials for oneself – and experiencing their immediacy for oneself also.

Take for example the account given by Jehan de Wavrin of the Battle of Agincourt (1415), written a few years after it occurred. 'I, the author of this work,' says de Wavrin halfway through his description of the opposing armies on the eve of the battle, 'know the truth about this, for I was in the assemblage on the French side.' Interestingly, this remark is made while de Wavrin is telling us how noisy the French camp was, and how silent the English camp, as the fateful night passed; but that on the French side 'one hardly heard a single horse neigh throughout the host'.

Imagine reading Ernst Jünger describing a German attack on British lines in the closing weeks of the First World War, historian Michael Howard's account of how his unit took up its position under mortar fire near Salerno in the Second World War's Italian campaign, or the Duke of Cumberland's dispatch reporting the events at Culloden Moor in 1746. The cumulative effect is that one gets a sense of when such descriptions ring true. When Jehan de Wavrin describes how the French cavalry churned the ground into a sea of mud at Agincourt, and could scarcely move because of the weight of their armour, and how the foot-soldiers were massed too closely together to be able to raise their swords and spears, the effect is cinematographic: here is the reality that was that event in all its horror. And when the French counter-attacked, England's King Henry ordered that all prisoners be killed so that his troops were unencumbered in meeting the new danger: the brutality of the past is before our eyes in ways that reconstructions cannot quite achieve.

A chronological reading of history's eyewitness accounts might begin with Egypt and Mesopotamia – the former in the wide-eyed and all-embracing curiosity of Herodotus, and the latter with a variety of sources including letters from the archives of the kings of Mari, dating to the centuries before 1750 BCE. These make better sense when combined with accounts by archaeologists of their finds – for example, Howard Carter writing about the tomb of Tutankhamen. The juxtaposition of funerary memoirs of Egyptian officials, and the wonderment of later ages breaking the long silence of their tombs, makes a striking mosaic of insights.

From these ancient civilisations one can advance through the antique Greek world, Rome, the Dark Ages in Europe, and their contemporaneously splendid eastern civilisations, in the words (among numbers of others) of Thucydides and Plato, Cicero and Suetonius, Marcion and Eusebius, Masoudi and Lady Murasaki – the litany of great names, and the anonymous recorders among them, offer a rich panoply. The Roman scholar Procopius pulls no punches in his uncensored account of Byzantium's lascivious Theodora 'cracking dirty jokes and wiggling her hips suggestively' and her early scandalous career before she became the Emperor Justinian's consort. Where that is titillating, Thucydides's account of the plague that struck Athens a millennium before in 430 BCE is excoriating; even the carrion birds that fed on the unburied corpses in the streets died of the disease which, in a matter of weeks, nearly snuffed out Western civilisation in its cradle.

Reading one's way from the crusades through the Renaissance and Reformation to the *Mayflower* pilgrims and the English Civil War and Restoration introduces us to sources ranging from Fulcher of Chartres, who witnessed Pope Urban II's declaration of the first crusade in 1095, to Pepys in a Restoration England where Roman Theodora would have felt quite at home. History speeds up as it becomes more recent because there are far more source materials to draw upon, so one gets an increasingly newsreel effect sometimes more potent than actual newsreel footage. Think of reading one's way through the epoch from Louis XIV's court in the late seventeenth century to the Boer War at the turn of the twentieth century, and on through the bloodied and dizzying century leading to today. That is a panorama of war and revolution, colonisation, urgent but faltering efforts at reform, industrialisation and industrial unrest, refugees in millions, death camps and gas chambers, mushrooming cities, tidal waves of emigrants, the fall and rise of empires, skies darkened with bomber fleets, the struggle and agony of whole peoples in welters of gore – and the ever-faster race of scientific and technological development utterly transforming the experience of much of mankind. It is a tidal race of tumult and suffering; to see it cascade past, bearing the flotsam of time, is a vertiginous experience: but a necessary one.

In every case the eyewitnesses' act of writing down what they experienced gives sharp definition to their reports. In the way of contemporary history, these sources often have a greater resonance because they reach out and connect with other events at other times. Such accounts bring home the recurrent reality of social problems and the fragility of human arrangements before nature's power – and remind us that neither is unique to our day. So we might read of small boys being sold to Moroccan soldiers in Naples during the Second World War, or the letters of Margaret Paston to her husband in the unsettled fifteenth century, as she feared riots were about to break out; or John Evelyn's account of the Great Fire of London, or descriptions of a volcanic eruption whether in antiquity or recent decades.

In every case past time becomes almost as present as it was to the diarist or correspondent of the day. We should read history as often in this form as in the more considered and organised form offered by the historians: remembering always Thucydides's dictum, 'history is philosophy teaching by examples'.

And how does one evaluate the worth of such accounts? The chief test is consistency with independent sources that provide confirmation. Other criteria include internal consistency and verisimilitude of detail, contextual knowledge of the author indicating likely motives of bias, plausibility in the light of general knowledge of the time, and understanding of human nature (here employing the kind of empathetic insight urged by such proponents of '*verstehen* theory' as Wilhelm Dilthey and Max Weber). One can be misled by the apparent sincerity of an author, or by the skill with which he weaves a narrative and embellishes it with persuasive detail; but that is a risk one takes in the search for truth about past times, which is also a search for the truth about our own time.

Love

If love is merely chemistry, does that devalue it?

It seems that the ancient Greeks knew better than we about the subject of love, at least in regard to distinguishing its categories. They identified several varieties: the love of parents for children, love between friends, the affection of comrades who have experienced much together, charitable love for humanity in general, obsessive love, erotic love, playful love – and gave each its own name and story. They thought that *mania* – what we call infatuation – was a punishment sent by the gods; and they prized *philia*, the love between friends, above all other kinds.

Interestingly, they did not single out the only kind of love that can be, and often is, genuinely unconditional – asking nothing in return and sometimes getting nothing in return: and which is unquestionably a matter of biology, and more accurately, biochemistry: namely, maternal love.

Without question maternal attachment has been a constant since our remotest ancestors lived in trees, for everywhere in mammalian nature mothers tend and protect their young until the latter are able to survive alone, illustrating how essential maternal attachment is to the continuance of life itself. One of the more poignant comparisons between human mother–child bonds and their existence among our relatives in nature is provided by chimpanzees: Jane Goodall discovered when she studied the chimpanzees of Gombe in Tanzania that some young chimps die of grief when they lose their mothers.

Although mother-love is biological, it is not universal because it is not guaranteed in every case, at least among humans. This is no contradiction: not all women have the instinct, and it is known that the processes of pregnancy and childbirth that fully activate the instinct can sometimes be disrupted. The way we have detached ourselves from the basics of nature in our lives – especially from death and childbirth, which our ancestors witnessed far more frequently and directly than we ever do, among themselves and among the farm animals most of them lived with – even makes some women disgusted by the thought of giving birth and what seems the equally primitive and animalistic act of suckling. For such, 'maternal instinct' is an empty notion.

But in the ordinary course of events nature's clever pharmaceutical mixtures that course through a pregnant woman's systems switch on a repertoire of behaviours that amount not merely to loving, but to being in love with, their babies when the latter come squalling into the world. And thereafter, again in the normal case, the baby, child, youth and adult that serially results can take a great deal for granted about the lengths to which his mother will go – sacrificing much, accepting much, enduring much, fearing much, hoping much, wishing much, trying much, sometimes weeping, sometimes feeling absurd quantities of pride and pleasure – and all with little thanks.

The Greeks really ought to have had a word for mother-love, though one suspects they would have needed to coin an entire phrase – perhaps 'a necessary and fortunate madness prompted by endogenous chemicals' – to do it justice.

The point of all this is to register the fact that although mother-love is chemical, it is obviously no less valuable and important for being so: there is no inconsistency between the chemistry and poetry of the best emotion we know. The same therefore applies to all the other kinds of love and their place in life. Oxytocin has been identified as the hormone that promotes bonding and trust between individuals, and it would be daft to say that trust and bonding are less valuable to us because a hormone is involved in the stimulation of the emotions in which both consist.

The fine frenzy of reciprocated lust is likewise a matter of chemicals so powerful that they can override caution and convention. This is the inheritance of nature's reproductive imperative; the lion, the mouse, the firefly all feel that imperative in its season; in bonobo chimpanzees it is the currency of social intercourse, in humans it is the maker, breaker and shaker of our most vital relationships. No wonder then that Lucretius begins his great poem on nature, *De Rerum Natura*, with a hymn to Venus, goddess of sexual love. She is an imperious deity, because through the instruments of venery, named for her, the whole future of the species rushes and thunders, demanding to be created in that blind moment of high and delirious consummation which is her reward to her servants. It is because of the urgency and self-oblivion of the goddess's rite that the Greeks described it as madness, indeed as a punishment, and why some of them welcomed the loosening of her grip on them as they aged. This is one of the respects in which one disagrees with them.

Stendhal on Love

How much light does Stendhal's On Love
throw on the subject of love?

Stendhal's strangely engrossing *On Love* is not so much about love as such as about three other things: infatuation, women, and a slice of the history of a section of European society in transition. It is informed by a highly literate sensibility, and by a temperament which, though on the one hand both romantic and Romantic, has also a tincture of the dispassion of eighteenth-century science. Analysis of a quite serious psychological kind crosses the weft of anecdote, memory, whimsy, eulogy and aspiration that decorates almost every page. A book like this could only be written by someone who fancied himself deeply disappointed in love, though all the evidence both internally and externally is that its author, who was in love with love far more than he was in love with his Métilde, was by no means disappointed in *that* love. On the contrary: the subject of love absorbed and pleased Stendhal, as a topic of research pleases the scientist; all appearances of the vagrant wanderings of this book to one side, *On Love* is an essay that could only be written by a man who really desired to spend time with his subject.

Stendhal – Henri-Marie Beyle – is an attractive presence in his book. One thing that makes him so is the one just mentioned, that he is a lover of love, or perhaps more accurately a lover of the infatuation stage of love: its early, romantic, passionate stage of courtship and conquest, with its refusals and yieldings and its first transports of pleasure. The word 'lover' must here be understood in its constructive application: Stendhal is not a roué, voyeur, seducer, rapist, despoiler, cynic: far from it. He genuinely loves the idea of the romantic passion, the rosy effulgences of desire and the sighs and urgencies that inhabit the condition. To be a roué and seducer requires a certain indifference to the human, personal, psychological aspect of the one seduced, for the roué's plan is to abandon after use. This is not Stendhal. For, more importantly even than being a lover of the idea of love, he is a lover of women, fascinated by them and observant of them, sympathetic and admiring, and all genuinely so, even if not always completely accurately so. But he sees that women are better at business than men, when given the chance; that they are excluded from theatres of activity that give the feeblest of men a right to a station above women who are in fact vastly their superiors. He sees and sympathises with their difficulties: they have more to lose in love, more risk of mockery and opprobrium if it overpowers them, less opportunity to distract themselves from it, fewer chances to check their jealousy or mitigate its corrosions when it occurs. Every disadvantage of their circumstances is as clear to him as the reasons why they are eminently worth vying for and dying for by men of true feeling.

Stendhal is in short a feminist, and when he has one of his alter egos ('Salviati') say in the text, 'Indeed, half – the most beautiful half – of life is hidden from one who has not loved passionately', the deep implication is that this is because encounter with the feminine in the special circumstances of courtship is valuable in itself, one of the life-enhancing experiences, and therefore a ripe topic for the kind of exploration Stendhal undertakes, even though the task of writing about love fully and coherently is difficult or perhaps in the end impossible.

Still, one should not fail to notice that Stendhal's tongue is firmly in his cheek at times. 'I cannot emphasise this enough,' he writes, 'the love of a man who is head over heels either *delights in* or *trembles at* all that he imagines, and there is nothing in nature that does not remind him of *her*. Moreover, delighting and trembling are a deeply absorbing business and everything else pales in comparison.' Likewise one should notice that his feminist sympathies do not prevent him from recognising – and condemning – the difficult, the proud and the false woman. Nor does he think that love, passion and erotic obsession are invariable goods; they can be painful and destructive, he knows that; he is not a fool. There is sharp perception everywhere in *On Love*, and a kind of genius in the structureless structure of it, which allows all the contradictions and qualifications to be resolved – like an Hegelian synthesis – into a justification for celebrating love by devoting a book to following as many of its intricacies as possible.

What has so far been said touches on two of the book's emergent themes – infatuation and women – which are the foreground to its background, which is the post-war transition from eighteenth-century aristocratic life to nineteenth-century bourgeois life. Emphatically, the book's sensibility is a product of the former, and although the gentry and aristocracy of France and Italy did not go so far as 'good' society took itself in the Britain of the Victorian age, still they were both a lot less sure of themselves and a lot less louche than their forerunners in the era of the *ancien régime*. But change was enough on the way for Stendhal to devote a section of the book to dissecting (in none-too-commendatory fashion) female 'modesty', and to employ a trope of the time, the inefficacy of 'cold reason' against 'imagination's fire' in writing of female jealousy.

It is just at the moments of apparent offhandedness in his generalisations that some of Stendhal's more interesting observations fall. 'The difference between the meanings of unfaithfulness for the two sexes is so great that a woman in love may pardon an infidelity . . . Here is an authoritative rule for distinguishing truly passionate love from that founded on *pique*: for women, infidelity will practically destroy the one but will strengthen the other.'

The most famous idea in *On Love* is that of 'crystallisation', the beautification spread over and around the loved one by the act of loving her (or him) itself. The notion is taken from the tradition of the 'Salzburg bough'; lovers in that musical city would suspend twigs down the shafts of salt workings until they were covered in glittering crystals, then draw them up and present them to their chosen inamorata as a love-offering. Stendhal has the smitten one project a crystal disguise onto the beloved's imperfections or ordinariness, making her (or him) seem to have dropped from heaven by a special dispensation. This is the essence of infatuation, indeed, and to the subtle workings of biology all thanks must be given for the continuation of the species even by the plainest of Jills and dullest of Jacks.

The kernel of this idea, as with that of love at first sight, owes something to an influence on Stendhal that he later acknowledged: to William Hazlitt, England's greatest essayist. Hazlitt and Stendhal became friends in Paris in the early 1820s and found much to share in their views about this great subject. That is unsurprising; the spark for some of what Stendhal thought about that matter was struck by his reading of Hazlitt's long essay in *The Edinburgh Review* for 1815 on Sigismondi's history of European literature. Stendhal's copy of the essay is annotated in the margins with observations and comments that found their way into *On Love*, in content if not in form. It is no coincidence that Hazlitt and Stendhal both wrote books on love – very different, to be sure; for where Stendhal's was urbane and speculative, Hazlitt's was painful and indeed ugly, a memoir of a helpless, humiliating and too quickly degrading infatuation with a much younger woman, whom he had crystallised so completely that he never saw her as she was – an ordinary enough pretty young woman who led him on a bit but never really gave him cause for the encouragement he gave himself over her. But the two books sprang from neighbouring roots; Hazlitt believed that love at first sight was a function of a prepared vision, a dream in the mind of a romantic who, when he saw something close to what he had imagined, was thereupon already in love, because long since in love with the dream. That is precisely what happened in the case of Hazlitt's tragic and destructive infatuation, and it is hard not to see the Salviati version of Stendhal as just one such lover of the idea of love, ready to fall and be tormented because that is his ready-made desire.

Stendhal and Hazlitt were tutored in youth by such inflammatory teachers as Rousseau and *Gil Blas*, even to the extent of Hazlitt echoing phrases from the latter in his own *Libor Amoris*. But the longer context for their respective views, and in particular their over-focus on the romantic beginnings of love, is the courtly troubadour tradition, and its resurgence in the warming pan of poetry. Stendhal's romantic milieu is the opera box, the salon, the chaise bowling along the paths of an urban park. The semiology of flirtation has its role as an element in the transactions that constitute courtship and the 'dissembling eyes' of passion. There is little or nothing of mature or matured love, of the mountain-high passion that endures long separations and many vicissitudes, and finds its reward in itself because it has no other consummation. These are terrains of love – there are others – that are not seen from the summer-house of Stendhal's preoccupation. But his preoccupation is with that segment of the experience of love which most novels, most films, most plays and poems address: the passage of experience that is incomparably heightened, that is thrilling, desired, suffered, yearned for, and regretted when over; and therefore which is the one most natural to write about, if one must write about it – because one is not living it.

Chief among the traits for which Stendhal's novels are praised is their insight into character. No doubt his career in the Napoleonic administration, and his life in the army, were among the sources of this, but the experience and reflection that went into *On Love* play their part too. The book began life as a novel, but Stendhal soon realised that neither fiction nor the formality of a discursive treatise could even half-do what can only be half-done anyway; and so the aleatory, divagatory, wandering method of *On Love* formed itself by accident out of the way Stendhal wrote it – out of notes and anecdotes, observations and ventriloquised 'diary' entries and reminiscences. The result works; this is a gem of literature, one of many possible windows into the human soul, a book one must at some point read and meditate upon, even if – in the larger scheme of things – it is more a comment by the way than the last and definitive word on its eternal subject.

Science and Rationality

Is science a 'faith-based belief system'?

In a *New York Times* opinion piece, physicist Paul Davies, Templeton Prize-winning believer that the universe is 'meaningful and purposive' (a claim that the very wealthy and religion-motivated Templeton Foundation uses its money to try to encourage scientists to make), asserts that it is a mistake to distinguish science from religion by describing the former as based on testable hypotheses while the latter is based on faith. 'The problem with this neat separation,' he says, 'is that science has its own faith-based belief system.' He does not seem especially clear about what he means by this, given that he begins by describing scientific faith as 'the assumption that nature is ordered in a rational and intelligible way', but soon shifts to describing it as 'belief in the existence of something outside the universe, like . . . [an] unexplained set of physical laws'. Either way the failure or refusal to explain the 'source' of physical laws is, he says, to regard nature as 'rooted in reasonless absurdity'.

The brevity of his piece does not allow Davies to offer his now familiar suggestion that the universe is 'self-conscious' or contains a 'life principle' which obliges the laws of physics to take a form necessary for the existence of intelligent life. There are half a dozen competing suggestions, most of them better than this one, as to why the universe's (or this universe's) parameters are as they are, and even the one that says 'it is just a bald fact that they are so' does not merit Davies's tendentious description as a commitment to 'reasonless absurdity', given that it is a perfectly consistent possible truth which only seems unsatisfactory to the pattern-seeking, reason-requiring impulse with which evolution has endowed the human mind.

Davies could not be more wrong in describing as 'an act of faith' science's assumption that the universe is orderly and intelligible. Patterns and regularities are a salient feature of nature, even to casual observation, and well motivate the assumption that they hold generally, or when they fail to hold do so for likewise orderly reasons. Once thus made, the assumption is then powerfully justified by the success of premising it in making testable predictions.

Making well-motivated, evidence-based assumptions that are in turn supported by the efficacy of their employment in testing predictions is the very opposite of faith. Faith is commitment to belief in something either in the absence of evidence or in the face of countervailing evidence. It is accounted a 'theological virtue' precisely for this reason, as the New Testament story of Doubting Thomas is designed to illustrate. In everyday speech we use the phrase 'he took it on faith' to mean 'without question, without examining the grounds'; which captures its essence.

If the assumption of nature's orderliness frequently or haphazardly failed to be borne out we would register the fact, supposing that we survived the mistake in the first place. True, this amounts to offering inductive support for induction; but not all explanatory circles are vicious, as shown by the fact that it is a mark of irrationality not to rely on the success of past inductions in a present one. To see why, imagine saying: 'Every time I have been out in the rain without an umbrella in the past I have got wet; but inductive reasoning is fallible, so perhaps this time I will stay dry.'

The public and repeatable testing of hypotheses distinguishes science as the most successful form of enquiry ever, and among other things shows that it is officially not in the business of accepting anything 'without question, without examining the grounds'. Davies and others who describe science as 'ultimately resting on faith' are thus not only wrong, but do much irresponsible harm thereby.

Education and the Internet

*Given that the Internet contains much error and
absurd opinion, how can it be made a reliable
resource for education and research?*

Speech, drawing, writing, mathematics, printing, photo-
graphy, telegraphy, film, radio, television, Internet: each
of these words denotes a seminal stage in the history of
information-transfer, each representing a large leap in power
and range over the preceding stage. The gaps between stages
have shortened from millennia to decades to years; the graph
representing the speed of development rises ever more steeply.

The extent of changes to human society and experience
promised by the Internet, and by mobile electronic
communication generally, is still unclear, although many that it
has already produced are now commonplaces – even necessities
– of daily life, such as email, Facebook, Google, Skype, Twitter.
All one's work, entertainment and communications can already
be concentrated upon one small portable device. Although for
good reasons many people still congregate in workplaces and
educational centres, how long will this last? Travel to one's
computer terminal in an office miles away, instead of working
on it at home, will soon become a comparatively rare thing as
transport difficulties and their environmental impacts grow.

One of the greatest promises of the Internet relates to
education. The benefits are obvious: one teacher online can
instruct millions of pupils. There are serious disadvantages,
involving the lack of individual teacher–pupil engagement;
but a mixture of online and traditional education can reduce
that problem.

The Internet will also be one major way of delivering 'digital immersion learning' to students. This is learning that uses virtual-world-creating devices to give students a sense of being fully and realistically inside an environment so that they can learn more directly by participation. They can 'experience' historical events, fly like a bird over continents, through planetary systems, into cells and molecules: Xbox games are a rudimentary indication of the possibilities.

But before the Internet can be confidently utilised as an educational tool, some of its more serious problems have to be addressed, chief among them the unreliability of so much of the information it contains.

Here is a minor but telling example. Suppose you wish to trace the author and context of a quotation you have encountered, 'Look thy last on all things lovely.' At the time of writing this, the very first web page cited by Google attributes it to the poet Austin Dobson. This mistake is soon corrected; it comes from a Walter de la Mare poem, and all the following web references say so.

The last stanza of this poem begins, 'Look thy last on all things lovely / Every hour. Let no night seal thy sense in deathly slumber / Till to delight thou have paid thy utmost blessing . . .' On the second Google page for this quotation this is rendered as, 'Look thy last on all things lovely. Every hour. Let no night. Seal thy sense in deathly slumber. Till to delight. Thou have paid thy utmost blessing . . .' There is what appears to be a solecism in this last line: should 'thou have paid' read 'thou hast paid'? – but the grammatical choice is the poet's, not the transcriber's; and some of the web pages silently change it according to the transcriber's own grammatical intuitions. (On standard views it is not a solecism, though it is at least musically unfortunate.)

Transcription mistakes abound on different web pages: 'let not night' for 'let no night', 'senses' for 'sense', and so on: a minor matter here, but not in a mathematical or chemical formula.

This example could be multiplied endlessly. The lesson is that if the Internet is to be confidently used as an educational resource, either its content needs to be audited for reliability, or its users have to be made skilful in evaluating the worth of what they find there. Given that the Internet is already the main resource for students, the need for one or both of these is beyond urgent.

The first might be done by the introduction of a system of classification. One suggestion is that an international consortium of universities should set up subject panels to check the worth of websites, endorsing those that are reliable. They should not censor, nor comment on matters of opinion; the price we pay for the Internet's open democracy is the rubbish it contains. But they could authoritatively identify some of the more worthwhile sites, and warn of factual error when it occurs.

The second might be done by – well, by educating students. The paradox here is an unavoidable one. Just as one is a better acquirer of knowledge if one is already knowledgeable, so one is a better evaluator of the worth of information if one is informed. Actually, as a moment's reflection shows, the paradox here is only a seeming-paradox; the point is that the knowledgeable and informed are thereby primed to become readily more so, whereas the ignorant and uninformed are disabled by being so from recognising and attaching new information. The more hooks you have to hang things on, the more things you will hang on them. By the same token, knowing a lot helps one to sort good websites from less good ones, because one will more readily spot errors, infelicities, unsubstantiated claims, improbabilities, nonsense, discordances, bias, tendentiousness, agendas, and the like, and one will know how to check facts, quickly and efficiently, because an education teaches one among other things how to get better educated.

Either way, without some such expert monitoring, whether provided by reliable bodies or by users of the Internet themselves, the Internet will increasingly be a problem rather than a boon, and limited in educational value therefore.

Knowing That and Knowing How

Which is more important: knowing facts, or knowing methods?

Philosophers thinking about the nature of knowledge – their starting questions in this connection are: what is knowledge, and what are the best methods for getting it? – have always distinguished between knowledge of facts and knowledge of techniques. Knowing that Everest is the highest mountain, and knowing how to measure the height of mountains, are respective examples of the two kinds of knowledge; and the interesting question is: which is more important?

Obviously enough, an education system worth the name should equip people with both kinds of knowledge, for both are important. But it is still pointful to ask which is more so, for the equally obvious reason that no head can first cram in, and then later recall at need, everything that passes as currently accepted fact; and anyway the number of currently accepted facts is tiny in comparison to what we know we still do not know, itself in turn probably a tiny fraction of what might be knowable.

So although everyone coming out of an educational system should at very least know what the periodic table is, the salient dates of world history, the fundamentals of geography, and other kinds of basic information, they are greatly more in need of knowing how to find things out, how to evaluate the information they discover, and then how to apply it fruitfully. These are skills; they involve a flexible and creative grasp of methods.

Acquiring information is now easier than it has ever been, because of the Internet. We still teach research skills in higher education, and in both the sciences and the humanities – though in ways particular to each – there is much that can be taught. In the sciences, laboratory technique and experiment design and methodology are fundamental; in the humanities, the use of libraries and archives, the handling of documents, and such arcane things as calligraphic decipherment, are part of the basic tool-kit. This is all part of the machinery of how information is acquired.

The trouble is that quantity of data, especially data available online, is no guarantee of quality. Especially with online data there is no expert filter that weeds out bad information and misinformation. The only protection against either is the care taken by Internet users themselves. In one way it is no bad thing that the Internet is such a democratic domain, where opinions and claims can get an unfettered airing in most parts of the world. Censorship could easily masquerade as expert filtering. But this increases the necessity for Internet users to be good at discriminating between high- and low-quality information, and reliable and unreliable sources of it.

Knowing how to get and evaluate information, therefore, is arguably the most important kind of knowledge that education has to offer. It involves skills of sifting evidence, interpreting it, reasoning about it, asking the right questions, and always challenging and thinking rigorously. The best seekers after knowledge have always had, by instinct or experience, the forensic ability to be sceptical and acute in assessing data. But it is no longer enough for there to be just some people who are good at it: everyone needs to be likewise.

The requirement is for education systems to include, as a central component, critical thinking and research methodology. The processes of alert enquiry are key; T. S. Eliot wrote, 'There is no method other than to be intelligent.' Of course people should learn the basic skills of literacy and numeracy, and the framework facts of history, geography and science; that goes without saying. But along with it, all the way to an advanced level, there has to be training in the forensic skills of enquiry, without which education is incomplete.

Robots

Should we be afraid of the approaching army of robots?

In this age of super-rapid technological advance we do well to obey the Boy Scout injunction, 'Be Prepared.' That requires nimbleness of mind given that the ever-accelerating growth of computing power is being applied across such a wide range of developments, making it hard to keep track of everything simultaneously. The danger is that we only wake to the necessity for forethought when in the midst of a storm created by innovations that have overtaken us already.

We are on the brink, and perhaps to some degree already over the edge, in one hugely important respect, which until now has been the province of experts only: robotics. Robot sentries patrol the borders of Korea and Israel. Remote-controlled aircraft mount missile attacks on enemy positions. Other military robots are already in service, and not just for defusing bombs or detecting landmines; a coming generation of autonomous combat robots capable of deep-penetration operations in enemy territory raises questions about whether they will be able to discriminate between soldiers and innocents. (Fears have already been raised that because such robots will refuel themselves by consuming biomass, they will do it by 'eating' the corpses of soldiers – or civilians – killed by their firepower.) Police forces are seeking to acquire miniature Taser-firing robot helicopters. In Korea and Japan the development of robots for feeding and bathing the elderly and children, sounding the alarm if they fall or cry, and performing various household duties, is already advanced. Even in a robot-backward country like the UK some vacuum cleaners sense their autonomous way around furniture as they clean. A driverless car has already made the journey through Los Angeles traffic.

In the next decades completely autonomous robots might be involved in many military, policing, transport and even caring roles. What if they malfunction? What if a programming glitch makes them kill, Taser, demolish, drown, overheat and explode, fail at the crucial moment? Whose insurance will pay for damage to furniture, other traffic, or the baby, when things go wrong – the software company, the manufacturer, the owner?

Most thinking about the implications of robotics tends to take sci-fi forms, in which robots enslave humankind, or in which beautifully sculpted humanoid robots have sex with their owners and then post-coitally tidy the room and make coffee. But the real concern is where the money already flows: to militaries and police forces.

A confused controversy arose in early 2008 over the deployment of three Special Weapons (SWORDS) vehicles carrying M249 light machine guns in Iraq. Coalition military authorities said that the robots were never used in combat and that they were involved in 'no uncommanded or unexpected movements'. But rumours abounded about the reason why funding for the SWORDS programme was abruptly stopped after the deployment of these vehicles. This case prompts one to prick up one's ears: news about Predator drones carrying out missile attacks in Afghanistan and Pakistan are now commonplace, and there are at least another dozen military robot projects in full development. What are the rules governing their deployment? How reliable are they? One sees their advantages: they save the lives of one's own troops, and can fight more effectively than human combatants in many circumstances and environments. But what are the limits, especially when these machines become autonomous?

The civil-liberties implications of robot police devices capable of surveillance work involving listening and photographing, conducting search operations, entering premises through chimneys or sewage pipes, and overpowering and guarding suspects, are obvious. Some of these devices are already on the way.

Even more frighteningly obvious is the threat posed by military or police-type robots in the hands of criminals and terrorists.

So there has to be a considered debate about the rules and requirements governing all forms of robot devices, not a panic reaction when matters have gone too far, which is how bad law is made. On this issue, midnight is already striking.

And yet the beneficial possibilities of robotics are obvious and many. It cannot be beyond the wit of mankind to harvest those benefits and guard against what the scare-stories and anxieties suggest. For we also have to guard against frightening ourselves away from beneficial developments by taking negative scenarios as the main prompt of our actions.

Gender and Sex

Is it not time to recognise the existence of a third sex: an intersex?

The story of Dr James Barry is an extraordinary one. Barry was a 'pint-sized squeaky-voiced' nineteenth-century British Army surgeon who was discovered on death to be a woman – or so claimed the charwoman who prepared the doctor's body for burial. If the claim is true, Barry's story represents one triumphant response to the sexism that kept women out of the medical profession which had in fact – centuries before – once been exclusively theirs.

Quite a few women have dressed as men to escape the social disabilities of their sex in their time. Some enlisted as soldiers: Ann Mills was a dragoon and Hannah Snell a Royal Marine, both in the eighteenth century, and journalist Dorothy Lawrence joined up in man's clothes to fight in the First World War. Others had other reasons; 1930s jazz musician Billy Tipton married five times and was discovered to be a woman only after his death, as happened also with singer Wilmer Broadnax.

Some of these cross-dressers might have had the further reason that although anatomically female, they felt themselves to be male in gender, as some individuals who are anatomically male feel themselves to be female. The distinction now made between sex and gender is a helpful one, because it allows us to accommodate the fact that humankind does not divide neatly into male and female, but in its protean diversity admits of a spectrum between.

This is a fact that has only recently come to be well enough understood to challenge the often harmful medicalisation of sex ambiguity and gradation which began in earnest in the nineteenth century and culminated in the 1950s with the 'optimum gender of rearing' system developed at Johns Hopkins University. This system encouraged 'gender assignment', including surgical intervention, at the earliest possible stage in life to encourage the effective socialisation of the resulting individual into his or her 'assigned' gender.

The sheer complexity of sex and gender is now well enough understood for the Hopkins 'optimum gender' system to be no longer acceptable. Anne Fausto-Sterling of Brown University studied the literature on sex variations (see her book *Sexing the Body*, 2000) and found that as many as one in 100 people have bodies that differ from the male and female standards, if one includes XX and XY chromosomal abnormalities such as chromosomal mosaicism and the Klinefelter and Turner syndromes, androgen-insensitivity syndrome, adrenal hyperplasias, ovo-testes (formerly so-called 'true hermaphroditism'), genital agenesis, 5 alpha reductase deficiency, gonadal dysgenesis (Swyer syndrome), hypospadias, iatrogenic influences (for example, medical mistakes in pregnancy), and more.

The fact that there is a spectrum of sex identities was brought home to me by a brilliant pupil I had at Oxford, who after studying philosophy there as a Dominican monk in the 1980s came to the realisation that she was not male but intersexed, yet not only could not achieve recognition as such, but paradoxically had to struggle to be redescribed as female for so mundane a purpose as getting a passport. On being informally advised to undergo 'genital disambiguation' surgery to solve the problem, she realised that she had in effect ceased to exist in law as a person. This prompted her resolve to fight for the rights of intersexed persons to be recognised as such. Her brave endeavour, like that of the members of the Intersex Society of North America, promises to change the simplistic stereotyping that hides from view the realities of life for one whole tranche of humanity.

Gender and Research

Is there a gender bias in medical research?

When the first kidney dialysis machines became available they were so few in number that access to them was unavoidably rationed. That meant decisions had to be made about who was to benefit from them, and panels were formed to assess the merits of candidate patients. Famously, a review of the decision-making process found that the patients who received treatment tended to be noticeably similar in age, sex and social class to the people on the selection panels.

This discovery was an educative one, and it increased awareness about the biases that creep into choice-making, not least concerning which research projects are worth pursuing and where research funds should go. For example, it is often pointed out that diseases that afflict better-off Westerners are more intensively researched than those afflicting people in what used to be called 'Third World countries', especially in sub-Saharan Africa. In fact it is not just tropical diseases that get less attention, but treatment of curable conditions and provision of prophylactic measures such as sanitation, clean water supply, vaccines and condoms.

But it is not necessary to travel to Africa to be reminded of how bias affects what gets researched. Many states spend more on 'defence procurement and development' – on arms – than on other forms of technology or on scientific and medical research. More telling yet is the fact that even in advanced economies relatively little research spending goes on health problems that are specifically female.

Take for example the sometimes severely life-affecting experience of 'hot flushes' (in the US, 'hot flashes') experienced by women undergoing menopause. This is one of the commonest features of the climacteric, and is widely recognised as such in the medical profession, and yet its physiology and aetiology are still not understood, and the best that can be done to help women who suffer from it is general advice about management of its symptoms.

Menopausal hot flushes are unlike other flushing phenomena such as blushing. Increased heart rate and peripheral blood flow are uniquely accompanied by decrease in galvanic skin resistance, which makes the combination of symptoms diagnostic. Such research as there has been implicates disturbance of the temperature control mechanism in the hypothalamus, and recognises the critical role of reduced circulating levels of oestrogen; but just how the latter causes the former, and what other mechanisms are involved, remain a mystery.

Matters are complicated by the finding that other factors appear to be in play also. Women in the Far East do not have hot flushes with the frequency and severity of women in Western countries, prompting questions about genetics and diet – is it either, or is it both? For example, tofu, derived from soy, and soy sauce are staples in the Eastern diet, and soy is high in phytoestrogens. A few studies have been done to see whether supplementing the Western diet with phytoestrogens could work as an alternative to hormone replacement therapy. Results have been disappointing, and claims about the benefits and disbenefits of phytoestrogens on other aspects of health have been ambiguous.

Women are left with the advice to drink less alcohol and coffee, to avoid eating curries, and (best of all, because it is said without irony) to keep cool. Such advice might help somewhat, but not nearly as much as a serious endeavour to understand the complex physiological mechanisms at work. It is too tempting to remark, 'If men underwent menopause . . .' but a major reason for the lack of attention is that hot flushes are not life-threatening as well as not masculine, a combination that too frequently makes for neglect.

As this shows, gender is indeed an influence on the allocation of medical research resources: it is Western males who benefit most.

Scientific Literacy

Does it matter whether or not the results and methods
of science are better known to the general public?

More than twenty years ago the American Association for the Advancement of Science (AAAS) published a book called *Science for All Americans* (1989) to address what it recognised as a pressing need for greater scientific literacy in the general population. Better awareness of scientific ideas and ways of thinking was required, it said, to help people understand how science and technology are shaping our world, because without that understanding they would be less able to take part in decisions about such challenges as climate change and the ethics of new medical advances.

The urgency felt by the AAAS two decades ago was prompted by alarming statistics about the decline in scientific literacy during the preceding quarter-century, as measured by high-school student performance and polling on levels of public informedness. That decline was not unique to the United States, and little has happened to reverse it, despite the fact that scientific and technological advances have accumulated with increasing rapidity since. Today the idea of democratic debate about the promises and perils of scientific advances is almost empty, or at best comes to life only when particular problems arise, usually in crude and simplistic form, about such matters as stem-cell research, genetically modified food crops, or surveillance technologies that threaten civil liberties.

Keeping abreast of what is happening in science and technology should be a matter of course for thoughtful people, no matter what their educational background or occupation. There is no excuse for people to be ill informed in view of the many quality magazines and books that make awareness of science possible for those without formal training in it. Active engagement in any branch of science of course requires expertise, but an intelligent appreciation of reports about the outcomes, significance and possible applications of research does not.

This is one part of what is meant by scientific literacy. Another is being able to use relevant aspects of science awareness in decisions about one's own health, exercise, diet and personal responsibility for the environment (such as domestic recycling and energy use). A third and equally important part is being able to take a responsible – because informed – stance on issues that vex society, such as reproductive technologies, public policy affecting the environment, use of certain kinds of military and security technologies, and ethical dilemmas over health-care resources and techniques – a stance that might, for example, influence how one votes.

In 1995 the US National Academy of Science defined scientific literacy as 'knowledge and understanding of the scientific concepts and processes required for personal decision making, participation in civic and cultural affairs, and economic productivity'. This is a good but limited definition, which only partly overlaps the one just suggested, and it leaves entirely out of account the biggest boon that scientific literacy can confer: the development of rational attitudes.

By this I mean the kind of healthy scepticism that asks for good evidence and good argument, that applies critical scrutiny to propositions or claims, that suspends judgement while the evidence is pending, and accepts what the evidence says once it has arrived, independently of prior wishes or partisan beliefs.

There is nothing idealised or utopian about this sketch of the scientific mindset, which simply describes it at its workaday best. In an age of resurgent irrationalism, in which assertive religious constituencies promote world-views and ethical outlooks that run diametrically counter to science – think creationism and opposition to therapeutic cloning – scientific rationality is at a premium. Yet fewer and fewer people can appreciate what that means: which is why promoting general scientific literacy has become more urgent than ever.

Personal Identity

What makes an individual the same person at any point in his life as he was at an earlier point?

After John Locke published his *Essay Concerning Human Understanding* in 1690 he sent copies to various savants of his acquaintance, asking for comments, and in particular for advice on whether he had left out anything essential – for if so, he said, he would add it to a second addition. His correspondent William Molyneaux of Dublin replied that Locke needed to say something about personal identity, that is, what makes a person the same person throughout life.

Belief in the idea of a substantial soul was waning; in the absence of this metaphysical entity as a convenience for underpinning personal identity, what – asked Molyneaux – makes the retired general continuous with the eager subaltern of forty years before, and he in turn with the red-cheeked baby in his nurse's arms twenty years before that? In response Locke added a chapter to his second edition – Chapter 27 of Book II – which instantly caused a storm of controversy, and has ever since been famous in the annals of philosophy.

In that chapter Locke argued that a person's identity over time consists in his consciousness (he coined this term, and thereby introduced it to the English language) of being the same self at a later time as at an earlier, and that the mechanism that makes this possible is memory. Whereas a stone is the same stone over time because it is the very same lump of matter (or almost, allowing for erosion), and an oak tree is identical with its originating acorn because it is the same continuous organisation of matter, a person is only the same through time if he is self-aware of being so. Memory loss interrupts identity, and complete loss of memory is therefore loss of the self.

The divines (represented by Bishop Stillingfleet) took umbrage, and attacked Locke for dispensing with the idea of an immortal soul. In 1712 *The Spectator* magazine ran a front-cover demand that 'the wits of Kingdom' should get together in conference to settle the matter of personal identity and selfhood, because the controversy was getting out of control. One result of their challenge was an hilarious (and rather obscene) spoof memoir by 'Martinus Scriblerus', written by the members of a group of friends including John Gay, Alexander Pope, Viscount Bolingbroke and Queen Anne's physician

John Arbuthnot, in which the problem of personal identity is explored through a court case over a pair of Siamese twins.

In 1739, when David Hume published the first volume of his *Treatise of Human Nature*, he stated that there is no such thing as the self, for if one conducts the empirical enquiry of introspecting – looking within oneself – to see what there is apart from current sensations, feelings, desires and thoughts, one does not find an extra something, a 'self', over and above these things, which owns them and endures beyond them.

Thus in fifty years the unreflective idea that each individual has an immortal soul as the basis of his selfhood had changed utterly. For millennia before Locke no one had so much as raised the question. But it was no surprise that the question should suddenly become urgent as the Enlightenment dawned, with its central idea of the autonomous individual who is a bearer of rights and who is responsible for his own moral outlook; such an idea needs a robust idea of selfhood, and the philosophers eagerly tried to make sense of it.

Hume's sceptical view did not prevail. Kant argued that logic requires a concept-imposing self to make experience possible, and the Romantics made the self the centre of each individual's universe: 'I am that which began,' wrote Swinburne in 'Hertha', 'Out of me the years roll, out of me God and Man.' Without a deep idea of the self there could be no Freud or psychoanalysis.

So fundamental is the idea of the self to modern human consciousness that one would expect developments in neuroscience to have a direct bearing on it. And that is exactly what is happening, with surprising and often disconcerting results. Some neuroscientists argue that there is nothing in the organisation of the brain, no structure or locus of activity there, which can plausibly be identified as the seat of a sense of self. Yet there is indubitably a phenomenological sense of self that neuroscience must somehow account for; we 'feel' that we are individual selves, centres of our experience and memory, owners of our plans and hopes, identifiable to others and ourselves by our interests, character traits, sense of humour and reactions. The fact that no single region of the brain has (yet) been identified as processing representations of the self does not rule out the possibility that there is one such. More likely is the possibility that if 'the self' denotes something discoverable in the brain or its activity, it is the result of co-ordination among multiple distributed brain centres.

Though workers in cognitive and social neuroscience are, at this time of writing, busy investigating what if anything in the brain or its workings gives rise to the vivid phenomenology of selfhood, critics and sceptics argue that the research tools they use, such as functional Magnetic Resonance Imaging (fMRI), are so far just a sophisticated form of phrenology, insufficiently fine-grained to capture the realities of subjective self-awareness. If nothing else, the barb shows that the jury is still out on one of the most important topics known to both philosophy and science.

Brain and Mind

Is the mind all in the brain?

Unquestionably, the brain is a marvel. In the most ordinary of heads it performs miracles of complexity every second. Equally marvellous is how much we have come to know about brains, though – as always with the growth of knowledge – we have also learned how much more we need to learn.

The great mystery remains, though: how the intricate, super-fast, vastly complex interactions of the brain's billions of neurons through trillions of connections give rise to mind. There are many familiar ways of describing the puzzle, but the simplest is to say that physical occurrences in the brain have physical properties – a position in space as well as a duration in time, a measurable intensity, the involvement of a specifiable set of physiological structures – whereas thoughts (say, about sub-prime mortgages or the political situation in Bulgaria) do not: they do not have a weight, or a colour, or a scent, or any other such physical property.

This was once taken to be a reason for thinking that mind and body are separate and wholly different things, creating the larger mystery of how they interact. Now hardly anyone seriously takes such a view, and so the mystery is, instead, how brain activity secretes the rich, brightly coloured phenomenology of experience, the tangled hidden world of unconscious mentation, and the enduring patterns of character and memory that make individuals unique.

According to one influential school of thought, some of the ways we think about minds have to go beyond our investigations of what is inside our heads to include the physical and social environment surrounding our heads. This idea is prompted by the thought that what we know when we understand a concept has to involve a connection between a brain event and something in the world.

For an obvious example: to understand the concept of a flower, and to be able to distinguish between flowers and other things – trees and buildings, say – the relevant physiological occurrences inside the head have to stand in a determinate relationship with flowers and non-flowers outside the head. This relationship, again obviously, is empirical: an actual perceptual encounter between the head's owner and flowers, or at least pictures of flowers, must have taken place at some point.

But a less obvious aspect of having a concept of flowers is that whenever we think or talk of flowers, the relationship between what is happening inside our heads and flowers outside our heads has to remain in some form, in order for our discourse correctly to be about flowers rather than some other thing. Nothing mysterious or magical is implied by this; it just means that to explain the thought of a flower, as distinct from a thought of anything else, reference to flowers out there in the world is unavoidable.

The idea that thought is thus *essentially* connected to the outside world is intended to illustrate the more general idea that 'mind' is not solely describable in terms of brain activity alone, but must be understood as a relationship between that activity and the external social and physical environment. Philosophers give the name 'broad content' to thoughts that can only be properly described in terms of their thinkers' relations to the environment, and some argue that there can be no such thing as 'narrow content' – that is, thoughts specifiable independently of their thinkers' environments but just in terms of what is going on inside the skull.

If it is right that there can only be 'broad content', the implications are very great: it means that understanding minds involves much more than understanding brains alone: it involves understanding language, society and history too.

This is a thought that seems obvious enough when exploring anything to do with culture and creativity. In seeking to understand an artist, say, we naturally look to the influences, the historical circumstances, the experiences that contributed to shaping him or her. Yet in thinking about how brains produce mental phenomena, we tend to downplay the significance of the environment of the head in which the brain is housed. Consider: even in connection with the psychophysiology of perception, the nature of the distal end of the perceptual relationship is specified only minimally, and the equipment inside the head – optic nerves, the visual cortex – is the main focus. Of course, to understand vision so it should be; and perhaps there is no more to be said about what stimulates the retina's rods and cones and the firing of the optic nerves than that incoming light vibrates with such-and-such frequencies. But understanding vision is not yet understanding visual perception. For note that we never just see, but always 'see as'; concepts are always deployed in visual experience; and these concepts are of what exists beyond the lens of the eye, out there in the surrounding world. Recognising this is the motivation for saying that understanding mind, as opposed to the brain that gives rise to it, requires a 'broad content' approach.

Climate Change

Why does climate change not prompt more alarm?

In the blue flicker of television screens in hundreds of thousands of living rooms, silently staring faces are told the news: we are at war with terrorists, so the government will subject us all to new surveillance measures; we are at war over drugs, but here is an advert for whiskey; if you cannot pay your mortgage you will be out on the street, but if you are a banker who has lost billions of other people's money, the government will bail you out – and so paradoxically on. Occasionally there is mention of the impending end of the planet as we know it, but somewhat in passing, as if it did not quite matter, or were not quite true.

Why has climate change not prompted more alarm? One reason is that we do not wish to believe it. Believing it means serious and inconvenient changes to our lifestyles. Another reason is that there are plenty of vested interests who do not encourage us to believe it, and do not encourage themselves to believe it either: they include commerce and industry, and governments aiming for re-election and reluctant to impose inconveniences on voters.

Also, we are all waiting for a miracle to happen, in the form of people in white lab coats coming up with a quick, easy, inexpensive technological fix. Or perhaps we hope to wake up one day and find it was all just a bad dream.

Advertisers and politicians know that the trick to influencing attitudes and actions is to find a way of communicating lots of meaning quickly and above all simply. Commercial marketing relies on the logo and the advertising jingle. Political parties rely on the sloganised message, and for their opponents a jibe or accusation that resonates with the public. For example, one of the most famous political advertisements of recent times was a picture of a dole queue and the legend 'Labour isn't working': a stroke of genius that won an election. For another example, critics of ex-President George W. Bush call him 'Dubya', instantly projecting the image of a clumsy and inarticulate fool stumbling about in a china shop.

Science needs to find ways of speaking to the world with the same impact, especially when it is trying to save the world. On climate change it needs a resonant image, accurate but simple, to achieve this. And perhaps at last it has found it: by dramatising the greenhouse effect for non-specialists in terms of 'the bathtub effect'. This likens the world to a bath into which water is pouring from open taps twice as fast as it can drain away. The water is CO_2 from burning fossil fuels and chopping down forests. The drain is plants and oceans. The drain is getting clogged – the plants and oceans are becoming CO_2-saturated. The bathroom is heading for a flood.

In fact things are worse. The carbon-emissions policies bandied about by governments of polluting countries appear to assume that if you turn down the taps, the water can be made to enter at a more manageable rate for it to drain, and all will be well. Alas, there is a significant point to be grasped: that the taps are stiff and take a long time to turn, and that because of the weight of water already in the bath, the drain is close to being blocked. Already, therefore, there might be no way of preventing a flood.

Even the most pessimistic climate scientists think we should try to reduce carbon emissions nonetheless. It might only moderate rather than avoid catastrophe: but it is not rational to do nothing. The bathtub analogy might be just what is needed to get attitudes, and especially habits, *really* changing at last.

Another way to drive home the dangers faced by humanity is to require parents to think about what their children will have to cope with when they are adults. We are living on their future, consuming it now at a potentially disastrous cost to them. No one would allow his or her child to pick up a viper in the garden; we are tipping vipers into their future bedrooms as they sleep.

It is claimed by some that the danger of climate change is a danger only to mankind and some other species, but not to the planet itself or life as such, which in one or another way will survive. Past catastrophes have seen different species arise and flourish at the expense of those that became extinct. Might it not, some say, be an advantage to the planet if greedy, over-consuming, careless and destructive humanity vanished?

Those who pose this question probably do not have children and grandchildren, even though, uncomfortably, they have a point. But it is a point that leaves out of account the value that humanity's existence has brought into being, which has to be counted along with the disvalue in a final summation of what humankind and its history is worth, and whether it is worth preserving.

Ape and Man

Should apes be treated the same as humans in ethical respects?

A few minutes at the zoo is enough to convince most people that apes and monkeys are close kin to humankind. Some say that a few minutes watching proceedings in any parliament is enough to show that humans are close kin to monkeys and apes. Either way, we know that the primate family is a genetically intimate one, and this is especially so for the great apes – gorillas, chimpanzees, bonobos, orang-utans and humans.

It did not take genetics to tell us this, or comparative anatomy. After all, genetics tell us that we share many of our genes with insects, and the anatomies of all mammals are just resized and repositioned versions of each other. The key to the true closeness of all apes, ourselves included, is ethology. When Jane Goodall first sat in the Gombe rainforest, with fortuitous naivety giving anthropomorphic interpretations of the chimpanzee behaviour she witnessed, she was initiating a rethink: about apes, about humanity's relationship with them, and ultimately about humanity itself.

A lot has happened since Goodall's first forays at Gombe: not only has primate ethology flourished in the last half-century, but it has influenced sociobiology and evolutionary psychology, and perhaps most importantly for apes themselves it has been a stimulus for the Great Ape Project, which aims to secure a United Nations declaration granting non-human apes entitlements to life, liberty and freedom from torture and experimentation.

The Great Ape Project was launched in 1993 with the publication of a book edited by Peter Singer and Paola Cavalieri, and among the distinguished scientists who supported it were Richard Dawkins and Jane Goodall herself. Central to the project's argument is the fact – established by the work begun by Goodall – that great apes have complex social, emotional and cognitive lives, with self-awareness and capacities for affection and grief. Their genetic proximity to humans also of course counts as relevant: chimps and humans differ in only 1.2 per cent of genes.

In 2008 the European Union published a long-awaited set of proposals about regulation of research that uses animals, and one main plank in it is that all medical research on great apes is to be banned. Studies of great-ape behaviour, and research that would protect great-ape species from extinction, will continue to be allowed; and there is an exception for circumstances in which serious epidemic disease might threaten humankind. But though there has been little experimentation on great apes for some time now, the ban is a remarkable achievement, and a marker on the road to greater protections for all animals used for research.

This last remark is not intended to imply that matters have not greatly improved in this respect, for they have. To see how dramatically this is so, consider: in one of his letters the seventeenth-century philosopher René Descartes recommends slicing off the apex of a living dog's heart and inserting a finger to feel the strong contractions of the cardiac muscle. For a long time his approach to the use of animals was the norm. He regarded them as automata, without sensation or emotion; the appearance of both, he claimed, was a function of the robotic activity of their central nervous systems, which, unlike that in man, were not connected to conscious experience. His views in this respect were partly motivated by theological considerations: animals do not go to heaven when they die because they have no souls; if they have no souls, they do not think and feel; ergo one can practise vivisection on them, and ignore their manifestations of agony and distress as mere automatic play-acting.

In our more enlightened age animal experimentation is governed by the 'Three Rs' requirement: Reducing the number of animals used in research; Refining experimental techniques to minimise animal suffering; Replacing animals with alternatives whenever possible. But no campaigner for animal welfare can be quite satisfied even with this, sensible and progressive though it is. For as knowledge increases, so do doubts about the ethics of using any mammal, and even crustaceans – evidence exists that lobsters and crabs can experience pain, which makes one shudder at the thought of those lobsters in the restaurant window, nippers held with elastic bands, waiting to be thrown into a deep pot of boiling water. It makes one think.

And once one starts thus thinking about ethical boundaries, one begins to see that they are best drawn as far out as possible.

Synecology

Humanity's relationship to the rest of life on earth is generally bad news for life on earth. But could that relationship itself save mankind from extinction?

It is old news to say that life on earth constitutes an intricate web of interconnections so mutually crucial to each of the many elements involved that disruption to one can be catastrophic to others. This is the basic concept of ecology, and especially of synecology (the ecology of communities of species living together).

But it is not old news to be reminded that there is almost no place on earth where we know everything about all the species inhabiting it, from its largest plants and animals to microbes and viruses, or therefore the relationships that exist between them – and, by extension, among all things in the biosphere generally.

We discover some remarkable synecological facts, such as the relationship between Africa's whistling thorn tree and the fierce 'biting ant' that lives upon it. In return for nesting sites and nectar, the ants defend the tree against grazing mammals by swarming to the attack when one approaches. Researchers found that if they simulated the extinction of grazing mammals, the ant–tree relationship ends, as if the trees were terminating their now unnecessary contract with their bodyguards.

Another remarkable mutuality is that between domesticated dogs and humans. At the Canine Science Forum in Budapest in July 2008 discussion of canine psychology revealed that what we often dismiss as merely metaphoric attributions of human-like mental states to dogs – a sense of guilt, of fairness, of grasp of social complexities in relations with humans – might after all be an accurate representation of what goes on in dog minds. And the suggestion is that this is a canine evolutionary adaptation caused by 10,000 years of close human–dog cohabitation and the selective breeding involved.

Whereas the ant–tree relationship is by now the kind of thing one expects to find in an ecosystem, the dog-psychology suggestion is more fertile ground for speculation. Mutuality is a two-way street: have humans been evolutionarily influenced psychologically and physically by their relationship with dogs? Humans have more and less close relations with a number of other animals such as cats, horses and cattle; what are the evolutionary reciprocities there? For millennia humans and domesticated animals have shared the same habitations, breathed each other's breath all night long, exchanged viruses and bacteria – influenza is an annual gift to mankind from China's pigs – and eaten each other's body products in different forms (we their flesh, they our excrement: this latter a delicacy for pigs, for example).

The net might be cast wider. Humans are what they are in important part because of the vegetation and climate of the period between 100,000 and 500,000 years ago. A glance at the landscape of Europe shows how hugely and quickly humans have transformed its ecology, and by extension their own place in its synecology. We are now discovering the unsustainability of this – for humans. Nature itself is not so lacking in robustness; the planet bears the scars of past catastrophes that annihilated many species, reshaped the land and changed its vegetation – but life adapts, continues and flourishes: it is not life itself that fails, only particular versions of it. Humans are busy endangering themselves and many other species in their suicidal plunge, but not life itself, which – for it has all the time in the world – will reassert itself in new forms when it is ready.

This contrast between the fragility of aspects of the present and the robustness of life overall is a hopeful one. But if we value any present life forms, ourselves included, perhaps we need to study synecology more carefully: those unexpected mutual relationships might offer some suggestions for survival.

Longevity

Can we cope with the dilemmas that will be posed if we find ways of postponing death?

From the ethical point of view, two scenarios offer themselves in connection with the future of death. One relates to a situation in which the average human lifespan grows ever longer, but without major solutions to ageing and its many attendant diseases and disabilities. The other relates to the simultaneous conquering both of death and the current downsides of ageing, so that people live healthy, well-functioning lives for 150 or 200 years or more.

In the first case there will have to be a debate about the moral legitimacy and manner of elective death, in the forms both of suicide and euthanasia, and the medical provision for them.

In the latter case there will have to be questions about restricting conception, pregnancy and birth, to avoid a global population catastrophe.

Either way, humanity will face even more severe versions of moral dilemmas that already vex us about almost everything related to birth and death.

Today, on the birth side of the question, we debate contraception, abortion, family size, childcare, suitability for parenthood, eugenics, sex selection, cloning, embryonic stem-cell use, and more.

On the death side of the question we debate physician-assisted suicide, voluntary and involuntary euthanasia, passive and active euthanasia (turning off life-support systems or electing not to resuscitate, withholding treatment for infections or cardiovascular crises when post-treatment quality of life is predicted to be nugatory), and more.

In these contemporary debates we have not reached a consensus, only some compromises, few of them stable and none of them uncontroversial. Longer lifespans will make at least one of these sets of questions vastly more pressing and more difficult. Are we ready for the intensified debate to come?

Prediction is of course a mug's game; remember the early days of flight, when people thought that because biplanes flew better than monoplanes, aircraft of the future would have twelve wings. But it is reasonable to suppose that lifespans will continue to increase dramatically as they are currently doing (by two years every decade) and that the conquest of ageing and its deficits will take time to catch up. So there will be a period when many countries have the burden of high proportions of diseased and disabled elderly people. In this period questions about the propriety and even the need for suicide and euthanasia, in most cases medically administered, will become agonisingly acute.

Then successes in gerontology will catch up, and negative aspects of longevity will diminish. Among other things this will refocus questions on reproduction. If women can have babies all through their lives until they are 150 or 200 years old, will there not be questions about how many babies each will be allowed to have? If birth is rationed, who will be allowed to reproduce, and who will have the authority to decide this? What effect will this have on women who will not be allowed to bear children? Will there need to be public policy decisions about, say, sterilising young girls whose genetic profile makes them unsuitable as mothers, to avoid accidents and subversive conceptions later? Such questions are every bit as agonisingly acute as questions about assisted death, and China has already illustrated the difficulties and the heartache that attend them.

In one way, questions of the former kind – about elective suicide and certain kinds of euthanasia (at least the voluntary and passive forms) – are somewhat less horrendous than questions about restricting reproduction, if only because many old and chronically ill people would prefer a medically eased death to a life that has become difficult, and certainly if it has become intolerable. The arguments for carefully legalised physician-assisted suicide are already overwhelmingly strong, and the practice of passive euthanasia is already widespread and largely accepted.

What one does not like the sound of, though, is the coerced deaths of old or ill people. Parity with forced sterility of women, a draconian-enough measure, raises the spectre of permission for suicide and euthanasia first becoming encouragement, then requirement, prompting chilling memories of Nazism.

In the light of deep qualms on this latter head, it is doubtful whether electively shortening lives in these ways will be an adequate solution to the longevity problem. The greater likelihood is that we will be faced with both the death and the birth dilemmas at once.

A third solution is to abandon our current practice of seeking to extend our lifetimes. Fried Mars Bars and a cigarette, anyone?

Water

Should there be an ethics of water use?

China is a country used to earthquakes, and it has often suffered very big ones. In July 1976 the coastal city of Tianjin was devastated by a massive earthquake, which cost more lives than any other earthquake in the twentieth century: in excess of a quarter of a million people died in the city and the Tangshan region surrounding it. The quake measured approximately 8 on the Richter scale; an aftershock of nearly the same magnitude sixteen hours after the main quake increased the death toll and further devastated weakened buildings, bridges and roads.

The Chinese province of Sichuan experienced an earthquake just as large in May 2008, also measuring 8 on the Richter scale. Seventy thousand people died, a quarter of a million were injured, and 4.8 million people were made homeless.

A look at the map provided by the United States Geological Survey Earthquake Hazards Program shows that the rim of the Pacific Ocean is the world's major earthquake zone. Indonesia, the East China Sea and the Japanese archipelago, the islands and promontories of the Bering Straits and Alaska, and the coast of California, are the hottest spots for earthquake activity severe enough to measure over 4.5 on the Richter scale. They are caused by tectonic movements around that vast ocean, illustrating how the earth's crust is a thin, fragile, mobile skin on the molten sphere of our planet, which is vigorous and alive within.

The Tianjin earthquake is probably attributable to the tectonic instability of the Pacific rim. The same explanation does not serve for the Sichuan quake, which occurred nearly 1,500 kilometres inland from China's east coast, and nearly as far from Lhasa in Tibet, which is worth mentioning because the Himalayas are themselves a focus of lively tectonic activity, for they are the result of the Asian plate being raised (at the same rate as one's fingernails grow) by the subduction of the Indian plate moving northwards beneath it.

The Sichuan earthquake, by contrast to both Pacific-rim and Himalayan earthquakes, might have a quite different cause. 'Sichuan' means 'four rivers', but the devastating quake there, together with its powerful aftershocks, dammed nine rivers and created twenty-four new lakes, which among other things immediately posed renewed threats of landslides and floods.

Sichuan's quake occurred on a known fault, the Longmenshan fault. The question is: what triggered it? The proximate cause is of course that stresses along the fault had built to a level at which they had to be released. But what exacerbated the pressures? Again, of course, they might have built through the natural process of the local movement of the earth's crust. But there could also have been a contributory factor: man's interference with nature, and especially with the effects of his activities on the distribution and use of water.

Some researchers have come to believe that the weight of water accumulated by the gigantic Zipingu Dam on Sichuan's Min River, just a few kilometres from the epicentre of the quake, was the tipping point that caused the fault to fail and rupture along a stretch more than 300 kilometres long.

Scientists know that seismicity can be triggered by what seem to be relatively small disturbances. Extraction of water, oil, rock and coal from the crust near a fault can cause it to give way. So can pumping waste fluids or carbon dioxide into underground caves and fissures. And so can adding the weight of water in a dam. Is this latter what happened in Sichuan?

The point is, however, a much more general one than the risk of causing earthquakes by damming rivers for electricity generation or irrigation purposes. When nature diverts waterways or creates lakes, no one can complain: nature's powers are often intractable, and when people choose to live on shorelines, flood plains, the slopes of mountains, known geological faults, or near volcanoes, they take a risk and cannot repine if the risk proves too great.

But when mankind is the cause of serious natural changes, as with plant and animal extinctions, river damming, and the drying of rivers and lakes through overuse – think of the River Jordan and the Aral Sea respectively – there is plenty of cause for complaint. These last two examples are telling ones: where the Jordan empties into the north of the Dead Sea it is a muddy streamlet, if that; abandoned ships lie in the sand of a desert that was once the bed of the Aral Sea.

We know the seeming-paradox all too well: the surface of our planet is mainly water, yet water – usable fresh water – is in short supply. In some parts of Africa people have to walk several kilometres every day to get water for drinking and cooking, and they are the lucky ones. There and in Asia the prospect of conflicts over water is increasing. A particular example is the scheme in Turkmenistan to build a huge lake in the desert and a man-made river through the capital city of Ashgabat.

Population increase and commensurate needs for increased agricultural output are the immediate prompts for this scheme. Turkmenistan is 80 per cent desert, and relies on water brought from the region's chief river, the Amu Darya, by the 1,100 kilometre-long Karakum Canal to Ashgabat and the cotton and wheat fields of the country's south.

The Karakum Canal is the largest irrigation canal in the world, and it is literally the lifeblood of the country, providing 90 per cent of its water needs. Without it Turkmenistan would be all desert, and practically uninhabitable. But the canal makes only 4 per cent of the country arable; because the population has increased tenfold over the last century, a new water solution has to be found.

The proposed answer is an immense new lake of 3,500 square kilometres, increasing the country's arable land by 20 per cent. The problem, according to critics, is that such a big new lake will further deplete the Amu Darya, harming neighbouring countries. They argue that it would be better for Turkmenistan to spend the money on relining the Karakum Canal, which leaks half its contents into the desert. Turkmenistan's government claims that the lake will be filled with run-off from existing agricultural land. Critics reply that to keep a lake filled in a desert, with unavoidable leakage into the sands, will require constant replenishment by massive amounts of river water.

Turkmenistan's exploitation of the Amu Darya is one of the principal reasons for the damage to the Aral Sea. Once the fourth-largest lake in the world, the Aral is now the tenth-largest, and it has become three times more saline than sea water. It no longer contains any fish.

The north-west of neighbouring Uzbekistan has been hit hard by the Aral Sea disaster, and even further off Kazakhstan is affected by the alkaline soil blown from the lake's desertified bed. Such problems are progressive and cumulative; the soil-blow is causing increased respiratory illness and cancer in Kazakhstan, as it has already done in the Aral region.

All this illustrates the difficulty that water presents when shared and in short supply, as it will increasingly be in many parts of the world. Happily, one thing is sure: this is a problem science can solve, though more resources are needed right now to make that happen before shooting versions of water wars start.

But it also illustrates the unwanted, but at least in some cases foreseeable, risks of diverting and damming rivers, as well as overusing water supplies, especially shared ones. In the case of China's Zipingu Dam, the existence of a nearby geological fault was known, as was the fact that even a modest earthquake would assuredly have devastating effects on so populous a region as Sichuan. The big question, as a lesson also for elsewhere, is whether these considerations were taken properly into account.

The Zipingu Dam's possible relationship to the Sichuan quake is only part of a larger story. There are nearly 26,000 large dams in China, more than in any other country in the world. The organisation International Rivers, which lobbies to protect rivers and the rights of those who live on and from them, calculates that ten million Chinese were displaced to make way for these dams, and to this day suffer problems of dislocation and the break-up of communities. One-third of China's rivers are severely polluted, and some of them no longer flow all the way to the sea. China's frantic rush to industrialise at the fastest and cheapest rate is to blame. Accordingly, a river of causes might run from political and economic ambition through the Zipingu Dam and the Longmenshan fault to the jerry-built collapsed schools and houses of the Sichuan towns, and the bodies that lie beneath them. It was the damming of a real river that might have been the final trigger for the disaster itself.

Stem Cells

Some object to stem-cell research on ethical grounds.
Are they not themselves being unethical in trying to
block medical research that will help many?

If the promise implicit in work on reprogramming adult skin cells into pluripotent stem cells is borne out, the chief gain will be greater simplicity, safety and straightforwardness in research and eventual therapeutic applications. That is welcome news. But press coverage of these developments has predictably focused on the fact that they will avoid ethical objections over the use of embryos, objections raised mainly by those who sympathise with a so-called 'pro-life' agenda.

It is not often remarked that those objections are themselves arguably unethical, nor is it pointed out that they are inconsistent with what their proponents' beliefs should make them infer from what happens elsewhere in nature. These points, taken in turn, are as follows.

Stem-cell research is aimed at providing help to people suffering from Parkinson's disease, spinal-cord injury, diabetes, muscular dystrophy, cardiovascular disease, hearing and vision loss, Purkinje cell degeneration, and more. The amount of suffering and disability that could be diminished among people who actually (as opposed to potentially) exist, with currently existing and established commitments, relationships, responsibilities, hopes, jobs and interests in full flow, is enormous: and genuinely 'pro-life'.

If the adult skin-cell work proves to be a dead end, and it turns out that only embryonic stem cells will do, the need will return to challenge the objectors' insistence that it is more ethical to privilege thirty cells in a blastocyst over the needs of ill, disabled or dying children and adults.

The blastocysts in question come from donors, many of whom are undergoing *in vitro* fertilisation procedures. Egg donation carries some risks, as all medical procedures do, so informed consent is essential. It is not clear whether all objectors believe that the blastocysts should not exist in the first place, which would entail opposition to fertility treatment for couples who profoundly desire children; but the thought that these endeavours, so positive in themselves, might have the additional benefit of leading to hoped-for clinical applications should strike unprejudiced minds as an obvious good.

Add to this the fact that nature is remarkably profligate in reproductive terms, and for a variety of good reasons. Of the millions of eggs laid by oviparous (which means: most) fish, only about 0.5 per cent hatch. Humans are not much less lavish: every year hundreds of billions of spermatozoa die before reaching an ovum, and billions of ova are expelled unfertilised in menstrual cycles. More than half of fertilised ova do not result in pregnancy; an estimated quarter of all pregnancies spontaneously terminate before the sixth week; and overall about one in five of all recognised (diagnosed) pregnancies spontaneously terminate before twenty weeks' gestation. Until the advent of modern medicine, made possible by research and intervention of which stem-cell work is a continuation, stillbirths and infant mortality further dramatically reduced the number of conceptions that successfully reached adulthood.

Objectors to embryonic stem-cell research ignore this context, which is one reason why they can take the ethically perverse step of putting blastocysts higher in moral concern than currently suffering people. People are precious; the profligate cellular sources that sometimes result in people are not people.

In actively opposing medical advances aimed at addressing the plight of the suffering, and on doctrinaire grounds, objectors to embryonic stem-cell research are thus in fact being positively unethical. The argument against them is not that the good ends of stem-cell research justify any means; it is that the good ends, the circumstances in which blastocysts become available, and the background facts of nature, jointly enter into a weighting of the interests at stake. To anyone without prior commitment to a view that makes small clusters of cells more important than people, it is perfectly obvious where the greater weight lies.

Cities

*Can the problems caused by mass urbanisation be
solved without losing the benefits it promises?*

Among the outstanding phenomena of the twentieth century are the huge migrations of population it witnessed. It is natural to think first of the effects of war, exacerbated by nationalism and beliefs about ethnicity. A major example is the forced displacement of millions of people in Europe and the Middle East in 1945 and afterwards. But these movements are dwarfed by the movement of rural dwellers to urban areas, a process whose origins lay in the pre-twentieth-century Industrial Revolution, but which in the last sixty years has turned from a stream to a tsunami.

The result has been the creation of urban agglomerations with staggering populations: Tokyo is said to have 35.1 million people in the overall urbanised area centred upon it (the official city population is 8.4 million); some other examples of such estimates are Mexico City 19.4 (8.6), New York 18.7 (8.2), Bombay 18.1 (13), Shanghai 14.5 (9.8). The process of urbanisation is increasing; over half the world's population now lives in cities, and in developed countries the figure is nearly 85 per cent.

It is no surprise therefore that much thought is being given to the future of cities. One anxiety concerns the implications of the Kuznet's Curve effect: as cities grow they suffer increased pollution and environmental degradation; only later, with further increases in wealth, does a clean-up begin, making city life less unsustainable.

But the insistent growth of urbanisation puts most cities on the upward arc of Kuznet's Curve, and the problem is worsened by the scale of energy required to supply, transport, educate and employ massive human numbers. The ideal city once hypothesised by planners was an urban area defined by commuting times of thirty-five minutes each way between home and work. The great urban agglomerations have long since exploded those limits.

The focus of attention understandably falls on air and water quality, total carbon footprint, the development of renewable energy resources, noise pollution, transport networks, and everything that goes under the label of 'livability' – provision of homes, open spaces, schools, shopping centres, leisure facilities, and more – as envisaged by planners trying to fit together all the pieces of the jigsaw in a maximally sustainable way.

That is as it should be. But it raises a question that seems to get too little discussion, concerning the non-physical factors that make some cities powerhouses in economic, cultural and political terms. It is reasonable to suppose that such cities have, in addition to background factors of geography and the power and influence of the countries in which they are located, a population size and mix that are causally related to their wealth and the facilities they therefore enjoy. A city that draws in talent and money is likely to draw in yet more of both in a self-reinforcing, cumulative process, generating the critical mass that eventually constitutes a world cultural metropolis such as New York or London.

But some proposals for remodelling cities in the eco-sustainability direction, particularly those that propose decentralisation, downsizing, and promoting online working from home, appear to run counter to what makes for a powerhouse city. The question that needs to be asked is: how can we ensure that the critical mass required for powerhouse status is enhanced rather than diminished by efforts to be greener and cleaner, especially if these efforts demand deconcentration and localisation?

At present the debate about urbanisation is mainly about the science and technology needed to solve the problems it causes. The social science that could explain the desirability and success of city life needs to be included too, in case the green fix does unanticipated harm to the positive things that big cities provide. But social science is also part of the solution to problems, which are not restricted to excessive energy consumption, pollution and disease, but obviously enough include crime and a variety of psychological and relationship stresses caused by the pressures of urban styles of work and private life. Given that the trend to increasingly dense urbanisation is an irreversible one now, the social problems have to be addressed equally with the structural ones to maintain the unquestioned benefits of scale and synergy that cities represent.

Unconscious Knowledge

Are there things we already know without realising it?

It is a commonplace of detective stories that the solution to a mystery can lie unnoticed in the facts until they are put into a new and at last revealing arrangement. There is a straightforward reason for this in logic: all deductive inferences are simply reconfigurations of the data in the premises, so the conclusion is already present in them, and they only need to be organised in the right way for the conclusion to appear.

Inductive inferences are quite different: they go beyond the data in the premises, and that is why they are fallible and even risky. Many inferences in life and science are inductive, which is why we sometimes find ourselves proved wrong by later facts, despite our best efforts to reason carefully from the best earlier data we possessed.

But the thought that answers lie hidden in current knowledge is an intriguing one, and often prompts researchers to review the literature in their fields in case something has been missed. Another technique is to put together unexpected juxtapositions of data, or to look for analogies between apparently unrelated fields. This endeavour can have the effect of jolting assumptions, suggesting possibilities, and sometimes bringing important discoveries to birth.

The justification for such out-of-the-box thinking is the obvious one that nothing exists in isolation, and that almost any natural phenomenon you care to think of is related to, affected by, and covaries with other phenomena. The development of ecological perspectives in biology is a vivid case in point: the sensitive interrelationship of all parts of an ecosystem is such that the entire chain can be disturbed, or anyway forced to adapt, when just one link ceases to function properly.

Human physiology is of course itself an ecosystem, and states of health and disease are similarly a function of relationships between its parts, with injury and pathogens playing the role of disturbers of one or more links in the chain of health.

But a recent discovery reminds us that what counts as pathological from one point of view might, from another, turn out to be an advantage. This is the implication of work done in Paris by researchers at the Institute of Development Research under Vincent Robert, who looked at the different responses of obese and normal mice to the malaria parasite *Plasmodium berghei*. They found that obese mice do not develop cerebral malaria when infected by the parasite, whereas more than half the normal mice died as a result of doing so.

Both populations of mice developed pernicious anaemia, from which all the obese and the surviving normal mice died within three weeks of infection. But the protective effect of obesity against cerebral malaria was striking. When the reason for this is established it will undoubtedly help in developing new treatments for human malaria victims.

For present purposes the interest lies in the fact that what looks like a problem from one point of view offers a boon from another point of view. One can think of other cases; but how many more such possibilities lie in wait out there for the right connections to be made?

That reminds one of the phrase used as a motto by the writer E. M. Forster: 'only connect'. In this computer age the connections can be made while we sleep, in the medical case by eliciting patterns in data about who has got what conditions while not having others. Quite a few of those hitherto overlooked correlations might turn out to be non-accidental.

While one standard trope of detective stories is the reordering of already known facts into a new pattern which suddenly reveals who did it, another is the discovery of one new and in itself seemingly innocuous fact which, like the twist of a kaleidoscope, makes everything else fall into place. The history of physics in the early decades of the twentieth century follows this pattern, with Planck's quantum solution to the puzzle of blackbody radiation giving Einstein his clue for the quantisation of light, and so on in a domino effect that resulted in quantum mechanics.

Strictly speaking, one cannot be said to know something without being aware that one knows it, no matter what psychoanalysts say about unconscious knowledge. Knowledge is not knowledge unless it is taken to be such: you have to know that you know in order to know – and there is no regress here, despite appearances. If a mental gestalt is required to see the right pattern in a constellation of facts, then obviously before the gestalt occurs one does not see the pattern, which is to say: one did not know what was there to be known once the gestalt occurred. The point therefore is that there could be much to be known that we do not now know, if we only we could rightly order the facts we already have.

A different point concerns the fact that we know that there is very much we do not know. The preacher of Ecclesiastes claimed that there is nothing new under the sun; contrast that attitude with Dr Johnson's view about what it means to be tired of London. He regarded his city much as Enobarbus viewed Cleopatra: as a thing of infinite variety. Consider: 95 per cent of the ocean floors of this planet have never been explored. And from the fractional glimpse that anyone has taken into the oceans' abyssal zone, we are enticed by the realisation that extremely strange things lurk there.

'The abyssal zone': the successive depths of ocean are wonderfully named. The twilight zone extends downwards to 3,300 feet, the bathyal zone to 13,000 feet, the abyssal zone to the deepest part of the deepest ocean trenches, which lie in the Pacific at 33,000 feet. What creatures of amazement swim or crawl in those inspissated deeps, miles below the light in the crushing pressure of the water's weight?

Each human individual is as a dot of plankton in an ocean. What even greater limitlessnesses stretch away on all sides in the physical universe, containing what endless fascinations to explore! If mankind can survive its own many and dangerous faults, it will find that it is just at the beginning of the adventure of knowledge.

Political Rhetoric

*Is it possible to judge the worth of a politician
from the rhetoric he or she employs?*

Reality has a habit of interfering with human hopes, as
President Barack Obama learned during his first election
campaign. Even in the run-up to the 2008 Democratic
Convention in Denver, Colorado, which rubber-stamped his
candidacy, he found himself in the unusual position of slipping
behind in the opinion polls for a time, as public attention
turned from selecting a candidate to fighting a real election.

The reason for Obama's stumble was that most of what he had
until then said in speeches and interviews contained a high level
of rhetoric and rather little substance. He had talked insistently of
change – 'change we can believe in' was his official slogan – and
of facing challenges, 'new hope' and 'common purpose'. He had
appealed to history, looked to the future, promised to be honest,
spoken endlessly of his 'journey' in life, the 'journey' of his
campaign, and the 'journey' that his presidency would be. Yet even
as the Convention in Denver approached, few could then say with
certainty what his policies would be if he reached the White House.

The stirring rhetoric of the early part of Obama's nomination
quest took its underlying rhythms and repetitions in part from
African-American church preaching, to which he subjoined
the high-toned tropes of political demagoguery typical in
America, where politicians talk in idealistic terms of 'dreams'
and 'defining moments' and 'crossroads', of 'carrying torches'
and 'new generations of Americans'.

The use of repeated vague phrases is of course not confined to
America, but is the stock-in-trade of all politicians everywhere,

even if in Britain the rhetoric is considerably more prosaic. Gordon Brown repeatedly talked of 'getting the job done', 'taking the difficult decisions', 'being prudent' and 'the long-term interests of the country'. He also talked about 'listening to the people' – though this listening was evidently due to take an unexpected form: under his administration the security services were to be given permanent powers to eavesdrop on everyone's phone calls and emails.

The point of rhetorically empty phrases is twofold. One is that they address the emotions rather than the intellects of hearers. 'Hopes, challenges, new (this or that), values, family, fairness, dreams, aspirations, democracy, freedom, the people' – these are feel-good terms, but their use commits a politician to nothing specific. This connects to the second reason, which is that feel-good generalities are useful when politicians do not yet know, or wish to reveal, what they propose to do about the various *challenges* that they *hope* will *fairly* be met in the *interests* of the *aspirations* of *all the people*. Commitments made at election times can prove to be albatrosses in the tough realities of office; politicians by nature therefore try simultaneously to speak as much and say as little as possible.

Novice politicians are given instructions by their parties on how not to answer questions directly, how to answer a question they have not been asked but prefer to answer, how not to answer at all by equivocating or changing the subject, and how to take every opportunity to say positive-sounding things about 'meeting challenges and aspirations' to fill up as much time in an interview as possible, radio and television interviews usually being brief.

By these means politicians endeavour to slide out of the awkward spots that most interviewers try to get them into. It is a gladiatorial contest, the interviewers either trying to ask the questions that the public would like answered, or at least the questions that will maximally embarrass the politician, and the politician – knowing this full well – trying to keep his cool and his credibility simultaneously. Perhaps the surprising thing is the belief on the public's part that, except on the rarest occasions, they might hear something frank and informative.

The grail for all politicians is a positive but vague word or phrase that will catch on and do them good. The 'new' in 'New Labour' was Tony Blair's election-winning inspiration in the approach to the 1997 election, which is what Obama successfully wanted 'change' to be in his campaign mantra of 'change we can believe in'. In all its many and desperate changes of leadership in the wilderness years of opposition, Britain's Conservative Party failed to come up with a workable catch-phrase, perhaps nervous about repeating John Major's mistake of 'Back to Basics' on the morality front, which was immediately followed by a flood of revelations concerning trousers-down, backhander-taking, perjured Tory politicians. (It turned out later that while extolling the moral basics, Sir John was himself adulterously consorting with fellow MP Edwina Curry.)

The example of John Major's 'Back to Basics' illustrates the danger of confected catch-phrases, which is that if they are too specific they can backfire explosively. 'Peace in our time,' proclaimed Neville Chamberlain. 'Read my lips: no new taxes,' asserted George W. H. Bush. 'Mission accomplished!' cried George W. Bush on the deck of an aircraft carrier. 'Education, education, education,' intoned Tony Blair. 'British jobs for British workers,' said Gordon Brown. 'Crisis? What crisis?' the *Sun* attributed to Jim Callaghan. The utterers of these words wished every single one of them back inside their throats before long. That is why it is safer to adhere to the nice-sounding empty stuff: hope, challenge, aspiration, democracy, freedom, security, change.

Politicians generally stick to these safer and emptier words despite wishing that they could produce the telling flourish that a Winston Churchill or a Franklin D. Roosevelt managed so effortlessly: 'This was their finest hour', 'We have nothing to fear but fear itself'. In fact a comparison of real and would-be stirring sayings is almost a mark of the difference between statesmen and snake-oil salesmen, despite the fact that sometimes, in their own day, it was not always easy to tell which was which: not even with Churchill. The final judge, as in all things, is history; and history alone.

Hope

To inspire hope and raise expectations carries
a big risk; is it better to do neither?

Among the numerous gems of eloquence with which Barack Obama strewed his path to the White House, one that quickly gained a footing in collections of quotations is this: 'We have been warned against offering the people of this nation false hope. But in the unlikely story that is America, there has never been anything false about hope.'

Because the resonant ideas of hope and its necessary correlative, change, inspired many Americans who had never voted before to vote in the presidential election that took Barack Obama to the White House, especially among the young and hitherto disaffected, an immediate reaction among observers is to ask: given the inevitability that not all, or perhaps even many, of the hopes that Obama then raised could be realised, surely he took a great risk in loading his presidency with such expectation? Why is it that people fail to realise how unlikely it is that all the hopes generated by an election campaign will come to fruition?

These are good questions, because they are prompted by one of history's clearest lessons: that almost all political endeavours end in failure and disappointment, whether or not they start in a joyous riot of welcome and relief. A minor forerunner of Obama's electoral success was Tony Blair's election victory in Britain in 1997, which reminds us of a painful truth: the higher the starting point, the steeper the eventual fall. Obama inherited a disastrous legacy of wars, financial crisis and poisoned alliances, an America divided despite the signal achievement of his victory as a black man, and surrounded by an unstable and uncertain world. Failure in some or most of the tasks that faced him seemed a near-certainty. Yet he was launched on those tasks on a tsunami of expectation. What place could the euphoria of hope have in this, other than to blight him eventually?

The answer lies not in whether those hopes would be realised in future, but in the catharsis of having hope in the present. Along with something to do and someone to love, having hope is one of life's essentials. It is an obvious but important fact that genuine hopelessness is a destructive, suicidal, terminal state of mind for an individual, and equally corrosive for a society. Even unrealistic hope is enough to get people out of bed in the morning, and to try again after failure or rejection. Hope is a psychological necessity, and perhaps it is a distinctive mark of humanity too; for alone among animals human beings have foresight which, informed by memory, would seem to give a truly rational individual good grounds for steeling himself against hope as much as possible – and yet most of us do exactly the opposite most of the time.

In describing second marriages as 'triumphs of hope over experience' the inimitable Dr Johnson exploited the central fact about hope: that it is an emotion, and moreover one of those emotions, like fear, greed, desire and love, that trump rationality far more often than not. Dr Johnson's contemporary David Hume, the philosopher, argued that reason cannot move people to act, only emotion can; unless we felt strongly enough to exert ourselves in one direction rather than another, we would do nothing, but would suffer the fate of Buridan's Ass, which starved to death between two bales of hay because, having no reason to eat from one bale rather than the other, it could start on neither.

Hope, however, is one of the strongest of motivating emotions. As a non-rational sentiment it has no interest in weighing the likelihood of success; it just adds more hope, that things will work out as hoped; that 'this time things will be different'; that the very strength of hope will itself surmount obstacles and alter realities. In the not infrequently self-fulfilling way of emotions, hope is thus its own best hope, because in sufficient quantity it can indeed be powerful. If proof were required, one has only to note that the hopes generated by Barack Obama's candidacy carried it to success.

Commentators writing at the time of Obama's election were careful to say such things as this: 'The hard realities of office over Obama's coming four years are of course a different matter. Even if hope continues to run at fever pitch, which it will not, it cannot by itself be enough. Others have hopes too: Obama's opponents, among them those who positively hate him and hate the fact that he has been elected, hope that he will fail, and some doubtless even hope that he will be assassinated. Like the intoxicating hopes raised by a liberal, eloquent, new force in American life, these perverse hopes also help some to get out of bed in the morning. Hope is no respecter of principle or morality.' And they were right to write in such terms; the implied warning is salutary.

The main point, though, is that although hope by its nature is a forward-looking emotion, its real effect lies in the present: it is what motivates and encourages now, it is what makes a difference to how the world seems to us even in the middle of difficulties. On the day of Obama's election, the cheering multitudes in Chicago's Grant Park and the streets of other American cities, who had both hope and a vote, to say nothing of delighted people around the world who had no vote but only hope, were reaping hope's benefits in the moment. The future was then only relevant as the site of dreams. One of one's hopes then was that their hopes would still sustain them when euphoria faded.

Renaissance Portraits

What does Renaissance painting, and especially portraiture, tell us about the history of ethics?

Since at least classical antiquity there have been portraits of individuals as opposed to generic representations of human faces. Apelles, antiquity's most famous painter, was celebrated for his portrait of Alexander the Great, and many of the luminaries of the Greek and Roman worlds, especially emperors, were frequently portrayed. The purpose was chiefly either propagandistic or exemplary – emperors' statues gazed over Rome's far-flung subjects with marmoreal authority, while busts of philosophers and poets celebrated cultural achievement.

Unquestionably the most striking ancient examples are Roman Egypt's Fayum mummy portraits of the first three centuries CE. Had those wonderfully warm, realistic, vivid depictions been known in later centuries they would assuredly have inspired emulation. As it is, the surviving portraiture of medieval times, largely restricted to illuminated manuscripts and recumbent tomb sculptures of knights and bishops, focused on a narrow range of individuals only.

The explosion of portraiture in the Renaissance is striking enough in itself, but its comparison with the preceding period of nearly a thousand years since the decay of Western classical civilisation makes it even more so. For suddenly it was no longer just nobles and churchmen who were portrayed, but individuals from right across society. Kings and popes continued to have official portraits, and princesses were painted so that possible royal spouses could inspect them; but it is the burghers, wives, children, artists' self-portraits, family groups, youths, beauties, scholars, artisans, old men and women – portraits known to us now by anonymous labels such as 'Portrait of a Young Man', 'Portrait of a Man with a Glove' – that appeared in large numbers, and with them studies of physiognomies and types, 'tronies', peasants, deformed faces, and even – as in the eccentric work of Archimboldo at the Prague court of the even more eccentric Rudolf II – portraits made out of vegetable still-lifes.

The reason for this efflorescence of portraiture is the same as the reason for the Renaissance itself. The late-medieval mind saw the world as a vale of tears, a risky place where one's soul was at risk of snagging on the everywhere-surrounding thorns of sin; one had to struggle through temptation, disease and danger, in the hope of heaven at last – the place pointed to by Gothic cathedrals trying to escape earth through their soaring spires and flying arches. Grim *contemptus mundi* literature bemoaned the fallen condition of man and the world, which latter it portrayed as the anteroom of hell.

Consider by contrast the beautiful hues and expansive, sunlit, airy temper of Renaissance art, with its picnic scenes and flowery landscapes, its exquisite faces and flowing garments, its musical instruments, books, and portraits of real people living in a world where joy and beauty are to be found. What a revolution in sensibility, philosophy and morality had occurred! It was the reawakening of the possibility of good in the here and now, a lesson taught by the poets and thinkers of the classical era whom the Renaissance not only rediscovered but accepted and applied, that took scales from eyes, allowing the world to be seen afresh, and celebrated.

And with it came celebration of the human individual, recovered and restored to central place in the literature and philosophy of the time, as always vitally interesting, often beautiful, and capable of good. Take Pico della Mirandola's *Oration on the Dignity of Man* as one of many examples, so different from the *contemptus mundi* tracts – and its very title reveals the new spirit that made portraiture not merely a central artistic genre of the time, but one of its quintessential expressions.

Shock Art

Is 'shock art' art?

'Art' might be our language's most controversially difficult word to define, but one thing that has never been a necessary part of its definition, whatever else is understood by it, is that something can count as art only if it is nice, soothing, pleasant, unshocking, good-mannered and safe. A crucified frog, a horribly jerking body in an electric chair, a waxwork of Hitler, goldfish swimming in a blender about to be turned on, are all in various ways and to various extents disagreeable or indeed horrible, some of them more so to some people than to others; but this fact alone does not prevent them from being art if they are art. For that decision, other criteria have to apply.

In the same way, it is not a necessary qualification for something to count as a work of art, if indeed it is a work of art, that it should be 'moral' in some way. Imagine a painter of the Renaissance presenting to a church a portrait of the Madonna that it has commissioned from him – a portrait of exquisite beauty and technical mastery portraying the Madonna nude at the moment of conception, perhaps after the fashion of Danaë receiving in her lap the shower of gold. Such a work would have been considered then, and still by many today, as immoral, blasphemous and offensive; and yet it might otherwise satisfy every traditional criterion of artistic excellence.

Yet again, something might achieve the status of art despite the fact that its maker was motivated by a desire to shock, or to draw attention to himself, or to upset people, or to make a brutal statement about something – such as capital punishment, say – which he felt the public does not sufficiently understand in all its implications. In fact, the role of art in educating both the emotions and the understanding of its public is a very ancient and respectable one: the lurid murals and altarpieces of medieval Europe, graphically depicting the suffering and death of Christ, the emotional agonies of his mother and disciples, the ugly monsters and devils of hell luring the innocent to destruction, and the punishments they inflict on the wicked, are a prime example of what might be called 'shock art' designed to drive home a point or evoke powerful emotions, not all (or even many) of them pleasant. Munich's Alte Pinakothek has huge images of this kind far more upsetting to anyone susceptible than a model of a frog on a crucifix, holding a mug of beer.

And (again!) yet again, it is not a necessary condition for arthood that a work should be 'in good taste'. No one could accuse Marco Evaristti of good taste; most people would think, with considerable justice, that not only does the contrary apply, but so too do accusations of puerility and gracelessness in his striving to effect, with each new project, something yet more disgusting or offensive than the last, at least partly for purposes of self-promotion. Well, grant all this; but then grant that even so he might be making art – or might one day do so, given that nothing in the abhorrence of the work, or the self-promotion or puerility involved in its making, can stop it from being art if it is art.

Familiarly enough, what one phase of history refuses to value as art might be highly valued at another time. Impressionist painting is the obvious case in point. None of the aesthetically offended viewers in Paris salons twelve decades ago could have imagined the daubs they disprized as commanding millions of admirers at exhibitions and millions of dollars at auctions. In a century's time art-lovers might expect innovative things to be done with cadavers, and might even pay high prices to have bits of them framed on their walls. Watching goldfish being liquidised is in most ways no different from watching cocks fighting or bears being baited; it is somewhat less cruel, though cruel it is, than lobster-cooking.

What all this adds up to is this: you might not like it, but it might still be art. Of course, it might not be art at all. A great deal of what is offered as art today, in the way of performance, installation, video or conceptual art, fully merits the telling description not so long ago given it of 'craftless tat'. Having offensive material rubbed into one's face in the supposed name of art does not, by that fact alone, or even because its maker went to art college, make it art. Emphatically there have to be other and far better reasons for that accolade to be awarded. But we do art and ourselves a disservice if we think that art can only be art if it is nice.

The Byzantine Idea

Does the word 'byzantine' deserve its negative connotation?

Of the two main uses of the adjective 'Byzantine', one describes the empire and the rich artistic and architectural heritage of Byzantium, the other denotes labyrinthine complexity – and by extension surreptitiousness, deviousness, duplicity. In this latter usage the word is usually written with a lower-case 'b' – thus: 'byzantine'. How did 'Byzantine' slide into 'byzantine' in this way?

It is no surprise that Byzantium should have added such a variegated palette of ideas to our culture, for it was a great city at the heart of a great empire, and its achievements and history are vast. For nearly a thousand years it was the preserve of the highest civilisation west of India, continuing and in some ways surpassing the Roman imperial tradition, at the same time absorbing the influences of Asia into it. The result is that 'Byzantine' and 'byzantine' are words that suggest many things, from particular types of architecture and iconography to general notions of intricacy, complexity and even moral twistedness.

An example of a specific use of 'Byzantine' to describe the city's fifth- and sixth-century style of architecture denotes buildings with a dome supported on pendentives – supports wide and curved at the top, tapered at the bottom – over a square space, the interior surfaces covered in marble and multicoloured mosaics on a golden ground, giving a gorgeous effect both in itself and when reflecting light either admitted through windows or emitted from lamps and candles.

Not much less specific is the expression 'Byzantine art' to denote the icon paintings, murals, mosaics, illustrated manuscripts and other works that have the instantly recognisable stamp of the civilisation they emerged from. Think of the supremely beautiful thirteenth-century 'Icon with Archangel Gabriel', exquisitely painted in tempera and gold on wood, or the Cambrai Madonna of the fourteenth century, with the lively baby wriggling in the Madonna's arms. Legend claimed that this icon was painted by no less a personage than St Luke himself, but the iconography itself places it in the late-medieval period: Byzantium invented the 'Virgin of Tenderness', of which this is a classic example with its *elousa* or 'sweet kissing' cheek-to-cheek pose.

These are examples of the capital-B 'Byzantine'. But the lower-case-b 'byzantine' stems from the tortuous, opaque, convoluted bureaucracy of government that the empire of many peoples, languages and cultures demanded. Under the *basileus* (the emperor) were many degrees of aristocrat and official, the latter divided into 'the bearded ones' (that is, not eunuchs) and eunuchs. Domestic citizens and foreign diplomats alike found dealing with Byzantium's bureaucracy almost impossible because of the labyrinth of departments and processes that had to be inched painstakingly through to get even the least thing done. Think of trying to do anything on the telephone today – for example: seeking help with a computer problem or setting up your iPhone on those badly misnamed 'help lines': those hours on the phone, being shunted from one faint far-off voice to another – then multiply it a hundredfold, add a dash of Kafka's *Castle* and a garnish of his *Trial* – and you are nearly there.

The use of 'byzantine' to describe this state of affairs began in the seventeenth century (some dictionaries give 1651 as the date of the first recorded use), but the reputation for complexity stems from the relationships between medieval European governments and Byzantium in the centuries before and during the crusades. A secondary sense of 'byzantine' to mean 'decadent' or 'effete' arose from the fact that the rough, barely civilised western Europeans who variously visited or sacked Byzantium on their rampages to the Holy Land found the polished manners, literacy and sophistication of Byzantium a rebuke, and reacted by despising and insulting it.

Among the insults was the entirely unwarranted one that Byzantium's history was full of intrigue, plots, poisonings and palace revolts. Of all the great civilisations, the Byzantine was probably the least like this, and correlatively the most stable. And this was a function of the highly developed system of government bureaucracy itself, in which due process, proper regulation and a rich framework of law and precedent enabled the vast empire to operate, century after century, with steady if slow efficiency.

But the jealousy of non-Byzantines ensured that terms which merely signified rank in the hierarchy of Byzantium came to have negative connotations. *Despotes* meant 'lord' in Byzantium, and was one of the emperor's titles; 'despot' has an unequivocally negative connotation now. Another of the emperor's epithets was *autokrator*, which as 'autocrat' now is a near-synonym of 'despot'.

A great power gets a bad name. Perhaps in a few centuries' time people will be insulting each other by saying 'you wretched washingtonian!', 'you scurvy whitehouser!', 'you ghastly congressman, you!' or 'what an american smell!', 'it was so american I couldn't touch it', and so forth. This would be linguistic history repeating itself.

The main use of 'byzantine', though, is 'very complicated'. Although the chief source for this idea has to be the bureaucracy already mentioned, one need only look at something like the mosaic portrait in San Vitale of the Empress Theodora holding a jewelled bowl, dating from the early sixth century, to see that the detail and complexity of Byzantine art could be part of the meaning too. The rendering of the folds of Theodora's robe draped over her arm is intricately done, wonderfully communicating the flow and weight of the cloth in subtle gradations of colour. That is a kind of byzantine complexity worth celebrating, a far cry from the sinister connotation of murky labyrinths, secrets and plots, deviousness, convolution and mystification.

Free Speech and Political Correctness

What can we say?

There are several questions of principle behind every furore involving the volatile mixture of free speech, censorship, offence and political correctness. This is a problem that keeps recurring, and it needs clearing up: every society needs to give itself some general guidance on what people can and cannot say if they are to navigate unscathed through the jagged rocks that those four concepts represent.

The central point, around which the others must revolve, is that free speech is a fundamental of such great importance that without it we could have only the most limited society and the most stunted possibilities for individuals. This is because without free speech we cannot lay claim to other liberties and rights, or defend them when they are attacked; we could not have democracy, which depends on the expression of opinion, debate, criticism and challenge; we could not have education worth the name, for it depends on the free exchange of information; we could not have any but the most pedestrian and formulaic literature, theatre, television and art; in short, without free speech our lives would be as closed as our mouths.

But we know very well that for all its vital importance, free speech is not an absolute. It has to be responsibly and maturely used, all the more so because of its potential for misuse. It can be a fig-leaf for doing damage and stirring trouble from motives that are not consistent with the other family of ideals in which free speech is a main member.

It is in fact not hard to draw the required line. To speak insultingly or act discriminatorily – even if you do it indirectly – with respect to the race, sex, sexuality, age, and disability if any, of other people, is unacceptable. These are things over which individuals have no choice or control. In respect of what people can choose, such as their political or religious commitments, how they dress, how they entertain themselves, it is open season: people must bear the consequences of their choices, including the disagreement, amusement, and even contempt, of others. 'Feeling offended' is no defence against attack on your political or religious views by those who do not share them, and indeed it is a vital feature of a healthy society that over matters of choice there should be a vigorous debate, of which satire and humour are a welcome and often revealing part.

Harsh things are often enough said in such debates, but here too there is a justification. Aristotle said that it is proper both to feel and to express anger of the right kind in the right circumstances, for example against injustice, unkindness, prejudice and greed. So angry words and condemnation have their place. Of course it would be far better if all disagreements could be peaceably debated, and if goodwill prevailed even in our differences: but it is not realistic to expect this in every case. Conflict and resentment are inevitable; it is when they happen that the line between the kinds of things we should not say and what we can say needs to be drawn.

So the rule is this: never asperse people for what they physically cannot help being. By all means attack what they choose to think or be; but even here it is better to attack ideas rather than individuals. Best of all, don't attack anyone for anything until you have given them a proper hearing. But if, having done so, you think they speak falsehood, folly or malice, do not be afraid to say so with all the eloquence and determination you can muster.

'Political correctness' has earned itself a bad name, because from legitimate and worthy origins it has mushroomed into folly. Its origins were that people unthinkingly and reflexively spoke in ways that denigrated and insulted others: 'nigger', 'wog', 'wop', 'Mick', 'Frog', 'Kraut', 'Chink', 'Nip': the first two denoted black people, the third Italians, the fourth Irish, the fifth French, the sixth Germans, the seventh Chinese and the last Japanese, all in negative and denigratory terms (and alas! only consider the etymology of 'denigration' itself: to blacken is to represent something as bad). There is an entire vocabulary of condescending and diminishing labels applied to women, such as 'chick', 'bird', 'dame', accompanied by stereotypes about their behaviour. Indeed, the hostile habit of lumping anyone different into crude and simplistic categories under a variety of demeaning labels, doubtless a hangover from our tribal past, meant that no one was exempt from being treated in these terms, and therefore from suffering discrimination as a result. For those at the top of the food-chain in economic terms, the fact that others call them names is a matter of indifference; but for those who are prevented by these labels – and all the prejudices that accompany them – from fair participation in society, they are not ignorable matters.

The home of humourless, inflexible PC-ness is said to be the American university, and what some call its Gestapo is a certain kind of feminist. What began as a demand for people to be treated with respect, and to use language thoughtfully so that the prejudices and injustices behind its discriminatory use can be avoided, has become a threat to free speech; it has become a form of censorship. And as it happens, the proponents of this form of PC thought and speech policing are also inclined to censor other forms of expression that they see as likewise discriminatory.

The trouble really begins when excessive PC-ness seeks to get itself onto statute books. That is when grown-up attitudes need to ally with the defence of free speech as a crucial liberty, and when we have to iterate the point that 'taking offence' is never a justification for depriving anyone of it.

To repeat: some of the impulses that underlie 'political correctness', before this pejorative label came into existence to denote their misapplication, are admirable. They consist not only in the conviction that no individual should be discriminated against because of facts about them that are not of their choice, but in the allied conviction that every individual – just in virtue of being an instance of the class of things worthy of moral regard – should be approached with courtesy, consideration and fairness, until or unless they give good reason why either of the first two should be withheld. (The third is non-negotiable in any circumstances.)

'Political correctness' is a misapplication of these latter ideas. Its legitimate beginnings lay in arguing that historically induced distortions in social relationships should be corrected by changes in both attitudes and practices, requiring that people be challenged to think differently about others they had previously regarded – and therefore treated – in disadvantaging ways, and by remedying the effects of negative discrimination by deliberate enactment of its opposite. This is 'affirmative action' or 'positive discrimination'.

This last is controversial, but arguably necessary, and for as long as it takes to effect a major corrective in the distortions at issue. But the self-appointed PC police are not content to remedy injustice justly. The salient example is their 'respect' agenda. For the PC police it is insufficient to require that one's default first approach to others be courteous and considerate so long as they merit it; one must respect them almost no matter what their choices and attitudes, their proclivities and associations. An assumption underlying this is a degree of relativism that puts any such choices beyond evaluation, and hence beyond criticism. So anyone who criticises or disparages across the sealed borders of difference is automatically indictable before the high court of PC.

The respect agenda completely overlooks the fact that respect is something earned, not claimable by right. The world pullulates with profoundly unrespectable people, views and actions, at all levels and in all neighbourhoods, and PC's reflex tendency to attack most of those who attack many of them makes matters worse. True discrimination – careful and fair-minded separation of worth from dross – is bundled by PC with all discrimination, and banned; hence the trouble.

What began as a movement to rectify relationships has become a minefield of suspicion and anxiety. Much of the anger that has made it so is understandable; none of the humourlessness and puritanism that keeps it so is acceptable. It is particularly a pity that its excesses have stained left-liberal thinking, of which it is a strand; but not, thankfully, the whole.

Altruism

Are altruism and self-interest irreconcilable opposites?

Prima facie it seems an open-and-shut case that altruism and self-interest are opposites. The majority view is taken to be that almost all, if not indeed all, human action is premised on the latter. Economists have long assumed that the only rational form of agency is self-interest, and cynics are quick to note that the long-suffering maiden aunt martyring herself for others is, subconsciously or in secret, greatly enjoying herself.

But there is, to use a shop-worn phrase, a third way in the argument. This is to domicile other-regarding and other-supporting actions in a form of acceptable self-interest described in debates about moral psychology as 'enlightened'. Simply put, agents recognise that benefits accrue to themselves in the longer run if at their own expense they benefit others in the shorter run. A more inclusive view has it that general benefits to the community are perceived by its individual members as yielding benefits for themselves in more and less indirect ways.

This latter accords well with biological accounts of the way many species are so organised that sterile siblings of fertile individuals sacrifice themselves for the benefit of the latter's offspring. The unit of self-interest is the species, whose individual members therefore appear to act with supreme altruism.

In familiar kinds of conventional morality, altruism is regarded as good, self-interest as (at least often) bad. In the cluster of concepts to which the former belongs one finds kindness, concern, self-sacrifice. In the self-interest cluster one finds selfishness, egoism and greed. This indeed is why the term 'self-interest' is deployed in moral psychology and economics, precisely to distinguish it from these other and obviously more disagreeable notions, from which it is genuinely different.

On this view, the responsible agent is one who takes care of his and his circle's interests before he takes care of others; altruism on behalf of distant strangers might sometimes be irresponsible if it involved neglect of proper duties to oneself and one's close circle.

An intriguing theory is advanced by William Hazlitt in his *Principles of Human Action*. He argues that all action is 'naturally disinterested' because it is relative to the future (whether seconds or years from now); but neither the future nor therefore one's future self exists, so the latter is on an ontological par with all other selves. Accordingly, to be able to act in one's own interest, one must in effect always act in the interests of another. So 'disinterestedness' or altruism is the default case.

There is more to this argument than first meets the eye. But it is not necessary to be persuaded that a capacity for self-interest is dependent on a capacity for altruism to recognise that the two are not contradictory. Taking an interest in one's own welfare and flourishing can indeed be regarded as a duty – as part, indeed, of self-reliance, independence, paying one's own way, not battening on others – which, if fulfilled properly, and consistently with the good of others, better enables one to help others and play one's part in the community. To be needy, poor and ignorant as a result of self-neglect and lack of self-respect is hardly a good ground for altruism.

Plastic Surgery

*When is it justified to be doubtful about
the value of plastic surgery?*

Far more women than men have plastic surgery for cosmetic purposes. In some cases they take the risk of a general anaesthetic and other possible complications such as potentially fatal post-operative blood clots, in order to enlarge breasts, change the shape of their noses or the lie of their ears, remove folds of tissue under eyes or chins, 'lift' and tighten facial skin to smooth out wrinkles, change the shape of stomachs ('tummy-tucks': the names of the procedures are so beguilingly innocent and positive) and buttocks; and more.

Critics try to distinguish this kind of plastic surgery from the kind that is performed to repair damage from burns or other injuries, or to improve birth deformities, or to solve problems such as heavy, over-large breasts that cause back pain. These latter, they say, are 'real' problems and the surgery performed to help solve or diminish them is life-enhancing; whereas surgery for reasons of vanity is merely frivolous, and a symptom of society's malign emphasis on appearance.

No doubt there are a few people with more money than sense who, out of boredom or whimsy, choose to go under the knife despite having no need to – just for a change, say, or because while out one evening they saw on a passer-by a nose or breasts whose shape they liked. But it is a safe bet that the majority of people who choose plastic surgery for cosmetic purposes feel a genuine need to do so, even in the absence of injury or medical reasons. Body image and appearance are not trifling matters, after all; they influence almost all our transactions with others, and have effects on our life chances that include career success and family life.

This is because, as empirical studies have repeatedly shown, others make judgements based on appearance in the first instants of meeting, and are influenced in their attitude and behaviour then and thereafter by what that judgement is. Politicians are told by their media advisors that by far the greater part of their effect on voters consists in what they look and sound like rather than what they say. That is a dispiriting fact; but it is a fact; and it is one that people, and especially women, are intuitively so aware of that it both explains and justifies the time, thought, energy and expense devoted to appearance, in all respects of shopping for clothes and accessories, applying make-up, dieting and exercising, and even in some cases choosing surgical adjustments to face and body.

Feeling bad about one's appearance might be an unjustified artefact of the effect had by the thinness and air-brushed exquisiteness of glossy magazine models who seem by their very existence to accuse 'ordinary' (that means: real) women of imperfection. But feeling bad about appearance is a serious feeling, and merits being taken seriously. The best remedy is of course to recognise that the glossy magazine idealisations are in truth deformities; advertising campaigns purposely showing real women in their attractive variety of shapes and sizes are one step towards that. It is an oddity that the type of woman portrayed in magazines for women, and those portrayed in magazines for men, are sharply different; in the former women are tall and thin, in the latter curvaceous and fuller in body. The latter shapes, typically shown nude in these magazines, are more attractive to men. Women yearn for the shape possessed by fashion models because it makes them look better in clothes, so they invest great effort in losing weight. And yet, paradoxically, when the imperative becomes being attractive to men and looking good naked – which they do not when thin – they seek breast enlargements, silicon lip injections, and procedures that remove signs of ageing, such as Botox anti-wrinkle treatment and face-lifts.

But in light of the pressures felt, and the real consequences experienced, by people who diverge – or think they do – from ideas of attractiveness, what right has anyone to complain about people taking the next logical step from clothes buying and cosmetics use, namely altering their physical features in the gym, at the hairdresser's, at the weight-watching class – and in the operating theatre?

This sympathetic attitude will not persuade those who see choosers of cosmetic surgery as victims of false consciousness. There is something to this. But while false consciousness still promotes anxiety and concern, the debate about the appropriate remedies for them will continue.

A special, and especially pertinent, consideration in the debate about plastic surgery is surely the matter of face transplantation. At the time of the first face transplant, undertaken by Professors Jean-Michel Dubernard and Bernard Devauchelle in November 2005 at the Amiens University Hospital, there was still considerable unease about both the technical and ethical implications of the procedure. On the technical front, its critics were concerned about lifelong immunosuppression with its attendant dangers, the risk of rejection despite it, and the difficulties of successful microvascular and microneural anastomosis (the joining together of tiny blood-vessel and nerve-cell branches respectively). On the ethical front, problems focused on the psychological challenges to recipients concerning adjustment, identity and attitudes towards the deceased donor, and on the sensitivities of donors' families.

These anxieties were not the same as those felt about solid organ donation in the early history of transplant surgery. Kidney and heart transplants can easily be justified on the grounds of prolonging life or enhancing its quality. Face transplants are not life-saving procedures, at least in the literal sense, and its critics therefore argue that reconstructive surgery using a patient's own tissues is medically and ethically preferable, even if the results are cosmetically far less good.

The debate has, however, moved on. Technical difficulties remain, but are not insuperable, and the medical value of face transplantation is now, and rightly, more widely conceded not just in cases of devastating disfigurement where conventional techniques would be ineffective, but in cases where victims of burns or trauma cannot (for example) open their mouths to eat, or close their eyes to sleep.

But this last thought is key, because it suggests that quality-of-life considerations apply in the same way as they do in solid organ transplantation; and once this is recognised, face transplantation cannot reasonably be restricted to approval on functional considerations only, but must be decided on the general psychological health of the patient as well.

This seems to me the overriding point once questions of technicality are set aside. Some victims of severe facial disfigurement might have or acquire the courage and self-possession to live flourishingly despite their appearance, or more accurately despite the inevitable reaction of people they encounter in the course of daily life – a reaction that will always be an at least initial barrier to normal interaction. There are any number of circumstances in which facial disfigurement is a bar to establishing relationships with others, and many careers that a victim of it cannot hope to pursue. So even the bravest victims will find that a severely compromised appearance is as much a disability as other more conventionally recognised disabilities.

But for many, if not most, victims of disfigurement the psychological burden can be profoundly life-affecting. Some become prisoners in their own homes, others are caused agonies of self-consciousness by the stares of children or the startled reaction of people in shops or buses on first catching sight of them. When one considers what a torture it can be to suffer in these ways, face transplantation becomes as urgently a quality-of-life issue as cardiac or renal transplant.

As argued above, there is a case for saying that even elective 'cosmetic' plastic surgery – face-lifts, breast enlargements, liposuction procedures, and the like – can be defended on the ground of the immense importance that appearance has to the flourishing of individual lives, and not just because, as some say, glossy magazines tendentiously manipulate attitudes to appearance and turn them into an obsession. There are good biological reasons why the well functioning of human relationships turns in part on appearance, and the fashion and cosmetics industries are a response to that fact. There are of course negatives here; eating disorders are a case in point; but the fact remains that appearance is a central determinant of life-chances, and severe diversions from the norm are such that they can, and very often do, trump other compensating considerations such as intelligence, experience and talent.

For this reason there seem to me no grounds for objecting to face transplantation once technical medical problems have been solved, for the argument is the same as one would use in justifying reattachment of a severed hand, namely, the restoration of a profoundly important function – the function of being able to occupy social space with a degree of normalcy, thus accessing the possibilities and utilities, not to say advantages, of doing so.

Appearance

Is a concern for looks mainly a female phenomenon?

Friday-night clubbing teaches how intimate is the link between sex and appearance. Almost-naked girls shiver in the autumn nights outside city clubs, asserting the triumph of beauty over temperature, making the night exotic with their appearance, silvery with their cries, heady with their perfume and promise.

The vision is of a piece with the rest of nature, except that there the order of appearance is reversed. Among birds, males have the most brilliant appearance, sometimes to excess: there is no more extravagant piece of sexual furniture in nature than the peacock's tail. Male frigate birds with inflated red gular sacs, and cockatoos with erectable head-feathers, are not so vulnerable to predators as the peacock, which seems to risk his all on display. With that burden of weight and drag, how shall he escape a determined predator? The small brown hens of the bird world, safer in their anonymity, choosily observing the strutting males and (according to genetic studies) promiscuously dividing their favours among them, have chosen the better part: safety over splendour.

For much of history human males have been as all males in nature: the gaudier sex. And because human lifestyles in what we call civilisation are inimical to the preservation of natural shape and form, creating a necessity for both sexes to resort to art to hide or enhance their appearance, this male gaudiness has taken the form of extravagant dress. Any number of historical examples could be adduced, from the wildly elongated penis-gourds of Papua to the beauty-spotted, bewigged, frothily laced beaux mincing along the corridors of Louis XIV's Versailles in their high-heeled silver-buckled shoes.

It is only recently that men have retreated into the conservatism of dark suits and ties, and for leisure-wear the same dull uniform of short-sleeved shirts worn outside jeans, thereby leaving all the decoration to women. It is an historical oddity, and the few dashing dressers among men – adding a touch of mascara to deepen the effect of something sardonic and Satanic in the sartorial – stand out the more for it.

Given that human males and females would, in the state of nature, have distinctively different shapes and proportions – a triangular arrangement from shoulders to hips for males contrasting with the hourglass of the female; the male's longer legs depending from a narrower pelvis, as against the long-body-short-legs of his broad-pelvis consort – it would seem necessary for each just to be healthy to be attractive. Perhaps this thought explains why men care less about dress than about physique these days, heading for the gym rather than the boutique in search of appearance. Women might do both, though they seem to find the latter more persuasive.

Not that one would like men to return to the peruke, the beauty-spot, the penis-gourd. It would be enough if they stuck to colourful ties and decent shoes. What we do not want is for women to mimic men (as they are doing in other things, such as binge-drinking and raucousness on nights out) by losing interest in dress likewise, or to revert to the hen-like monochrome of their Victorian ancestors. Only think how dull today's world would become if women cared as little about their appearance as men.

Education

What should education really be for?

We have come so far down the trail of thinking that people go to school in order to become foot-soldiers in the economic battle, as if paid employment were the sole meaning of life, that we scarcely understand what Aristotle meant by saying 'we educate ourselves so that we can make a noble use of our leisure'. In contrast to this remarkable view, today's dull-witted, pedestrian, pragmatic view seems to be that the educational minimum must be whatever is enough in the way of literacy and numeracy to operate a check-out till.

Not that I agree with the apparent implication of Aristotle's remark that a noble use of our leisure is the only reason for education. I think that, in addition, education makes better workers, better voters, more thoughtful, informed, engaged and therefore responsible citizens, healthier and happier people, and a more mature, flourishing, open and progressive society. All these benefits do not accrue from limiting education to equipping people with functional skills adapted to the eight hours a day they are destined to spend at the economic coal-face. It comes from drawing out their capacity for reflection, from helping them to develop skills of enquiry and criticism, allowing them to recognise what they need to know, to find it out, to evaluate it critically, and to apply it.

Moreover, a true education provides people with a broad knowledge of culture and history, enabling them to appreciate the amenities of civilised life, to understand what they encounter in their experience as citizens of the world, and to relate with greater insight and generosity to others. Like any appetite, the appetite for finding out, and thinking about what is learned, grows by feeding; and with the nourishment it provides come other goods of mind and heart.

These are admittedly utopian aspirations for education, but they are only so because we fail ourselves in two important ways in our expectations and what, as a society, we are prepared to grant ourselves. The first is that our mass education system exists almost exclusively for people in the first two decades of life, and in them we seek to download a national minimum curriculum into heads in step-rank fashion, each age cohort passing uniformly through the sausage machine to a quantifiable outcome. The resulting pressure for aiming at common denominators is inexorable, and as numbers increase and budgets erode, expectations follow the latter.

The second is that we think education stops round about the end of the second decade of life, and that people will then get on with the next stage of conformity, as both cogs in the wealth-production machine and consumers of its outputs.

But education should be a lifelong endeavour. When it is, it is a richly satisfying one, which keeps minds fresh and flexible, and maintains interest in the possibilities of the world. By one of those incomprehensible acts of stupidity of which governments are so frequently capable, our own has decided no longer to fund 'equal or lower qualifications' in higher education, meaning that if you have a bachelor's degree in English literature and after twenty years in the workplace wish to study for one in computing or nursing, the government will not fund it. So much for the tens of thousands of people who, part-time, continue with or return to higher education to extend and refresh themselves by taking up new subjects and opening new horizons.

This act of folly followed an earlier one, some twenty or more years before, when the then government decided that it was only going to fund extra-mural evening-class provision if it resulted in certificates and diplomas, requiring written work by those attending, and exams at the end. Before them, for a long time, evening classes were more relaxed affairs, and thousands enjoyed and profited from them who were driven away by the more banausic and pedestrian requirement – actually, of course, a way of cutting budgets – that they should result in a piece of paper at the end. The value of evening classes lay so far away from the production of certificates and suchlike that presumably those responsible for emasculating it did not even understand what it was. Those elderly folk who kept their minds going, socialised, had an evening in the warm with others doing something interesting: did it save money to drive them away from that resource? All those who, in the unthreatening environment of a literature or history evening class might have been inspired to try for university – or merely to read more – but never attended because they were put off by the idea of essays and exams: do they represent money well saved?

There are those – surely, in other countries and times only? – who would like most of the population to be drones, not too questioning or well informed, not too apt to criticise, and easily persuadable about things, especially at election times when a few promises about tax cuts and the like can get the inconvenience of asking people to think something (in this case, who to vote for) out of the way. The reason why such a reductive and manipulative view is wrong is precisely the reason why a broad liberal education, an education for life and not just for work, matters.

Intelligence Pills

Pills are being devised to enhance human mental capacities and skills. Would their use ever be justified?

Almost any magazine one opens contains advertisements for diet pills and electrical belts that tone the stomach while one sleeps. Newspapers report athletes being caught for taking drugs that make them run faster or jump higher. It's well known that people take other kinds of drugs to make them happy, or forget their sorrows, or to liven them up at parties.

It is now claimed that there are pills that make people more intelligent, improve their memory and generally sharpen their faculties.

One standard reaction to this is to think that chemical quick-fixes for improvement in body, mind or mood are lazy at best, dishonest at worst, and certainly not natural. Oddly, we appear to be more accepting of the many kinds of pill already in use to help people suffering mental-health problems. But the fact that large numbers of children – nearly half a million in Britain – are prescribed drugs to calm them down at school and help them concentrate, adds to our instinctively negative reaction: it seems wrong to control children's behaviour and stimulate their learning with drugs; there seems to be something sinister and manipulative about it. We are reminded, on the negative and troubling side of the equation, of the terrible mistake of lobotomy (still practised in China) to turn violent or lunatic individuals into zombies, as in *One Flew Over the Cuckoo's Nest*. What opposite kinds of monsters might we create with pills, and perhaps procedures, aimed at doing the opposite?

But it is in fact wrong to lump all the proposed enhancement possibilities together. Viewed rightly, some of them are good, such as memory-enhancers, and they can be so too even in the controversial cases, such as medicating hyperactive children. Each has to be examined on its merits.

It's clear that making people smarter with better memories is a good thing in itself. We have always striven to do this, as it happens – by training and education, and by healthy regimes of diet and exercise. It has always been known that what we ingest has an effect on our minds; think of what excessive sugar, or alcohol, does to our moods or our thought processes respectively. They act like drugs, but negatively. Well: compare a drug that acts positively. Ingesting a drug like Modafinil to sharpen one's mind before giving a presentation at work is another way of achieving the same effect as that produced by good sleep and careful preparation. When neither of the latter is possible, as so often in our world of busy schedules, Modafinil is one possible answer.

The standard response of insisting on a preference for nature over pharmacology is an understandable form of conservatism. But mind-enhancing drugs are already here, and more will come; their intended effects are desirable, so they will be used;

and therefore the real question before us now concerns how we can use them responsibly, and fairly, and how we manage the new enhanced world that will result.

Genius

What is genius?

There is variety in genius as there is in talent and beauty. Some geniuses are innovators, some are deep thinkers, some are people of extraordinary skill, some have remarkable imagination or oblique ways of seeing things, some are highly intelligent, some are passionately curious; most are a combination of at least three of these things, constituting a volatile mixture of intellectual gifts and character traits. The intellectual gifts are an ability to see things from highly unusual angles, to overlook what is not essential, and to understand the true significance of the obvious. The character traits are persistence, obduracy, a capacity for taking enormous pains, and indifference to the ridicule or hostility of any who might think that the pursuits, the aims, the innovations in question are crazy.

Geniuses have something of a child's openness and readiness of mind, that ingenuous ability to see things afresh, to make imaginative leaps and to combine seemingly unrelated things into novel wholes. The deep thinkers among geniuses – Plato, Aristotle, Newton, Kant, Einstein – see into the place where the roots of quite different things meet and entangle underground. Some geniuses are hardly conscious of their powers, but create out of an overflowing abundance of skill: Mozart was one such. Skill is also the genius of painters and sculptors, and of the best surgeons, craftsmen, gardeners and architects. There is quiet genius too: the genius of poets and outstanding novelists, and there is visionary genius in the greatest statesmen and generals. Some geniuses owe their successes to care, study, unyielding effort, dedication, focus, determination and courage. Some owe their success to a flash of lucky eccentric inspiration at exactly the right time and place for it.

Genius is more common than people think. In its different forms it runs through the human species like a linking flame, and from it springs the magnificent achievements of civilisation and science. It does not depend on the right circumstances to express itself, though obviously it is much helped by them; but it rarely goes unnoticed in the long run, because part of human genius is the ability to recognise its own best examples for what they are.

The more we know, the more knowledge it is possible to acquire; the more we can do, the more we are able to do. Much that distinguishes the modern Western world's advances in science, technology and society is the result of a dynamically increasing accumulation of skills and information. When we consider the technological advances of ancient times – think of early China, for example, where coinage was introduced in the ninth century BCE, crop rotation was introduced in the sixth century BCE, revolving windows were devised in the fifth century BCE, crossbows with bronze triggers were made in the fourth century BCE, anti-malaria drugs were discovered in the third century BCE, the distinction between arterial and venous blood was noted in the second century BCE, winnowing machines were invented in the first century BCE, astronomical clocks were devised in the first century CE, folding chairs were made in the third century CE – the list goes on and on, ranging far more widely than the 'gunpowder, magnetic compass and printing' trilogy usually cited as examples of early Chinese discoveries. They are all products of genius of various kinds, illustrating the fact that human beings are the genius species, something we see clearly enough when we have got over our admiration at a chimpanzee's employment of a twig to fish termites from their nest in order to eat them, and compare this with a space rocket and an MRI scanner as an example of tool use. As Unamuno said, 'We are all heroes and geniuses' – if we have the will so to be, for that is the nature of our kind at its best.

Symbols

All societies use symbols. Is there a philosophical reason for their significance?

The paradigm of a symbol – by which is meant a simple or relatively simple device designed to convey an instantly recognisable meaning – is the Red Cross. Interestingly, there are at least two major paradoxes in this important and universally liked symbol. One is that while it is the sign of succour, of aid, of rescue, representing brave men and women risking themselves in the roar of battle to alleviate suffering, it is also – and therefore – a sign of failure: the failure of human beings to stop fighting and killing each other. This persistent inability of humanity to grow out of its adolescent desire to solve problems by violence makes the Red Cross necessary, whereas maturity in humankind would make it unnecessary.

Think of the contrast: think of the huge investment in technology and equipment designed for the mass murder of enemies; then think of it actually being used to effect this barbaric end, while in among the explosions and whistling bullets hasten ambulances with Red Crosses on the sides and roof, and medics with Red Cross armbands – and the absurd hangover from a chivalrous past, which makes you shoot a man and then, because he is wounded rather than dead, respectfully not shoot him again as the Red Cross hurries to save his life.

The second paradox is that although in its inception the Red Cross had connotations of the charitableness that Christianity sometimes professed – though by far it did not always practise that – it soon came to enjoy a neutrality, a lack of partisanship, that detached it from that quasi-religious root. It was the sign of medical help, not of a faith or a party. While it was the single universal sign of neutral non-partisan aid it transcended every boundary, and existed on all sides of all disputes with unquestioned authority.

But in 1983 the international Red Cross movement, in a bid to remain neutral and inclusive, and evidently deciding that the cross of the Red Cross had too Christian and too Western a connotation, decided to rename itself the League of Red Cross and Red Crescent Societies, adding the Muslim equivalent of the Red Cross in the form of the waning-moon symbol of Islam's successful military past. So the very divisions that the Red Cross societies ignore in hastening to the aid of all have become a permanent allusion of its symbolism.

When Henry Dunant hastened to the aid of the wounded on both sides in the 1859 Battle of Solferino between Austro-

Hungarian and Franco-Sardinian troops – this was the founding moment of the Red Cross societies – he was not concerned about symbols. Symbols come to have a life of their own, sometimes bigger than the movements they symbolise, as the equivocation of the Red Cross symbol shows. But for all that, the Red Cross remains one of the best of the humane advances that our immature species has managed.

But another meaning of the Red Cross lies in the activities of the movement it represents, off the battlefield and away from the refugee camp. This is its work in the conference hall, and it is here that its greatest contribution will be made: in bringing about a future with fewer wars or none, where disputes are rationally resolved, with arbitration instead of kicking and biting. For the Red Cross, its staff conscious of how paradoxical and yet how urgent it is to do the work of peace on the battleground, is the world's chief anti-war movement also. Pessimists, who always call themselves realists, think that the Red Cross will never be able to stop bandaging wounds among the bullets and bombs. Optimists think that they will help win the argument for peace one day. I am among them.

Why? Only think: the Red Cross symbol, two blunt red arms crossed on a white circle, was designed for visibility, to stand out at a distance even in drifting smoke and the murk of conflict. One day mankind will wake from the bad dream of its immaturity and see, as distinctly as one can see a Red Cross on a vehicle driving down a bombed street, that it must make the Red Cross unnecessary by agreeing with it at last.

Perhaps the most taken-for-granted symbols in the world are those used in airports worldwide to indicate the presence of toilets. There is a set of them, constituting a little language:

the male and female symbols, the disabled sign, the nappy-changing facility. Reflecting on them has the same kind of effect as physicists say explains the early universe: a sudden vast expansion of unexpected ideas and realisations.

Leave aside the fact that the male toilet symbol is a beautifully simplified version of Leonardo's study of human proportions – though this is interesting enough as a theme for meditation – and reflect on the fact that larger airports in developed countries provide unisex nappy-changing rooms. That marks a sea-change in the relations of men, women and children. A Victorian father would have been horrified at the idea that he might change a nappy. Now the signs tell us it happens frequently enough for the nappy-changing table not to be reserved to the women's toilet alone.

Much more striking, though, is the very idea of a public toilet. If you take the 'Himalayan Queen' train from Delhi to Chandigarh in the early morning, you pass through dawn fields in which hundreds of men are squatting a few yards from one another, fertilising the soil. This impactful image lingers against one's will. It raises a compelling and equally unpleasing thought: it explains why girls in developing countries drop out of education – if they are in it at all – when puberty arrives. The absence of toilets where they can manage personal hygiene makes the mud-hut schoolroom an impossibility for them.

Both public and private toilets are safeguards against the epidemic diseases that devastate poorer communities. In London one nineteenth-century summer, the sewage in the Thames backed up so far that it reached the Houses of Parliament, and with such noisome effect that the legislators at last – after centuries of disease and death in the poor East End of the city, caused by the infected river – passed an Act for a proper sewage system and clean water. This story leaves a bad smell: in answer to the question 'What does it take to force rational government?', the answer seems to be 'Politicians' self-interest'. Can that really be true?

The most important thing about the universal toilet signs in airports is the promise they hold for the future. These simple, clear, unambiguous symbols remind us of something so profound that we easily forget it: that human nature and human experience are fundamentally the same everywhere and at all times. We share the most basic urgencies; we all need the facilities that make a life of simple decency and comfort possible. They include respect for basic rights, security for our lives and property, a human share of the world's wealth, the freedom to form relationships of our own choosing, liberty of conscience, help from our fellows in times of need, access to possibilities of education and self-improvement, and the chance to exercise our legitimate talents either for the joy of self-expression or to improve our standing and income, or both.

Only a minority of people in the world enjoy these facilities. Are any of them less needful than a toilet in an airport? Not at all. They are basics, as the various human-rights instruments in international law show, for these are precisely the key features of such instruments. Declarations of human rights state the conditions which, if satisfied, hold open a space for individuals to make something of their lives if they will apply themselves to doing so. Without these rights people are the property of others or of chance merely. Their situation in life is as uncomfortable as that of a man with stomach trouble in an airport without toilets.

It takes an act of faith to think that as people from all round the world sit waiting for their flight announcements, their gaze will fall on the toilet symbols, and they will after a while begin to think: yes, we are all the same; we are one; we have the same needs; the little simplified-Leonardo man up there over the entrance to the male toilet is any man, anywhere, irrespective of colour, creed and ethnicity; and this sign, like music, has a message that speaks to all.

It might seem an odd thing to wish to liken the future to an airport toilet, but only think: it is an utterly democratic place, open to all without prejudice to any, speaking a universal language, answering the most fundamental needs.

Now even Eden has a serpent in it, proved by my speaking of the male toilet sign alone. The female toilet sign has an obviously Western look to it, because the image is of an unveiled female in a short stiff summer skirt, making a gesture of invitation to embrace. Oh dear. So this is a sign of scandal to some; to that billion or so human beings who think, in this opening decade of the twenty-first century, that women should be hidden, draped, chaste, secondary, limited, repressed.

Well, that means that the female toilet sign is a summons to the next great act of liberation that the world needs, because the world's future peace and prosperity centrally depend on women being educated and participatory. A translation from the universal language of airport toilet signs thus says: we are all the same at (so to say) bottom, women too: the future must be a place that, like this place, recognises that one great fact – and acts on it at last.

Employment

Is unemployment a curse or an opportunity?

When we talk of being employed we invariably mean having a paid job. There is something defining about employment; when we are told people's occupations – accountant, teacher, businessman, surgeon – we feel that we know something central about them; we have a handle on their identity and status.

The identity-constituting aspect of a job explains why unemployment can be a devastating blow, for it is not just the loss of money that hurts, but the loss of meaning and self-worth. This is not automatically related to the kind of job in question. A laid-off factory hand can feel as bereft as a redundant administrator. Having a job, paying one's own way, benefiting from the structures of working life and its social aspects, are not incidentals, given how large a part of each week is devoted to one's occupation.

Retirement can have the same effect, making some people feel marginal and reduced if they are not quite ready to hang up their working clothes and retreat to a rocking chair. But it is much worse for people in mid-career who lose their jobs and have difficulty in finding new work. It can take the proportions of tragedy to be forced into idleness and reduced circumstances; it can feel like rejection, and an insult, when one is fit and willing, yet is obliged to become a dependant.

It sounds like a cliché to say so, but this is an important truth nonetheless: that there is opportunity in unemployment. Money and status might have been wrenched away, but something valuable comes in return. The newly unemployed are understandably irritated by efforts to console them with remarks about their now having time for art galleries, evening classes, pottery club, walks, volunteering at the local charity shop, learning a language, reading more, and all the other easy-sounding nostrums that still-employed people airily suggest. But the plain fact is, this is true: and makes for a different sense of 'being employed' – and sometimes, indeed, better employed. For as Emerson said about any difficult circumstances rightly faced, 'They are opportunities no good learner would wish to lose.'

Confucius

*What might be learned from a study of
the ancient sages of the East?*

Confucius – Kong Zi – is a figure so wrapped in legend that he sometimes seems to be a legend himself. But he has a birthplace – one can visit it in Qufu, in China's Shandong province – and his dates are precisely enough given as 551–479 BCE, placing him a generation before Socrates. Certainly the few details that remain of his life have such an alloy of fable in them that it is hard to sift fact from fiction – the fiction resulting from the admiration of a culture which, in so many ways and for so long, has been influenced by him.

That is why Confucius's name continues to have the taint of legend about it. According to the historian Sima Qian, whose *Shiji* ('Records of the Grand Historian') gives a biography of Confucius, he was descended from a noble family in the state of Song, which had fled in a time of turmoil and become impoverished. His parents had gone up a holy hill – a *qiu* – called *Ni* in order to pray to have a son; and when he was born they therefore called him Kong Qiu Zhongni. So says Sima Qian; and the magical coincidences all look a little contrived. Even his age at death – seventy-two – is a special number in Chinese numerology; he was also said to have had seventy-two disciples who, out of the 3,000 he taught, understood him best.

One feature of Confucius's biography that does not seem invented is the fact that although he spent much of his adult life trying to get a ministerial post in different states – variously in the states of Lu, Wei, Chen, Song, Chu and Cai – he was signally unsuccessful, holding office only for short periods and only in middle-ranking ministerial positions. He wanted to put his ideas into practice and it was a major frustration for him that he was never able to do so. Late in life therefore he dedicated himself to teaching and, so the legends have it but on doubtful authority, editing classics, among them the *Book of Songs* and the *Spring and Autumn Annals* which give the history of the state of Lu.

What we know of Confucius's teachings is based on the *Analects* (in Chinese *Lunyu*), a collection of his sayings compiled from what was remembered by his disciples. More accurately, there are several versions of the *Analects*, and their respective compilations took place considerably after Confucius's death, which is a first hint that they require to be read with caution. A second and more serious such hint is that the *Analects* is so full of obscurities and contradictions that scholars judge it to contain many interpolations and almost certainly mistranscriptions too, requiring yet further caution in interpreting what some of its sayings mean.

Despite this, the *Analects* is a fascinating and important document, and even the ambiguities it contains are vital prompts for thought. As Paul Valéry said, *une difficulté est une lumière*, and it often happens that obscure philosophy is a fountain of inspiration for those who grapple with it seriously. At the same time, there are tracts of the *Analects* that are not in the least obscure, and have had a significant impact on how the Chinese regarded right conduct. Book X, for example, is a compilation of remarks about how Confucius behaved – they might have started as general prescriptions on how a gentleman should behave, and then been applied biographically to Confucius himself; but they came to constitute a potent outline of how the Chinese gentleman-scholar (the mandarin) should comport himself. Thus, it enjoins a courteous ceremoniousness and scrupulosity in dealings with rulers of states, mourners, messengers, and fellow officials, and it describes how to sleep, prepare for sacrifices in the temple, and eat. Confucius set great store by the 'rites' (*li*) – meaning the ceremonies constituting the due order of how things are to be done, not least in affairs of state and its festivals, around which public life and community cohesion revolved, making the proper observance of the *li* essential to the well functioning of the social and personal orders.

The central concept of Confucius's philosophy is *ren*, meaning benevolence. (The word *ren* also means 'gentleman' in the sense of someone who behaves with authentic respect and consideration for others; the two senses are intimately connected.) The cultivation of benevolence does not only mean acting rightly, justly and compassionately towards others, but ensures that one will oneself avoid being arrogant, unjust, ingratiating or tyrannical. There is a form of the Golden Rule implicit in this – 'do not do to others what you do not wish to be done to yourself' (*Analects* XII). The other-directed right action and self-directed restraint and self-mastery that follow from it are enhanced by a careful study of the *li* governing the proper way of doing things.

A ruler who is *ren* will be a good ruler, because he will govern with benevolence, and set a good example in his own life and behaviour. People led by virtue, said Confucius, will be good subjects; those ruled by laws enforced by punishments will do everything they can to avoid punishment, and will not be governed by a sense of shame (*Analects* II). Confucius believed that none of the states he visited had rulers who were *ren*, because the essential ingredient of *ren* itself, which is *de* or virtue, was lacking. Once again the *li* are significant in this connection; *de* is a kind of moral force or energy which, Confucius says, an individual possesses because of correct observance of the *li*, so these latter are again shown to be essential to the good order of things. And it is *de* that makes *ren*, and *de* that guides the subjects of the *ren* ruler to serve him well.

An outstanding feature of the Confucian ethos by which China was influenced for long periods of its history is the system of scholar-civil-servants (the mandarins) who ruled under the authority of the Emperor. Long periods of study and a graduated system of imperial examinations, open to everyone with talent and brains (and the funds necessary for such a long education), produced scholar-administrators for provinces, counties and cities in the hierarchy of imperial government. Becoming a mandarin carried great rewards and status, and because it was achieved by competition rather than birth it ensured a supply of quality administrators for the empire's vast reaches.

The imperial examination system is well described in the novel *The Scholars* by Wu Jingzi, written in the eighteenth century CE, more than two millennia after Confucius's death, thus illustrating the length of time that the tradition (though with many changes, adaptations and intermissions of course) lasted. The source of that tradition was Confucius's own emphatic notions about the importance of study. A good teacher, Confucius said, would teach his pupils the wisdom and practices of the ancients, in a course of instruction including ethics, rhetoric, literature, the arts (the traditional 'six arts' were ritual, music, archery, chariot-driving, calligraphy and arithmetic) and the science of government. His method, as exemplified in the *Analects*, is a model of one kind of instruction: he did not lecture, but asked questions, quoted classics, and employed analogies and parables – and let his students find the answers or see the points he was guiding them towards.

At the centre of this educational endeavour lay the importance of moral and personal striving towards *ren*, and for this reason the *Book of Songs* was very important in the Confucian scheme of things. The *Book of Songs* is a poetry anthology, containing works which Confucius regarded as inspiring and educative because they are full of insights combined with beauty. No doubt it is because he extolled its virtues as a pedagogic and ethical classic that he is said to have edited it into its traditional form. Whether or not he did so, it is a striking fact that he saw poetry and the arts as an integral part of the education of gentlemen and rulers, and equally integral to achieving the good society.

Another great figure of the Confucian tradition, Mencius, wrote, 'Ever since mankind came into this world, there has never been anyone so great as Confucius.' His teachings touched the minds, hearts and loyalties of many generations of his countrymen, and anyone reading the *Analects* – even a Westerner in the twenty-first century – can recognise the presence in them of a great teacher and an essentially good man. It can be said that a better acquaintance with Confucius and his views has been too lacking in the Western tradition; it is both right and timely, as the globalised world becomes one village and different traditions meet and mingle, that the insights of China's great philosopher should become more widely known to all.

The Moral Worth of Truth

If it is sometimes good to tell a lie, what does this imply for the moral worth of truth?

For all but those who place their own purity or faith above the welfare of others, to lie is assuredly sometimes good. The Church of Scotland has an apt and pointful teaching, which says that it is a sin to tell an untimely truth; and one can multiply examples in support. What would we think of Abraham Lincoln, who could not lie, if he were a French farmer with a baled-out Spitfire pilot hiding in his shed and the Gestapo asking questions at his door?

Yet truth is a precious commodity, and its absence is usually an evil in itself, and usually leads to evil. How could anyone think of falsehood as the basis for good, or knowledge, or progress? If truth is sometimes dangerous or destructive, would silence not be better than lying? Or, best of all, should we simply not have the courage to accept all the hard consequences of truth-telling, if they come?

One possible answer, and rather a common one, is to say that all moral goods are relative to circumstances, and take different weightings depending upon the circumstances' details. So in some cases truth trumps other possible goods, and in others is trumped by them. For example, loyalty to one's own side in a war justifies lying to the enemy, so there truth is trumpable by loyalty; but in reporting the outcome of scientific experiments truth is never trumpable, not by loyalty to one's provider of funding or to one's laboratory chief or to anyone or anything else.

Despite the attractiveness of this answer, a certain disquiet might be prompted by its apparent relativisation of moral value. Of course, there is a persistent line of thought that takes this to embody the correct view of moral value anyway; but it would decidedly be an advantage if a case could be made for saying that there is an absolute value that always settles whether or not to speak truth in the circumstances of any case. This absolute value is *the good* itself; so that the decision whether or not to speak truth rests solely on the grounds of what would best serve to promote the good.

This might look like a mere redescription of what the relativist means when he says that circumstances dictate weightings of competing goods, but note this view's implication: my total circumstances (say, my culture) can make something good that another's total circumstances (say, his culture) make bad. Hence the impasse of relativism, which threatens to evacuate the idea of moral value itself. If there were a stable conception of the good available, matters would be otherwise.

Obviously the next question therefore is 'What is the good?', so that we can know whether speaking truly or falsely will serve it. This question, equally obviously, is the big one.

One significant aspect of the relationship between truth and the good concerns the way that what is strictly speaking not true can serve the good: the case of fiction. Plato said he would banish all poets (that is, all tellers of tales) from his ideal republic because they make things up, their stories are not true, they are fabricators; and in his ideal republic there would be nothing but truth-speaking. Apart from the fact that this overlooks the many ways in which what we say is neither true nor false but has other functions ('would you kindly close the window?' – 'hurrah!' – 'I do thee wed' – none of these is either true or false – and so on for very many utterances with uses other than fact-stating), it also overlooks the way that fiction can state 'higher truths' and be educative, informative, enlightening, insightful – all these things lead to better understandings of truths – as well as inspiring, moving, solacing, cathartic – all of which can lead to truer emotional states and thus are also servants of truth, albeit here of a different kind. So, Plato is comprehensively wrong on this point; not only can fiction serve the good, but it is one of the major ways of doing so.

This should not give comfort to defenders of the idea of 'noble lies'. Fiction is not a lie; it is not true, but 'non-truth' is a broader category than 'lie' and 'falsehood', which latter two are non-truths that mislead, typically in a deliberate way. Fiction does not only not deliberately set out to misinform or mislead, but can (in addition to entertaining) inform and lead as just shown.

To explain this, note that 'true' and 'false' do not exhaust the options between them, for there are also the categories of 'non-true, but not false either' (as in fiction) and 'neither true nor false' (as in 'please close the window'). The 'noble lie' idea is that the rulers, or priests, or anyway those in charge, should tell and sustain a lie to the general populace in the supposed interests of the latter, such as that there are gods who will protect them, or reward them for obeying the priests and punish them for failing to do so. The 'noble lie' can comfort, maintain good behaviour, and encourage soldiers to fight bravely because they think they will be rewarded in an afterlife.

Almost all, if not indeed all, the tropes of demagoguery about the motherland, the gods, the revolution, our forefathers, the honour and glory to be won in battle, and so forth, have a good chance of being ignoble lies, as history – that nursery of truth and the higher truths – repeatedly tells us.

Relativism

How does one argue against the relativist?

Aristotle and Einstein have different views about the universe's size, Torquemada and Richard Dawkins differ on religion, St Theresa of Lisieux and Cora Pearl differ on sexual morality. Some will think that the first in each pairing is wrong and the second right, others will think the opposite. Both sides at least agree that there is a right and wrong in each case. But there are those who think that all of them are right, in their own individual ways. These are the relativists.

Relativists thus deny the existence of objective truth. There is no truth, they say, only truth-for-me; and what is true-for-me can be false-for-you. And this, they say, is just as it should be, because the validity of what we believe is always a function of our standpoint.

Postmodernism finds this view attractive for various reasons, among them the otherwise commendable one of giving everyone a place in the sun. Members of a Stone Age community can stand proudly by their beliefs, says the relativist, which are as valid in their own terms as is Western science for Westerners. This example is extreme; more plausible is the thought that moral and religious commitments can vary across time or cultures, with no independent way of adjudicating their comparative merits. Although relativism more usually takes this latter form, the more extreme form has been embraced by some; a notable example is the philosopher Paul Feyerabend, who thought that native rain dances were as valid a way in their own terms of making clouds shed their rain as seeding those clouds with silver iodide from an aeroplane.

The first way to argue against the relativist is to point out that if there is no such thing as truth (or validity, or justification for belief, and so on) except from a given perspective, then one has to accept one of the following three assertions: the claim 'there is no truth except from a given standpoint' is true only from a given standpoint, or it is self-refuting, or it is a very special kind of truth in being the only one that is true from all standpoints. Each of these alternatives makes a nonsense of the claim that there is no truth except from a given standpoint, so the relativist position is incoherent.

The second way is to point out that when people assert that their beliefs are true, they typically do not mean 'only for me'. This phrase applies in cases of taste or preference, and sometimes when there is known to be no fact discoverable to settle a choice of view. But if I say that it is true that camels have humps, I do not mean to imply that it is simultaneously true that camels have no humps because someone else believes as much.

The third way is to point out that if relativism is true, enquiry (in science and elsewhere) is pointless, because if there is no objective truth, there is nothing for enquiry to look for. If fairy tales and physics are equally true 'in their own ways', one might as well rest content with whatever one currently happens to believe, and seek no further.

Each of these responses to relativism was given by Plato in his *Protagoras* 2,500 years ago, a fact that attests yet again how hardy a perennial relativism, like most kinds of nonsense, is.

One of the better motives for relativism is to challenge the snobbishness and contempt shown by denizens of 'superior cultures' such as the contemporary West to 'inferior cultures', such as those variously described as backward, primitive, Stone Age, and the like, in such places as sub-Saharan Africa, Papua New Guinea, the Amazon rainforest and the Arctic. It is politically incorrect to insist that peoples with high levels of technological development, literacy and political organisation are more 'advanced' than hunter-gatherer communities living in straw huts. The blunt and obvious fact is that they are indeed more advanced in the respects mentioned, but this is not an answer to the different question – the one that the relativist is thinking about – namely, whether it therefore makes them 'better'. Well, of course not: until one has specified the relevant points of comparison. As it happens, I would rather live in a contemporary Western society, especially if I were a woman, than in most of the alternatives, and to make a case for saying so; the dispute then becomes one that is not about 'different truths' which are nevertheless each genuinely true – a non-starter – but about preferences. And preferences are assuredly but innocuously relative.

Doing Ill to the Bad

Is it acceptable to do bad things to bad people?

In the field of moral aphorism there is no more contradictory a swarm of injunctions, observations and resolutions than those concerning what we do, should do, or should not do to others. Some British soldiers in Afghanistan wore caps inscribed with the legend 'We do bad things to bad people'. This remark or claim is an entrant to the debate about justifiable ways of treating others, and it is severely at odds with Christianity as regards what to do to bad people; for, familiarly, the latter says we should offer them the other cheek (though I suppose there is an interpretation of the soldier's cap that would agree, provided the cheek is below the belt).

A perennial debate surrounds the 'do unto others' cliché: is it 'do unto others as you would have them do unto you' or 'do not do unto others what you would not have them do unto you'? George Bernard Shaw famously advised against the former, on the grounds that others may not like having done to them what you would like them to do to you, and the latter is therefore claimed to be superior. Think about it, though; might it too not come under Shaw's stricture? For they might like what you do not like, just as they might not like what you like.

214

In fact the 'unto others' injunction in either form misses a point: that the most enlightened and generous moral attitudes are premised on the possibility that others can be very different from oneself, so that one's own likes and dislikes are not much more than a self-regarding and limited basis for thinking about the needs, interests and desires of others, and of how to adjust one's behaviour towards them accordingly. One needs to be able to see and accept otherness in order to be an effective moral agent.

This is why literature and the arts are so important, in (among other things) educating our moral insights and sympathies, so that we can recognise and respect differences from ourselves, and act appropriately. Human diversity is great, and failure to grasp the true texture of that diversity is the cause of much narrow-mindedness, self-centredness and unkindness. The key moral attitudes are generosity and tolerance, where tolerance is not mere indifference but active acceptance that others have a right to their choices, whatever one thinks about them oneself.

At the same time, to be overindulgent and over-tolerant is just as harmful. Bad people do bad things for lots of different reasons, some meriting concern and help, others meriting a robust kicking. In war the folk on the other side are this latter kind of bad by definition – they are trying to kill you – and what they do accordingly invites robust kicking first and discussion, if any, afterwards. That is the context for the 'we do bad things to bad people' legend on the soldier's cap.

The cap's legend is thus an understandable exhortation to its wearers and their comrades, as well as a threat to the bad. But as a general principle – well: no. Doing bad to the bad should not be a preferred first step, even if to some of the bad it ends up being a necessary last step. There are obvious prudential reasons: to do bad things to the bad might well make them behave yet worse, and other approaches might be more effective in making them less bad. The moral reason is that we owe it to ourselves to try the latter tack first, if it is feasible: to ourselves, note, as well as to the bad, whose reasons for being so might be complicated ones with which, if we understood them, we might sympathise. We owe it to ourselves because one of the constraints in the moral life is the answer each of us gives to the question 'What sort of person am I?' The point in all the above is that the answer to this question has to be coupled with all the different answers given every time to the question 'What sort of person is he?'

Smoking

Smokers say they have the right to smoke; others say they have the right not to have to breathe their smoke. Is a smoking ban the best solution?

Among both our legislators and ourselves there continues to be muddle about the degree to which a state can intervene in the lives and practices of individuals before it crosses the boundary into nannying and, eventually, unjustifiable diminution of individual liberty. Smoking is only one of many examples where the question of the boundary arises; others range from raised car seats for children and seat-belts in general, to drink, drugs and prostitution. Yet in fact the underlying principles are clear, and there are fewer grey areas than people think.

Isaiah Berlin is as good a place as any to start. In distinguishing between *positive* and *negative* liberty he defined the former as the freedom to seek and realise various goals, the latter as freedom from external compulsion. He favoured the latter because he thought the idea of the former could tempt the state to prescribe and even enforce behaviour that it believed would be in citizens' best interests – and therefore what every citizen should desire, whether or not in fact he does so. By contrast, negative liberty defines the area within which people should be left to their own choices and preferences without interference from others. It is the classic conception of liberty as formulated by John Stuart Mill.

The equally classic constraint on the 'negative' conception of liberty is of course the Harm Principle: in exercising one's own liberty one must cause no harm to others. It is the conjunction of these two ideas that settles the location of the nannying boundary. Where the exercise of given choices and preferences can harm others, and where restraint is an insufficient safeguard against its doing so, the state has a role in providing protection to possible victims. Where any harm that might occur is to the freely choosing individual himself, alone, the state has no place intervening.

Banning smoking in public places is legitimate because it protects the health of others. Banning smoking as such would not be legitimate. Legally requiring car seats for children is justifiable because children are not competent to ensure their own safety. Outlawing certain drugs (heroin, cocaine) is not justifiable, though it is justifiable to place the same kind of conditions on their use as are placed on that other major drug, alcohol, to protect bystanders from the effects of their use and abuse. And so on: the principle is clear enough.

Grey areas remain, and have to be matters for decision. Legally requiring motorcyclists to wear helmets, and everyone to wear car seat-belts, are two such. Each is certainly prudent, but that is the wrong motivation for a law enforcing it. Saving NHS bills is a better justification; but then that entails a justification for outlawing obesity. The latter is harder to enforce; evidently the (British) state chooses its battles, and nannies where it can – usually too far over the boundary, as drugs and other matters of private choice show; but smoking in public places is not one such.

Here is a real problem for actors and directors of feature films: how do you convey human emotion without the aid of a cigarette? Before cigarettes changed from being the ultimate symbol of cool to a dangerous bad habit, they provided a hook for every conceivable important movie moment: mystery, suspense (the face between the upturned collar points on the dark street, momentarily illuminated by the flare of the cigarette lighter), lust, seduction (Lauren Bacall asking Humphrey Bogart for a light), anger, disappointment, rest, elegance, relief, tension, tranquillity – in short: the human condition in the glow at the end of a little tube of rolled-up intoxicant leaf.

The most famous cigarette advert in the world says it all: the lean, tough, good-guy cowboy out on the range, leaning across the horn of his saddle in the late-afternoon light when the herd has been rounded up, drawing luxuriously on his cigarette, Stetson tipped slightly back, the wrists of his soft leather gloves folded negligently down. Ah, man, you can just see how good that smoke tastes, how good life can taste, how the hit of the nicotine gives a satisfying buzz, everything relaxes, the world turns mellow.

And what better accompaniment to this easy little piece of paradise than a glass of whiskey? Though the real accompaniment, in the long run, is the oxygen mask for the emphysema sufferer, struggling for breath, or for the lung-cancer patient who at first thought he just had a niggling cough or an odd local twinge in his back like someone pushing a pencil-point into the same spot, over and over, all day long.

Because of the rich cloud of meanings, the great majority of them cool, adult, sophisticated, tough or sexy, that floated around the cigarette in movies and adverts, almost everyone reached for a pack of twenty as soon as they could escape adult eyes. The kids grouped around a single fag, passed from hand to hand with much puckering of lips, watering eyes and spluttering, thought they were on the road to becoming the best-looking Hollywood stars in history.

And the truth is that cigarettes taste good, feel good, and when they were acceptable they looked good too: they were the ultimate stage prop, they quelled nerves both in giving smokers something to do with their hands and by soothing the neurology within. It seems amazing now that we sat in cinemas in a dense fug of tobacco smoke rising from dozens of cigarettes, all of us so used to breathing in the carcinogenic motes that we did not even notice – except that the beam of light from the projector to the screen swirled thickly with exciting blue mysteries.

It has to be acknowledged that the speed with which Paris has shed its Gauloise-wreathed aura is amazing. No one believed that a smoking ban in public places would stick. How could those earnest intellectual discussions continue in smokeless cafés? Yet they do: it is a sort of miracle. It makes one half-believe that the cigarette could be stubbed out of human history by the combined big fingers of health awareness and social disapproval.

But the cigarette has not been stubbed out of human history. Hundreds of millions of them are consumed every day in China, the most-smoking country in the world, and there is no sign of much reduction there. Even in the more health-enlightened advanced world, millions do the equivalent of setting fire to banknotes and inhaling poison at the same time. Economies the world over creak under the burden of smoking-related ill health, but are addicted to the tax revenues that partially defray that expense – though one can never quite put a price on cancerous death and family grief as one can quantify lost man-hours.

Flick the lighter and a tough big question is lit up by the flare: who has the right to tell anyone what to do and not to do with his own life? You can justify a smoking ban in public places to protect people from the secondary effects of tobacco smoke, because we accept that even in the most liberal society there is a requirement that the exercise of one's freedoms should not harm others. But it is tyranny to force others to behave as one thinks they should, even if one knows for sure what is in their best interests. The critics of this liberalism say: but no man is an island: if he smokes, he damages others – even if there are no passive smokers in his vicinity, he adds to health-care costs and lost productivity. You can answer: he keeps tobacco farmers and cigarette manufacturers in work: swings and roundabouts. The answer will come: the same can be said of the heroin addict feeding the Afghan poppy-farmer's family. You can reply: yes, you have a good point there.

No, the cigarette has not been stubbed out of history, and it will be a long time – all the way to never – before it is. One can say this with assurance because the human animal craves its mood- and mind-altering substances: all the drugs from alcohol and nicotine to heroin and cocaine – all of them dangerous, all of them potentially though not invariably destructive – are a human food, and no quantity of advice, laws, vilification or 'drug wars' will ever stop them. Society would do better to apply the alcohol lesson: that is, learn how to manage it by accepting its ill consequences, trying to encourage more responsible use by the majority, sweeping up the pieces – car crashes, broken marriages, cirrhosis of the liver, fights outside pubs and bars – and otherwise being stoical. The alternative is to reprise the futility of King Canute, who stationed his throne on the beach and ordered the tide not to come in. I imagine Canute, the waves breaking round his ankles, responding to the inevitable by lighting up a king-size filter cigarette and taking a long, deep, philosophical draw on it – if he had lived in our own smoky times.

Hypocrisy

Is it not hypocritical to charge people with hypocrisy?

When former governor Eliot Spitzer of New York appeared before the media after being heard, on an FBI wiretap, arranging a tryst with a prostitute, he apologised for having 'acted in a way that violates my obligation to my family and violates my or any sense of right or wrong'. This form of words implies that his fault was to seek paid-for sex, and no doubt plenty of people agree, chiefly those who are for marital fidelity or against prostitution, or both.

But what made it impossible for Mr Spitzer to remain in office, despite trying to describe what he did as a private matter, was that throughout his public life he presented himself as a moral crusader, gaining a reputation as an anti-corruption campaigner who in two terms as New York State's attorney-general not only exposed financial shenanigans on Wall Street, but dismantled two major prostitution rings, in the process proclaiming his revulsion and anger at their existence.

In short, Spitzer's chief crime was hypocrisy. If anyone ever needs a clear-cut example of this failing, Spitzer provides it – as does 'Praise the Lord' preacher Jim Bakker, brought down by scandals about alleged rape and fraud, and even more so preacher Jimmy Swaggart, who exposed Bakker and described him as a 'cancer in the body of Christ', only to be himself found consorting with prostitutes. (Memorably he told his congregation, following the revelations, that 'The Lord told me its flat none of your business.')

In all these cases public professions and private behaviour not only contradict one another, but do so in a particular way. The public professions are claims to virtue and high standards, yet the private behaviour consists of what the public professions proscribe. If someone publicly supported prostitution, but privately did not engage the services of prostitutes, no one would call him a hypocrite. It is the twofold fact that virtue is claimed, but dishonestly and consciously so, that is the key.

In its original Greek meaning, 'hypocrite' meant an actor, and was a morally neutral term; it has gained its pejorative meaning because the acting in question is more than acting, it is a gross lie.

All this said, Spitzer-type cases have the unfortunate consequence that many examples of failure to live up to ideals are misidentified as hypocrisy, and – even less fairly – the word gets misapplied to examples of human frailty (or just to human nature expressing itself in all the naturalness of its needs and desires) when in fact there was no claim to special virtue in the first place.

Politicians and preachers are the prime targets for accusations of hypocrisy, almost exclusively in matters of sex and money. True, they have only themselves to blame if they pretend to live by high moral standards and then find the front pages of newspapers covered with photographs of themselves sucking toes not attached to their wives. But there is a difference between people who lay claim to such virtue but who practise what they themselves define as its opposite, and those who make no such claims. Many people assume that certain public roles automatically carry with them expectations of traditional sexual virtues, and in some cases they are right – for example, clerics, school teachers (at least as regards school children), doctors – and in some cases not right – for example, politicians (unless they proclaim themselves squeaky-clean), city traders, bus drivers.

If the charge of hypocrisy is bandied about too much it masks the important fact that there is no dishonesty, and no shame, in sincerely wishing to attain certain ideals, but not getting there. That, after all, is a common human experience. The philosophers of classical antiquity endlessly discussed the problem of 'knowing the better but doing the worse', which some thought of as a product of weakness of will, others as self-deception, still others as a fact about the difficulties, constraints, temptations and complexities in the human condition.

The key word is 'sincerely'; the central feature of hypocrisy is precisely the lack of sincerity. And of course it is easy for people insincerely to claim sincerity, as yet another layer cloaking their hypocrisy. But although people can hide from the nastier truths about themselves for long periods, there is some satisfaction to be had in knowing that not everyone can do this completely, and that especially includes hypocrites. Knowing that one has been hypocritical about something is no small punishment in its own right.

In their relentless pursuit of sensation and scandal the media are always too quick to describe ordinary failings as hypocrisy. There are familiar cultural differences in this; French newspapers would only label a married politician a hypocrite because he or she has a lover if that politician had publicly advocated marital fidelity. In our Anglo-Saxon world with its adolescent, sniggering and apprehensive attitude to anything sexual, it does not matter whether a politician has said anything at all about sexual morals; a mistress, a prostitute, a visit to a gay bar means open season.

It would be refreshing if the Spitzer case focused attention on the real meaning of hypocrisy, thus putting a limit on the hypocritical use of 'hypocrisy' as a blanket witch-hunting term in the moral sphere. We might all be able to think more clearly and judge more fairly as a result.

There is a general social hypocrisy about prostitution or, as it should better be called, sex work. It is a serious wrong for anyone to be coerced into sex work, or while in it to be subjected to ill treatment; but this is not because of the sex in sex work, but because of the coercion and ill treatment itself, which are wrong in every kind of work. Moralists refuse to believe that some people engage in sex work willingly – but indeed some do – and the mere connection with sex is enough to make them brand sex work as intrinsically evil. It is no more so than any other kind of work if willingly and safely undertaken. For a variety of reasons, as a clear-eyed view of the matter would show, when sex work is willingly and safely engaged in, it can be a significant and valuable service: a prop to marriage, a safety-valve for natural urges that society devotes a lot of energy to limiting and controlling, and a source of straightforward pleasure. It is not sex work per se, but the endless efforts at repression of sex work, that represent the symptom of a sickness somewhere in the moral economy of the world. A large part of that sickness is hypocrisy.

Parental Rights

*Is there a 'right' to have more children than one can
feed and care for? And, if so, does it create a duty
on the rest of us to feed and care for them?*

According to one familiar outlook, one does not have a right but a duty to have children, whether or not one can provide for them. The Old Testament injunction to 'go forth and multiply' is held by Catholic moral theology to be trumped by St Paul's teaching on the preferability of celibacy, but still incumbent on those who had better marry than burn. For these lesser members of the flock, the accident of conception, no matter what the consequence for the resulting numbers of children, has to be borne with patience – by all concerned.

The question itself, though, has a steely edge to it. Should the poor be allowed to have children if they cannot feed and wash them properly? This has become 'any children', not just 'more children', but the implication is already there. Perhaps the real question is: Should we allow any children to be born and raised in poverty and want? – intending by this not to deny the maternal instinct when it rises, but the indifference of society to the needs of children (and their mothers) once they are born.

There are two reasons for wishing to switch the matter round this way. One has to do with the imperative felt by many, and probably most, women towards maternity. Any dispensation that denied motherhood to women on the grounds that they do not meet certain economic or other socially imposed criteria would be an unjustifiable one. If the idea of a 'natural' right has any grip, it applies in the sphere of biological fundamentals such as this.

The other reason has to do with the obligations that any decent society owes those who are not in a position to fend for themselves, and who need a range of familiar helps to become so. Children are paradigmatically in that case, and so if they are not sufficiently circumstanced, we indeed have a duty to provide for them. This applies as much to children accidentally conceived by such of the feckless poor as have no real prospect of being good parents, as it does to poor people who strongly desire children. Wanted children are at something of a premium in the world, but the needs of the unwanted are as great.

When it comes to 'more children than the parents can afford', though, the question introduces the idea of responsibility to already existing children, to say nothing of society at large. If you have children and cannot afford more, have you not exercised your right to have children already, and are you not trespassing on their interests by having more?

Answer: Yes. But does this remove society's duty to both the children irresponsibly born and the children they thus deprive? Answer: No.

Money

Can money ever be an end in itself?

One of the things that most marks off human beings from the rest of the animal kingdom is their genius for getting the wrong end of the stick. Nothing illustrates this better than the subject of money. Consider the inconvenience of taking a cow to town, and butchering small bits off it in exchange for a pair of shoes here, a haircut there, a newspaper, a beer at the pub on the corner – and so rather bloodily and (for the cow) distressingly forth. Thus it was that our distant ancestors invented tokens of exchange to represent the value of bits of cows and pairs of shoes: much less distressing, much more convenient.

But no sooner had this stroke of genius been struck than humanity began to make money an end in itself, a fetish, something so desirable that some even murder for it. The token had become mesmeric in a way that a steak or a radish could only be to a starving man. When it comes to money, in short, we are all starving men.

The rational attitude to money is of course to wish for lots of it, but only because of what spending it provides. Consider: a man who has ten million dollars in the bank and never spends a cent is a very poor man indeed. A man who has a hundred dollars in his pocket and spends it on a good time is a rich man indeed. Accordingly, one should estimate an individual's wealth by what he spends, not by what he has; for in this short life of ours – one should never tire of pointing out that the average human lifespan is less than a thousand months long – wealth is experience, endeavour, enjoyment, energy. It is emphatically not a bank balance, a sheaf of investments, a pile of bricks and mortar, for none of this goes into the grave with its owner, and while it exists in that illiquid form it is of little real use, except as a promissory of what it can be turned into: travel, laughter, learning, expansion of spirit through the acquisition of delights and memories.

But until it turns into these things, money is valueless. Once upon a time money was itself, independently of its instrumental utility, valuable: a pound sterling was a pound weight of silver, so its exchange value equalled its intrinsic value. That could not last; people clipped bits off the edge in ways you could not notice, to make more pounds out of the accumulated snippets, reducing the true value of the official coinage in the process. When we started using intrinsically valueless metals and paper – mere tokens therefore – we at last seemed to accept that it is not money but what it can buy that matters. And yet even that deep truth has not sunk in everywhere, meaning that too few know that the real definition of 'being rich' is 'having enough' – not of money, but of what you want to buy.

Few people share the sentiment of the song whose refrain is, 'And I don't give a damn about a greenback dollar', but they go along with its second line, 'Spend it as fast as I can.' All round the world the influence of the almighty dollar has made it the paradigm of money, and therefore everything that money in sufficient quantity implies: status, freedom, opportunity, pleasure, security, the good life.

Dollars became green with Abraham Lincoln. He chose green ink for the reverse of the dollar bills he printed to finance the Union in the Civil War. The intention was to distinguish them from the varieties of other notes in circulation, issued by many banks in many states. It was the beginning of a legend.

Even though the rest of the world's currencies were not valued in terms of the US dollar until the 1944 Bretton Woods Agreement, it already by then had its 'almighty' status. It figures in uncountable numbers of narrative songs, its potency in film images is enduring: think of a James Cagney character in a gangster movie, peeling off a greenback from a fat billfold and stuffing it into someone's top pocket as a bribe: the message is that the greenback means everything and can buy anything.

The appearance of the US dollar bill has changed several times since Lincoln's day, but its green remains a central feature of its iconic power. It represents opportunity; its message is: 'You can have me if you work hard enough, or if you are smart or beautiful or talented enough.' In the minds of many the greenback is more than a currency note, it is a marker of human value: people are measured by how many of them they have. In that way the greenback dollar not only has two literal sides, but two philosophical sides too, standing for ambition or debasement, depending on how you choose to see it.

Will the dollar last as the world's currency? Many blame the Gordon Gekko greed of Wall Street for the global economic downturn of 2008–9; if the huge US economy sank under its own weight in its vastly debt-increasing effort to revive itself, the Gekkos would have sunk the dollar too. And within the lifetimes of the children of today's bankers in Frankfurt, London and New York, the world currency could be the renminbi or the rupee, if what is happening today more speedily alters the fundamental balance of the global economy.

But – for what this opinion is worth – one expects that the dollar will survive for decades to come as the world's cash, for as long again as it has been the world's cash *de jure* as well as *de facto*. US dollar bills are accepted tender in almost every country, and universally in the developing world; and it is the currency quoted in the invisible electronic transfers, counted in billions, of the world's daily tradings. With a status like that, it will take time for it to be replaced by another currency, if ever: like an oil tanker turning round at sea, it has many miles to go before the turn begins, and a long way round before it points in the other direction.

And while this is so, the symbolic power of the greenback dollar, that small oblong note that quickly loses its new-printed crispness and becomes limp and soft-textured in the hand, will continue to have more power over people and circumstances than anything apart from epidemic disease and all-out war. So the likelihood is that it will remain the world currency for a long time, and the foremost American symbol, and there will be more songs, and more films in which the appearance of the familiar greenback note will not have to be explained because everyone without exception will recognise it for what it is.

And therefore it will also remain the symbol of ambition, and of corruption; of success, and of envy; of desire, and of greed: because money is the repository of all these things, and the greenback dollar is the paradigm of money.

Shakespeare the Thinker

Can Shakespeare be described as having a philosophy,
an identifiable point of view on life?

It is often observed how mysterious is the phenomenon
of genius, even if we no longer think the word denotes a
creature who sits on poets' shoulders and whispers messages
from the Muses into their ears. It is one thing to accept that
some people can be stunningly inventive and clever, another
to fathom the nature of the gifts that make them so. But
in the case of Shakespeare, familiarly, all resources fail: here
was an individual whose capacities and achievement literally
transcend explanation.

Some perhaps grow weary of the pieties collectively
indulged about Shakespeare, until they reread him and are
electrified all over again by the language he uses, the insights it
conveys, the universality of understanding and sympathy that
informs the insights, and the vaulting power of imagination
that drives all. The fact of his genius has to be accepted as a
given. A different point – and one addressed by my former
tutor, the late and much-lamented A. D. Nuttall – concerns
something else: Shakespeare's intelligence. Nuttall discusses
it, and through it Shakespeare as philosopher, in his book
Shakespeare the Thinker (2008).

Anthony Nuttall was well equipped for this task. He was as
much a philosopher as a literary critic – and, unusually among
critics, he was well read in Anglophone analytic philosophy.
He did not have much time for the intellectual posturings of
'theory' in literary studies, and maintained an independence
of thought about what most moved him and mattered to him

in literature, especially in Shakespeare. He preferred the shift to historicism over the fashions for post-structuralism and deconstruction in theory, but against both he asserted the claims of authorial intention, not least in so alert, profound and deliberate a mind as Shakespeare's. One might even say that his reading of Shakespeare is a refutation of the view that the academic critic knows better than Shakespeare himself what he thought and meant; a reader who gives an author credit for knowing what he, the author, wishes to convey, is a reader Nuttall can get along with. To read his illuminating commentary on the plays, premised on this respect for their author's mind, is therefore to be in educative company.

Nuttall makes use of two interesting points in establishing his approach. One is a question about the significance of a certain historical event that occurred during Shakespeare's youth in Stratford. This was the death by drowning in the Avon of a young woman, followed by an inquest that left a question mark as to whether the drowning was suicide. The connection with Ophelia's death in *Hamlet* is an obvious one. The other is the degree to which the Shakespeare family, and in particular William himself, were caught up in the grim affair of the recusancy, in which Jesuit secret agents sought to unsettle the English state, and many in Stratford clung more or less secretly to the Old Religion. Was Shakespeare a Catholic, a recusant, secretly more loyal to God and the Pope than to Queen Elizabeth and King James?

The second matter is all the more interesting because Shakespeare set all his plays in a pre-Reformation past that made reference to the appurtenances and practices of Catholicism – friars and hermits' cells and attending the mass – entirely natural. But there is no hint otherwise of his taking sides on the burning (literally) question of the time; rather, he writes as if above it; and these two facts, jointly with the widespread lingering attachment to Catholicism in so many of his neighbours, relations and friends, plus gossip ('he died a Papist', wrote one near-contemporary), have been fertile in generating speculation.

For Nuttall, Shakespeare's detachment in handling this question is a mark of conscious indifference, where 'indifference' has its literal and positive meaning to denote an encompassing, universalising neutrality of viewpoint among the possibilities and passions that all human affairs involve. Whatever Shakespeare personally thought about anything, in the plays all sides of those thoughts are given sympathetic articulation; he represented the total picture, as if he looked down from the clouds (and with X-ray vision), exemplifying the French saying that to comprehend all is to forgive all. If there is a single thing one were to nominate as characteristic of Shakespeare's mind, it is this indifference, this embracing neutrality that saw all sides and allowed each of them their best expression.

The accidental or suicidal drowning in the Avon that stuck in Shakespeare's memory underwrites Nuttall's case against the historicists that writers are not merely the conduits of the influences of their time, but conscious responders to them. To those unhampered by theory the point seems clear: in the alembic of a great imagination the particular takes on universal significance, and lends itself to transmutations that serve the author's chosen purpose. But Nuttall applies this in his analysis of Shakespeare as 'the philosopher of human possibility', by drawing out the way Shakespeare goes beyond the given in his sources, and well beyond his memory and influences, to venture into an exploration of how things can be, and might have been, for people in the circumstances in which his dramas place them.

For Nuttall, this makes Shakespeare's dramatic universe 'a forest of flourishing but imperilled "might-be's" or a web of provisional essays'. He was 'too intelligent to be able to persuade himself that the problems [addressed in the plays] are completely solved', but he went further than anyone else in portraying how they felt to those experiencing them, and why they tried to solve them as they did. He was, in short, truly a philosopher of possibility: he saw the open texture of lives and their accidental nature, as well as the ideas, principles and necessities that acted as deterministically and fatally in individual lives as if determinism and fatalism were metaphysical truths.

If anything, this moves Shakespeare further away from recusancy, for it is a theological tenet of Catholicism that individuals have free will, without which the notions of sin and works cannot make sense. It was the Calvinists who embraced determinism, as inflexibly as the supposed operation of predestination itself.

At this juncture therefore it is pertinent to glance at what recent biography makes of Shakespeare in these respects, for example in René Weis's *Shakespeare Revealed* (2008). Weis joins the brave company of those in search of this extremely elusive human individual, but with an advantage: there is now a vast wealth of material available to be minutely combed-over, most of it circumstantial detail concerning matters related to Shakespeare's home town, his neighbours, his fellow players, people known to be connected with him, people possibly connected with him, the history and politics of the time, and a million other facts, clues, hints, possibilities and suppositions, very few of which definitely and conclusively settle the questions that wrap Shakespeare the man in such thick veils, but which anyway provide tantalising suggestions. Weis takes an interesting tack through these details, which is to assume that the plays richly reflect details of Shakespeare's early life in Stratford-upon-Avon, which can therefore be explored as if it were a map to his life and mind.

The idea is ingenious, and not without merit. But it actually serves to deepen rather than dispel the mystery, for the more one learns of the Catholic recusancy of so many of Shakespeare's neighbours, and the danger of the 'cold' religious war that beset England during Shakespeare's formative years, the more surprising is the way his work simply ignores the fact of the Reformation and the subsequent religious strife altogether.

Weis gives a detailed picture of the setting of Shakespeare's life, and a judicious one; there is no falling for the more speculative romances that have Shakespeare hiding with fellow Catholics in Lancashire in fear for his life, or being part of an alleged Arden plot to murder Queen Elizabeth. But on the central question of Shakespeare's religious sympathies or sensitivities, not even this much fine-tooth-combing yields an answer, any more than a fine-tooth-combing of the works themselves.

It is no criticism to say, therefore, that the result of Weis's exploration results in no diminution of the usual 'must haves', 'could haves' and 'probablies' that litter the pages of every Shakespeare biography. Weis's exhaustive familiarity with every inch of Stratford-upon-Avon engenders the feeling that he must have a familiarity with the poet's ghost that few others share. Interestingly, Nuttall took some of the same walks in Stratford and its neighbourhood, and had some of the same sensations of closeness to the poet's presence; not literally, of course, but figuratively; and remembers seeing a line of hills in the dusk that Shakespeare certainly saw, offering one of the few if rather unexciting definites in the fog of mere possibilities that hides him from view.

It is a striking thought that, as the philosopher of possibility, Shakespeare the individual is himself no more to us than a series of possibilities, so obscure is the tale of his life.

Shakespeare's Humanism

In what sense was Shakespeare a humanist, and what does it mean to describe him as one?

Shakespeare's ability to inhabit a great diversity of outlooks – he writes from Othello's point of view, and Iago's; from Hamlet's and Claudius's; from Tybalt's and Juliet's – makes it hard to attribute a consistent philosophical view to him, except in one respect: he was profoundly a humanist in the Elizabethan sense of this term. In Renaissance England humanism meant commitment to three things: the idea that human beings share a universal essence – a 'human nature'; that governing and improving society require an understanding of human nature; and that this understanding is best achieved through art and letters, which involves education and practice in the disciplines of civilisation.

He also employed, if only for the convenience of being able to rely on his audience's beliefs in relevant respects, the tropes of Elizabethan metaphysics, which sometimes conflicted with humanism. This metaphysics included the idea that royalty is a divine endowment, that oaths are sacred and their breaking punishable by hellfire, that magic is of the devil, that distressed spirits appear on midnight battlements or in dreams, and that the nature of the macrocosm can be disturbed and agitated by upsets in the human microcosm, if the individuals concerned are noble or royal.

Both humanism and this metaphysics of superstition appear in *The Winter's Tale*, the latter to a far less extent than in *Macbeth*, *The Tempest* or elsewhere. In fact in this play the metaphysics is only glancingly invoked: a meaningful dream and a meaningful storm are the only touches of the supernatural. Humanism, however, is fully present. The story, remember, is that Leontes, King of Sicilia, has become insanely jealous of his wife Queen Hermione, and believes that she has been made pregnant by his erstwhile closest friend, King Polixenes of Bohemia. When Hermione gives birth, Leontes orders his faithful servant Antigonus to carry away the child, a girl, and kill her. Antigonus cannot bring himself to do so, but leaves the baby with much money and fine cloth in a wood 'on the shores of Bohemia', where she is found by a kindly old shepherd and his son, who take her in, name her Perdita ('lost'), and care for her.

The two supernatural events are minor. Antigonus dreams that Hermione's spirit visits him, on the night before he leaves Perdita on the shores of Bohemia; and he does the latter in a shipwrecking storm, denoting the elements' upset over this unnatural outcome of Leontes's jealousy. But the dream is almost incidental. The play is otherwise and wholly an essay in the humanist conception of man's frail and divided nature, and of how it can betray itself and therefore others by falling victim to destructive passion – in Leontes's case, jealousy and the trouble it causes.

As usual in Shakespeare there are mirrors and contrasts to the main theme in other characters and the subplots that involve them. Polixenes's initial anger at his son Prince Florizel's love for Perdita, and the conscious roguery of the comedy figure Autolycus, are likewise disruptions to the relationships that constitute society, the more pronounced for the background of trust, kindness, good-heartedness, loyalty and truth of everyone else in the play, these being the bonds on which social order depends. Autolycus exploits the goodness of others in order to cozen them; all the other characters – the clown, Antigonus, Camillo, Paulina, Florizel and Hermione – suffer because they are faithful, though they are rewarded in the end.

This therefore is a humanist drama of morality and how it fares when powerful people's powerful emotions smash the fabric of connections that keep society's balance. An immediately obvious fact about Sicilia, and by extension Bohemia, is that prior to Leontes's jealous fit they form a well-ordered world in which mutuality and trust prevail. There are no evil people in *The Winter's Tale*; not even Autolycus succeeds in being deeply morally corrupt in the way that a Iago or a Lady Macbeth is, and this despite the fact that characters in this play are types rather than people, representatives of a moral position rather than personalities. They are what they are in order to mark out positions; they are tokens in a humanist essay on moral symmetries.

The symmetries in the play are the symmetries of humanistic optimism. An outburst of destructive emotion causes flight and loss in the play's first half; Time the Chorus carries us sixteen years forward to another outburst of destructive emotion that causes flight and loss in the reverse direction. This latter then sets to rights the harm done by the former, and the cut threads of relationship are rejoined into their proper tapestry thereby.

In both cases what preserves the possibility of rectification is loyalty. The courtiers Antigonus, Paulina and Camillo are central components of the play's machinery for this reason, for without them the tyranny of emotion in the two kings would instantly have expressed itself in murder. Both kings bluster, threaten, rage and accuse when roused, and had they been left unrestrained – indeed, had they not been saved from themselves by what one must call faithful betrayals – they would have consigned innocents to death. Leontes wished to kill Polixenes and Hermione, and fling her baby Perdita into the flames; Polixenes threatens the old shepherd with hanging for permitting Florizel's courtship of Perdita, and threatens Perdita with facial disfigurement because she has bewitched his son. All this emotional mayhem has to be restored to moral proportion, and the play is a demonstration of how this is to be done.

The play is carefully arranged in its moral shape, if not in its cavalier treatment of time – the suddenness of kingly rages, the speed with which messengers travel, the giant leap of sixteen years between Acts III and IV are all bold strokes of Shakespeare's late impressionism, subservient to the point that The Good is the product of right emotion. And this, a quintessentially humanist concern, is the play's central theme.

For a humanist, morality is the achievement of human endeavour when educated to its best ends by love and trust, and this in turn is a service performed by art. Love and trust are what Paulina wishes Leontes to recover, though not before he has thoroughly learned how the lack of trust destroys love. Art in the sense both of artfulness and artifice is brought to bear on the restoration of the play's severed bonds in a variety of ways; the good artfulness of Camillo in saving Polixenes from Leontes's wrath and later in saving Florizel from Polixenes's wrath; and most of all in Paulina's disguise of Hermione as a statue, and the artifice of the statue's coming to life.

The loving friendship of Leontes and Polixenes in their youth is presented as an Arcadia, a paradise from which the former's fit of jealousy drives everyone in catastrophic upheaval. The restored Arcadia of Perdita's upbringing – and of course, speakingly, the scene of her romance with Florizel – is the necessary route back. But the key to the story lies in its turning on two fixed facts: that human nature is defined by a set of universals which constitute its essence, and that this essence is disruptable by passion. It also turns on the idea that the individual expression of this essence is hereditary. Perdita's royal nature shines through her shepherdess's homely dress; Florizel is a 'print' of his father; the goodness of the old shepherd is instinct in his son the clown; the Sicilian courtiers – the 'well-born' – are civilised gentlefolk who stand up (in Paulina's case, with ferocious eloquence) for the good in the face of power perverted by passion. In every case, even in the roguery of Autolycus which is all too human in its own self-serving way, Shakespeare is committed to an essentialist view of human nature, and *The Winter's Tale* is an exploration of its strength, its frailty, and its recovery.

Within two centuries of Shakespeare the humanism of the Enlightenment had extended the humanism of the Renaissance into a theory not just about individual human nature but a philosophy of politics and society. On this later view, if there are universal human traits then there are universal human rights, and the social order must reflect that fact in its institutions and laws. This is not a conclusion Shakespeare drew, given that the metaphysics of his day saw the social order as constructed around the divine election of kings and a pre-ordained hierarchy reflecting the difference between noble, gentle and common birth. But he drew an analogous conclusion, if not about the rights of man then about the right way for men to relate. *The Winter's Tale* is full of disquisitions on loyalty, fidelity, trust, honour and truth, and is an extended parable on the consequences of mistrust and anger. All this centres on the vital question of social bonds, of what makes and sustains relationships, and its fundamental assumption is a typically humanist one: that the proper way for this to work is something that human nature itself tells us, for it is written in its essence. When Autolycus says, 'Ha! ha! what a fool Honesty is! and Trust his sworn brother, a very simple gentleman!' (IV.iv.596–7), he is telling us by opposites, as he shows us by his actions, what humanism would have us remember as we pursue the good.

Haste and Speed

Is the contrast here 'haste bad, speed good'?

At first it seems that a liking for speed is prompted by one of two motives: the exhilaration it produces, or the fact that it is – or at least feels – necessary in our bustling and impatient world. But perhaps what is in play here is a contrast, in which speed is the exhilarating thing, but haste is the less admirable condition that modern demands make necessary.

Take the exhilaration point first. Aldous Huxley rightly pointed out that speed is a distinctively modern pleasure. Before trains, cars and aeroplanes, the fastest available vehicle was a galloping horse. The first steam trains were capable of going at thirty miles per hour, which scientists of the day said was so fast it would kill passengers, who would not be able to breathe because of the rush and pressure of air.

Now the speedboat, the car, the motorbike, the express train, the jet aircraft can arrow through the world at speeds unimaginable then, and the thrill of swift passage has become commonplace, though no less exciting for being so. Just a few decades ago automobile advertisements emphasised such performance factors as top speed and o-to-6o acceleration; motorbike adverts showed goggled riders leaning round corners at high velocity, their hair flowing behind them; trains and planes appeared in adverts as blurred streamlined objects streaking through space.

The world has grown more cluttered and glutinous since then, because of the sheer numbers of people and vehicles moving about. Advertisements no longer extol speed because society has by now too often suffered the consequences of its dangers.

So, speed has changed its nature in our view of it; it has become hurry instead. Most people have to, or at least feel the need to, hurry from various As to Bs; a stressful sense of urgency pushes people along; they experience haste, rather than swiftness, all the more so as they chide the taxi-driver stuck in traffic. Likewise, if the computer does not boot up quickly, or one has to wait on a telephone listening to long-winded recorded instructions, impatience is the inevitable result.

There is little to choose between speed and haste regarding which is more likely to prove disastrous. Speeding in a car not only causes accidents, but makes them worse when they occur. We forget that the metal skin of a car is as tissue paper at high speeds. In the same way, writing a fast, angry email and punching the 'send' button before better thoughts supervene is another form of crash – a moral one. We know that what we do in too much of a hurry we often spend a long time repenting; but we still ignore the old Latin tag *festina lente*, 'make haste slowly'.

There is an Arab saying that a person's soul can only travel as fast as a camel can trot. This charming metaphor might explain jet-lag and many other downsides of too much speed and hurry. What it does not explain is Schopenhauer's telling observation, that once you are over the hill you begin to speed up, and do not stop speeding up until the end of the last day.

In general, though, the cluster of ideas that congregate around speed – swiftness, celerity, promptness, flight – connote better things than those relating to haste, hurry, lateness, out-of-breath struggles to catch a train or plane or to finish a task by a deadline. 'Speed slowly' is nonsense; but 'haste slowly' is good advice.

Protest

Is protesting worth it?

One mark of a healthy democracy is that its people not only have the right to protest when they perceive a wrong, but the will to do so. A democracy is moribund if its members do not exercise their right to challenge each other and the authorities when they are concerned about something. Writing to MPs, taking legal action, marching in the streets, are all forms of protest. Protest is a duty in certain circumstances, just as much as the duty to vote, to be informed, and to play one's part in promoting the general good.

It should hardly need saying that protest is more effective when it is peaceful. That is not a truth that angry protestors regularly remember. The impact of protests that take the form of demonstrations and marches is too often weakened by the minority who are there primarily to break windows and scuffle with the police. If I wished to undermine a protest march, I would hire thugs to join it and start some violence. All the press would converge on the stone-throwers, and the argument of the protest itself would be lost.

The police prepare for protest marches by arming to meet the violent minority. Too often, as a result, they end up clubbing people who are demonstrating peacefully. So the hooligans who ruin the case that the protesters wish to make are responsible for a double wrong.

In non-democracies, mass protest is the only way that injustice can be opposed or political change effected. The courageous demonstrators in Tiananmen Square in 1989 might have failed to achieve democracy for China, but they inspired the protesters of Czechoslovakia, East Germany, Poland, Romania and elsewhere. The result was the collapse of the Berlin Wall and all that it represented. Nothing could so well illustrate what protest can achieve.

If one does not complain about the fly in the restaurant soup, or the poor service in the shop, or the inefficiency of the utility company, or the faultiness of a product, or the effect of ill-thought government legislation, or the neighbours' inconsiderate levels of noise, one will not be doing a favour to oneself or anyone else. Too often we pass over what is unsatisfactory, not wishing to 'make trouble', thereby bequeathing further trouble to the next person who comes along. As Abraham Lincoln said, silence is a sin when protest is called for.

Of course no one wishes to be one of those killjoys who can find nothing right with anything and endlessly say so; but it is surely possible to tell the difference between justified and unjustified complaint. If everyone made a stand and protested against the shoddy, the inefficient, the unacceptable and the wrong, the world would be, and we would each feel, considerably better for it.

Philosophy in Education

Should school children be taught philosophy?

Dictionaries correctly, inspiringly, but unhelpfully, define 'philosophy' as 'love of wisdom', but a better definition would be 'reflective and critical enquiry'. Philosophy is of course a subject as well as a process, though a very comprehensive one: its two great questions can be said to be: What is there? and What matters in what there is?, which jointly and immediately invite the central range of more specific questions about knowledge, truth, reason, value, the mind, and more, which constitute the core of the enterprise. Efforts to gain understanding in these matters require the kind of thought that is distinctively philosophical: questioning, probing, critical, reflective, exacting, restless, accepting that there might be several answers or none, and therefore accepting the open texture of enquiry where there is rarely a simple solution to a problem, and hardly ever closure. Minds experienced in this kind of thinking are generally resistant to quick-fixes of ideology and dogma, and are healthily prone to examine, with a clear and when necessary sceptical eye, everything put before them.

Enquiry of this kind is obviously a highly exportable process; practice in it constitutes what is now called a 'transferable skill'. For this reason alone philosophy ought to be a central and continuous feature of the school curriculum from an early age, because it immediately potentiates students' work in other subject areas. There is a view that education should be as much, if not more, about teaching children how to get and evaluate information as it is about imparting pre-digested information to them – at least, after they have the literacy, numeracy and framework knowledge that provides the necessary basis on which a training in thinking and research can build. Philosophy is *par excellence* what offers the evaluatory part of this desideratum.

And because philosophy is not only about critical reflection and the construction of good arguments, but also about substantive questions – in morality, in epistemology, in logic, and judicially in relation to the claims, assumptions and methodologies of all other more specific areas of enquiry in the natural and social sciences and humanities – the training in thinking brings with it a rich furnishing of insights and understanding in many fields besides. In a curriculum devoted to acquiring knowledge and technique, there has to be time for reflection on what it all means, what it is for and why it matters, for almost any 'it'; and this too is distinctively the province of philosophy.

I have talked about philosophy at primary schools and sixth forms both, and found exactly what one would antecedently expect: that young minds are naturally philosophical minds. Inviting a class of primary-school children to discuss how they can claim to know that there really is a table here before them – that hoary old example – is an exhilarating and instructive enterprise. The question seems to them, as indeed it is, a good one; and they are quick to appreciate the force of sceptical defeaters to the standard evidence adduced in favour of the claim, and the countervailing force of the standard evidence itself. This openness and readiness to engage with ideas that adult minds might resist on the grounds of obvious silliness (which often means: unobvious importance) is a fertile thing. In view of this, and of the instant exportability of the methods and insights of philosophy to almost everything else in the curriculum, the case for placing it at the curriculum's heart makes itself.

Students of philosophy gain a possession that enriches them as individuals and social beings for the rest of their lives. As Aristotle said, 'we educate ourselves so that we can make a noble use of our leisure'. But they gain even more than that, for there is the harsh reality of economics and the world of work to be considered, and here too a philosophical education proves its worth. Our age is one in which people have to be flexible, adaptable and well equipped to meet and handle a constant stream of new ideas, techniques, technologies, complexities and problems. Contemporary economies may still have a use for people trained in a single practical skill, but this is rarer than it was and it is not the way of the future. A training in critical and reflective thought, a training in handling ideas, is of the essence in this new and demanding environment. Philosophy thus provides both for individual development and enrichment, and a bright set of apt intellectual tools for meeting the world's challenges.

Goodness

What is the good life?

Everyone wants to live the good life; most people also want to live a life that is good – *morally* good. The phrase 'the good life' has come to be associated with pleasures and attractive possessions, and people of a more austere outlook assume therefore that 'the good life' cannot be a life that is morally good. They think this because they believe that pleasures and possessions interfere with doing the right thing in circumstances of moral dilemma, where – quite often – sacrifices have to be made.

In the history of Western culture there has been a long-running conflict between the two strands of thought here at issue. Roman banquets, Renaissance feasts, risqué Restoration comedies and Regency excesses stand in sharp contrast to world-renouncing monks, Calvinist ministers, Puritans and sober-minded Sabbath-observing Victorians. As this shows, the contrast always exists within the history of our own society, with sometimes one and sometimes the other viewpoint in the ascendant, usually to the great annoyance of its opponent.

Underlying the contrast is a deep philosophical difference of view about the nature of human beings, and about the nature of goodness itself. For most of history people believed that human beings are quite different from the rest of nature because they possess reason and language. They unquestioningly assumed that humanity was created by a deity, and that each person has an immortal soul. In medieval times man was thought to be the knot that tied earth to heaven, standing right at the centre of the Great Chain of Being rising from the lowliest worm to God himself. Like physical things, man was made of the four elements – earth, air, fire and water – but he also had a fifth element, the 'quintessence', which he shared with angels.

Given this view, it is no surprise that what was regarded as good was whatever would take man away from his base, beastly, physical nature and prepare him for the true felicity of life after death. Pleasures and possessions were therefore a mortal danger, because they averted man's eyes from his heavenly goal and gave Satan a chance to damn him.

There is a great difference between that view and one which says: humanity is part of nature, and the beauties and pleasures of everything natural are part of humanity's inheritance. This was the view of the ancient Greeks, who saw in the exercise of man's reason the source of his ability to recognise goodness. The Greeks extolled friendship, the quest for knowledge and the appreciation of excellence in all things, as the source of the greatest pleasure that humans can have. They sought to understand what would make a good society so that individuals within it could enjoy flourishing lives. The focus of their attention was on this world and its benefits, and they debated intelligently about how to enjoy them, share them, and get the best from them.

Such was the view, differently expressed, of Aristotle, the Epicureans, the Stoics, the poets and the historians of the classical and Hellenistic world. Aspects of their views were taken up by Christianity in the centuries after it had assumed dominion over most of Europe, mainly because the simpler early Christian outlook, suitable only for a brief period of waiting until the Second Coming, was in need of supplementation once it was clear that longer epochs had to be endured.

But the major strand of classical thought that had to wait for the Renaissance to rediscover it was the enjoyment of this-worldly pleasures. For during the long centuries of the Church's dominion over the hearts and minds of people in Christendom – say, from the fourth century to the thirteenth century CE – the prevailing outlook was that the world is a vale of tears, a place of devilish snares, of trial and test, of suffering and woe. This outlook was expressed in *contemptus mundi* literature, in murals and altarpieces depicting the agonies of punishment for sin, and in the soaring towers of Gothic churches struggling to rise above the dirt, disease and decay of the physical world to the pure ethereal realms above.

The leading spirits of the Renaissance thought very differently. They were so conscious of the contrast that one of their earliest luminaries, Petrarch, coined the term 'Middle Ages' to describe what he saw as the dark period between the bright civilisation of antiquity and the rediscovered joy taken by his own day in art, nature, music, poetry, love and the human form, all celebrated in the splendours and variety of ancient literature so long obscured by the dominance of Church teaching.

The Renaissance's thinkers recognised that man is a natural being, and that it is equally natural therefore to delight in all the objects of the five senses – in colours and tastes, in scents and sensations, in music and the lover's touch; and so on for all aspects of the sheer exhilaration of being part of a world in which so much beauty resides, and such opportunities to enjoy it.

It is interesting to note that in our own present day the debate about what human beings are has confirmed the Renaissance intuition. Renaissance humanists followed the Stoic injunction to 'follow nature' always; today we know from biology and genetics how right this is, because we know how much we are part of nature, and how much all the things that were once thought to be distinctive of humankind – in the literal sense of distinguishing us from other animals – are widely shared, in different ways, by many of them. This realisation first fully came with Darwin, and has been overwhelmingly attested from a thousand different directions since. It tells us that the range of this-worldly things people find to appreciate in life, and the things that give them joy, are as natural to them as the desire for food and water.

Almost all the things people find pleasurable are things that naturally evoke responses from our complex human nature. It does not take much, therefore, to see that there is nothing wrong with pleasures and possessions in themselves, provided that they are not enjoyed at the expense of someone else's suffering or loss, and so long as the business of acquiring them does not become an obsessive end in itself. The first point obviously matters because in a good world everyone should have the chance to make a flourishing life for themselves, and no one should be treated as a mere stepping stone for someone else's benefit. This is a far-reaching thought, and once one begins to think it through one sees that all the law and prophets turn on it.

The second point matters too because the purpose of pleasure and possessions is to enhance the quality of one's existence, and to make yet further satisfactions and achievements possible: among them the greatest being successful relationships with friends, family and community. People think that this-worldly good lives tend to be selfish and debauched. Why? A selfish and debauched life is very soon a miserable one, because its pleasures are quickly exhausted and its achievements few. Worst of all, it is unlikely to result in the building of deep, lasting relationships with people one cares about. And a life in which this is the major achievement is a good life indeed: and an entirely natural one.

Human Beings

Are humans the most dangerous animals on the planet?

There is something deeply paradoxical about humanity. Look at a city and all the appurtenances of civilisation it contains: homes, businesses, schools and clinics, water supply, sewerage, transport, places of entertainment and recreation, art galleries, concert halls, sports fields, parks and gardens. To produce these things takes time, co-operation, stability and the accumulation of resources. An anthropologist from another planet would infer from a modern city that its human occupants are rational and peaceable beings, who work together for the common good in wonderfully sensible ways.

The alien anthropologist would be right, but only half-right. Let the spaceship land on another day in another zone – a war zone – and the inference would be that mankind is lunatic, destructive and dangerous. War is a chronic disease in mankind; aggression and violence are endemic to human beings and the societies they form. Some of the greatest investment of the world's energy and resources goes into devising instruments of war and training millions of people to kill each other.

This, then, is the paradox: outside the peaceful and flourishing city is the barracks where the soldiers drill, and the factory where the guns are made; far beyond the horizon are the smoke and din of battle, where humans kill each other in horrifying ways – ways that, in the course of the last hundred years alone, have resulted in nearly 200 million violent deaths.

The prevalence of organised conflict throughout history and in the present makes it obvious that war is somehow rooted in human nature. Philosophers, social scientists, novelists, historians and general enquirers perennially try to substitute for that word 'somehow' a detailed account of why and how humans are so wedded to conflict, even though they are also so wedded to peace and co-operation. Most such enquirers do it by navigating a route through the best understanding we have of the development of human psychology and the structure of the mind. The first aspect provides an explanation of how propensities to both organised violence and organised peace arise in the human psyche, the second aspect provides an explanation of how these two impulses can co-exist in the same mind. A notable contribution to this approach is made by David Livingstone Smith in his book *The Most Dangerous Animal: Human Nature and the Origins of War*.

The first aspect is perhaps the most familiar. Humans are social apes, and since our chief adaptation is intelligence rather than strength or sharp fangs, planned co-operative action is among the benefits that evolution has bequeathed us. This can be directed either to constructive or aggressive ends; and since both are needed, both are to be found in us. Livingstone Smith adds the suggestion that because females undoubtedly favoured pugnacious males in circumstances where protection was at a premium, genes for aggression would do best in the reproductive stakes, which would explain their prevalence among us now.

As to the second aspect, Livingstone Smith offers a more novel idea. According to a currently influential theory in philosophy and cognitive science, human minds are 'modular', which means that they are built out of many interconnected sub-parts, each specialised for a different type of task. It is due to the fact that the mind is compartmentalised that humans can deceive themselves, self-deception being, says Livingstone Smith, a highly necessary tool for managing the intricate business of occupying a complex social universe of many competing demands. But one thing that self-deception does is permit those modules of mind related to aggression and hostility to separate themselves from those related to sociability and especially – among these in turn – taboos against killing others of our own species.

Among the tricks we play on ourselves to overcome such taboos are those that involve dehumanising our enemies, convincing ourselves that they are monstrous or sub-human, and more similar to dangerous germs or disease-carrying rats than they are to ourselves. Speaking of our enemies as 'targets', or speaking of the business of killing them in terms drawn from hunting or cleansing, helps to override the taboo reflex. And to avoid the unnerving necessity of actually seeing the human beings we kill in war, we develop artillery, missiles, bomber aircraft, weapons that make the enemy anonymous and distant; we do not have to hear their cries of agony, see and smell their blood, be witness to the death we cause.

And even so, says Livingstone Smith, for all but the tiny minority of psychopathic personalities who feel no remorse because they have no moral sensitivity towards others, the majority of people who see action in war are psychologically harmed by the experience, proving the depth of the species bond that contradicts the urge to gang up on the out-group, the other, the enemy, and attack and annihilate it.

Given the fact that both war and revulsion against war are inescapable facts of human nature, an explanation is certainly needed of the paradox this represents. The best such explanations are sure to draw heavily on current results in evolutionary psychology, animal ethology, and the modular theory of mind, and they stand or fall with them. The first and third are controversial, and the second becomes controversial when people extrapolate too readily from animal to human behaviour. But the explanatory power of these theories is considerable, and given that we need to understand our human impulse to conflict, we need to make use of them.

One troubling consideration that remains is the fact that hot individual aggression is one thing, while the cold calculating business of organising and conducting a war is quite another. Individuals fight, states and armies – organisations – wage war. What is the interface between these facts, the mechanism that translates one into another? For whereas politicians ordain that there shall be war, the soldiers who obey them do not sustain hot aggression over the months and years of training and marching to battle. One wonders whether accounts that draw on evolutionary psychology and ethology do not tend to conflate these two things, and whether other more traditional perspectives in examining the phenomena of conflict – politics and history especially – should not be part of the theory too.

Travelling

What is the difference some see between travel and tourism?

In this age of air travel that takes you across continents at less than the price of a train fare between towns in Britain, the tidal waves of mass tourism that drag backwards and forwards across the world have grown to staggering proportions.

Critics of mass tourism say that its only redeeming features are these: that it redistributes wealth between countries, though not always from richer to poorer; and occasionally an individual is awakened to new knowledge, understanding or sympathy by encounter with difference. Otherwise the whole thing is, they say, an exercise in emitting carbon, wearing everything out, and vulgarising what is left.

Such critics might further say: grit your teeth and spend an hour at a 'tourist attraction' in a big city like London. Large school groups of foreign teenagers swarm through them, infinitely more interested in one another than in the 'attraction' in question. They are followed by uncertainly milling parties of Japanese tourists, whose motto is *photo ergo sum* and who interact with foreign lands through camera lenses only, as if needing protection behind thick glass to keep off the overwhelming sense of everything's non-Japaneseness. Appreciative Americans read aloud from guide-books, while other Europeans – having much better 'tourist attractions' at half the price at home than most of the places they visit – are politely puzzled.

The critics' caricature of tourism is not wholly inaccurate. It makes one think that it would be better, as well as different, if people travelled instead. The difference between travel and tourism is vast. For one thing, travellers stay longer, prepare better, are more discreet when there, and make an effort to know something of the language. Tourists move about in crowds from one must-see to another, typically looking but not always seeing, often photographing instead of thinking, invariably devoting more energy to worries about finding a lavatory and somewhere to eat than being open to fresh experience.

Worse, some tourists imagine that because they are abroad they are no longer subject to the restraints of home. The cliché of the drunk English youth burned lobster-pink by the sun, yelling and brawling, dressed in nothing but Union Jack shorts and a can of lager, is alas too true; though admittedly his degree of restraint at home is not much greater.

The classic exemplification of all but the last point is Venice. On the main routes from St Mark's Square to the Rialto Bridge and the Accademia there is not room to breathe, let alone walk, so congested is the porridge of tourists oozing noisily and sweatily along. Turn aside down an alley into a little *campo* thirty yards away, and there is quiet and solitude.

In the small tangle of canals neighbouring St Mark's, constituting an effortless half-hour route for gondolas, the tourist tropes of 'O Sole Mio' and water-borne accordions are repeated all day. Yet around the Ghetto Nuovo or on the Giudecca there is Venice for the traveller: a different place at a different pace.

It's all very superior, no doubt, to disdain tourism and extol travel, but the fact is that they are indeed different enterprises in attitude and practice, as anyone will see if he tries. And those who try rarely revert to tourism afterwards: the world becomes too genuinely interesting for that.

Any kind of travel is therefore something more than just a transition from one place to another; it could be an odyssey, the intention of which is the making of discoveries. As St Augustine said, the world is a book, and to stay at home is to read only one page of it.

Travelling has its supporters and its opponents. Among the latter are those who say that what you meet at the end of a long journey is yourself, and since you regularly meet yourself at home you might as well stay there. There are those who say that most people are surrounded by a little opaque bubble of ignorance wherever they go, and whatever does not conform to the patterns on it they simply do not see anyway; so they too might as well stay at home, to explore the inside of their bubbles without uselessly adding CO_2 to the environment.

And then there are the grave philosophers who say that the longest journey anyone can undertake is from his emotions to his reason, which is to say: the eighteen inches between his heart and his brain. And that, they point out, can be done in an armchair.

But the supporters of travel point out that we know little if we only know our home patch. So long as we travel with open eyes and minds, we stand to gain a great wealth in the form of insights into the lives, ways and experience of other people and their countries. Travel can thus expand our appreciation of things, educate our tastes, and introduce us to novelties. And at the same time it can teach us tolerance and patience, for travel, as Mark Twain aptly put it, 'is fatal to prejudice'.

The best form of travel is by sea, because the pace is right. The Arab saying has it that one's soul can only travel as fast as a camel can trot, which explains jet-lag. In our hasty age we have to suffer airport queues and weary hours as human sardines; but this is only the motion rather than the true travelling part of travel. So even by budget airline one can still be a traveller, in the real sense of one who goes to see and enjoy, and who comes home richer for it.

Civil Liberties

Why do they matter?

Civil liberties exist to protect individuals against the arbitrary use of state power. They include rights to individual freedom, privacy, the secure possession of private property, the expression of opinion without prior restraint, and freedom to hold and exercise personal beliefs provided doing so does not harm others. Central to civil liberties is the idea of a due process of law, consisting in a set of procedural formalities and restraints that protect the innocent, assure equal treatment to everyone, and require the authorities to show good cause why they exert state power over citizens, not least the powers of arrest and detention.

Tyranny exists wherever civil liberties do not exist. Think of a typical police state such as Soviet Russia in the period of its worst excesses, where men in leather coats knocked on doors in the darkest hours of night and took people away to torture and imprisonment without trial, or worse, because there was no regime of civil liberties, no institutionalised protection for human rights, to stop them doing it. The modern democracies of western Europe are of course a long way from being tyrannies, but from Germany to Ireland too many of them are going down the alarming road of compromising civil liberties in the supposed interests of fighting terrorism and crime.

The price of liberty, it is said, is eternal vigilance. Authorities in all countries and at all times, even in Western democracies, find themselves inconvenienced by civil liberties because civil liberties make the job of policing society more difficult. In particular, and to the great irritation of governments everywhere, they interfere with the authorities' ability to detect, arrest, prosecute and convict bad people.

But there is a good reason why civil liberties make the work of the authorities more difficult in these respects, quite deliberately so: namely, to protect the great majority of people who are not bad. The inconvenience of the authorities is the freedom of the people, and it is a price richly worth paying for all that matters to individual freedom and open societies.

The civil liberties that until now have served to define the open democracies of the Western world are taken for granted until something like the Criminal Justice Bill comes along to call them into question. People forget how very far from easy it was to achieve these civil liberties in the first place. It took centuries of hard and often bitter struggle to get them. Think of what had to happen in order for the ordinary twenty-first-century Western citizen to attain the position of a free citizen protected in his rights by law. The process began in the sixteenth-century Reformation; first, the hegemony of a single church over the minds and lives of individuals had to be broken. Then absolute monarchy had to be challenged, and replaced by more representative systems of government.

Both processes were sometimes revolutionary, but mostly evolutionary. They were plagued by setbacks, and made painfully slow and difficult by the reluctance of those in power, both ecclesiastical and temporal, to give anything away. Many died in furthering the cause of liberty – in fire at the church's stake, in chains in royal dungeons, on the battlefield. Their story is the story of the price paid for the civil liberties enjoyed today.

It is astonishing to think that the ordinary citizen of a democracy today enjoys rights, freedoms and possibilities that a few hundred years ago were only available to the very few: to aristocrats and senior churchmen. We are all aristocrats now in the degree of our liberties and opportunities, because we have replaced the rule of might with the rule of law. No arbitrary ruler can throw a citizen into prison at whim; there are institutions and practices that buttress the individual's liberties. Among them is trial by jury, the need for proof to be brought before a court where it can be tested properly, and a presumption of innocence for anyone accused by the state of committing crimes.

Any society that goes into reverse because it is facing hard times betrays the long history of struggle for institutions and a way of life according to ideas of rights and the rule of law. It betrays itself by betraying the principles on which it has come to be based. The test of a society's strength and maturity is whether it can stick to its principles in the face of difficult challenges.

The main point of civil liberties is to make, and to hold open, a space for individuals to choose their own way of realising what they choose to value, consistently with not harming others. The highest good for an individual is autonomy and the relationships freely nurtured within that autonomy. Without the protection of civil liberties, individuals are all too likely to have to live lives chosen for them by others.

A Good World

*What would count among the fundamental
conditions for a good world?*

If one were asked to prescribe the fundamental condition for a good world, it would be: peace for all and freedom for each, where 'freedom' means personal autonomy and mental liberation from prejudice, superstition, ignorance and fear. Cynics will no doubt think this a saccharine sentiment merely, if only on the grounds that it is unattainable and that one had better stick to the realities of a world in which the majority of people are trapped in economic and intellectual prisons made by history (and its bequeathment of superstition, ignorance and fear), perpetuated and promoted by demagogues and the greedy and powerful.

The cynics are of course right about the realities, but that does not mean one should shrug one's shoulders and capitulate. There is something one can do to fight back, by taking part in the battle that underlies it all: the battle (to put it in Voltaire's terms) between those who seek the truth and those who claim to have it.

On one side are those who enquire, examine, experiment, research, ask questions, propose ideas and subject them to scrutiny and test by themselves and others, proportion their intellectual commitments to the evidence in support of them, change their minds when shown to be wrong, accept that they do not know all the answers, and live with uncertainty and open-endedness while placing reliance on the collective, self-critical, responsible and rigorous use of reason and observation to further the quest for knowledge.

On the other side are those who espouse a belief system or ideology which pre-packages all the answers, who have faith in it, who trust the authorities, however ancient, and their priests and prophets, and who either think that the hows and whys of the universe are explained to satisfaction by their faith, or smugly embrace ignorance by hiding behind the finitude of their own minds and the inscrutability of their gods. Note that although the historical majority of these latter are the epigones of one or another religion, they also include the followers of such ideologies as Marxism and Stalinism – which, just like the religions, are all-embracing monolithic ownerships of the Great Truth to which everyone must sign up on pain of punishment, and on whose behalf their zealots are prepared to kill and die.

Examples of these opposing mindsets and their operation in history and the contemporary world are obvious and legion.

In the aftermath of the Reformation in the sixteenth century, Ignatius Loyola founded the Jesuit Order as an army of defence against the attack on the One True Church. The Jesuits saw that the reformers had learning and intelligence on their side; they were translating the Bible into vernacular tongues, and encouraging lay people to read it, and when laymen did so they could see in how many respects the doctrines and practices of the Roman Church varied from its teachings. The Jesuits aimed to be an army of clever and very well-informed casuists and propagandists, skilful in rhetoric and argument, trained to counter the reformers' charges, not interested in finding truth so much as in defending Catholicism's version of it.

It is said that the ignorant are condemned to repeat history, but it is equally true that those who know history can repeat it on purpose. In the United States the proponents of intelligent design and creationism have taken a large leaf out of Loyola's book of strategy, and are training a new breed of jesuitical defenders of faith against the onslaught of science. Only look at the exam set by creationist William Dembski for his Intelligent Design and Christian Apologetics course at Southwestern Baptist Theological Seminary. The Final Exam questions are as follows (and can be seen at: www.designinference.com/teaching/2006_spring_ID_primer/Final_Exam_28677_Spr06.pdf):

1. You are a panelist at the premier showing of Richard Dawkins's BBC production debunking religion titled *The Root of All Evil?* Richard Dawkins is there on the podium with you. After the showing of this program, you are asked to present a brief response. Throughout the program, Dawkins emphasizes that evolutionary theory is confirmed by overwhelming evidence whereas religious belief is as a matter of blind, unthinking faith. Challenge him in your response on both points: spend half of your response showing that evolution is not nearly as overwhelmingly confirmed as Dawkins makes out; also, indicate how, at least when it comes to the Christian faith, religious belief can be well-supported evidentially (e.g., indicate lines of evidence supporting the resurrection and the reliability of the Scriptures).

2. You are an expert witness in the Dover case. You've been asked to summarize why you think intelligent design is a fully scientific theory. Do so here. Sketch out ID's method of design detection and then show how it applies (or could apply) to biological systems. Further, indicate how ID is testable: what evidence would confirm ID and what evidence would disconfirm ID?

3. Barbara Forrest and Paul Gross have characterized intelligent design as part of a vast right-wing conspiracy to undermine our democratic institutions by substituting religious dogma for scientific theory. Accordingly, they see intelligent design as part of a 'Wedge Strategy.' Briefly recount the history of the 'Wedge' and indicate why Forrest and Gross may be wrong to paint it in conspiratorial terms. Is the 'Wedge' a legitimate cultural movement? Explain.

4. You've been assigned to teach six Sunday school lessons on intelligent design over six consecutive Sundays. Each lesson is an hour and fifteen minutes. Outline how you would conduct these lessons. What would you have people read? In what order? What would you present? What would you want participants to take away at the end of the six weeks?

As this shows, the training at the seminary is aimed at producing infantry for a religious war against science and reason; proof of this, and in Dembski's own words, lies in another of his exam questions for the same course:

You are the Templeton Foundation's new program director and are charged with overseeing its programs and directing its funds. Sketch out a 20-year plan for defeating scientific materialism and the evolutionary worldview it has fostered if you had $50,000,000 per year in current value to do so. What sorts of programs would you institute? How would you spend the money?

This makes as clear as day the tendentious purpose of an 'education' at the Southwestern Baptist Theological Seminary.

When the faithful of any faith win – whether religious or Stalinist-like: the structure is the same – the doors are open to horrors, ranging from inter-religious violence, oppressive theocracies, reactionary social policies, prejudice against gays and women, pogroms against Jews, slaughter of kulaks, starvation of millions as a result of ideological nostrums such as collectivisation, to wars and communities separated by walls in Israel-Palestine and Ulster – the litany seems endless. Someone once said: by their works ye shall know them. Indeed. Religion's apologists venture the fig-leaf of charitable works: but the non-zealous do these too, and for better motives. The true contrast is with antibiotics, surgery, television, lighting and heating, air travel – the litany is equally endless. And again, by their fruits we know them. Religion's apologists venture the canard that science produces atom bombs and mustard gas, as if mentioning them justified the atrocities committed by faith on the bodies and minds of multitudes; but these applications of science are the result of political and ideological decisions about how the findings of science are to be used. Scientists do not start shooting wars with each other over different theories of nitrogen fixation or whether black holes or boson stars lie at the heart of galaxies. Theologians, however, have committed many murders over the word 'and' in the formula 'the father and the son': if you want a lesson in lunacy, go and find out why; it makes all my point for me.

To summarise: the battle for peace and freedom is a battle about mindsets. The battle lines are clear. It is fought on many fronts: against faith-based schooling, against the overweening privilege accorded religious lobbies in society and in the agora of public opinion. It would be easy to take the next step of showing that the mindset that looks for and tests the facts rather than shores up ancient edifices of authority is likely to make the world a fairer one economically and in power relations too. But that discussion is for another time.

A New Ten Commandments

Given that at least half of the original Ten Commandments do not have much force these days, what might replace them?

It is three and a half thousand years since Moses lived, according to the standard reckonings of Bible scholars. That means that the tables of moral law he allegedly brought down from Mount Sinai, the Ten Commandments, are nothing if not ancient. Does that mean they are hopelessly out of date? Would a new set of commandments fit modern times better?

Our less-religious age certainly has little use for the first four commandments, which command everyone to love the deity, not to take its name in vain, to make no images of it, and to keep the Sabbath as a day of rest. Our age is not only less religious but more consumerist and lubricious, so the proscriptions against coveting your neighbour's ass and committing adultery have also become less carved in stone since Moses.

But four hold up well: proscription of the nasty deeds of murder, stealing and lying, and the injunction to honour one's parents. None of these is obeyed enough, alas; some think they would be, if only the first four were also obeyed – these are the folk who think religion is essential to morality. A short visit to the Old Testament will reassure them that murder, theft, lying and dishonouring parents – not to say adultery and coveting; think of King David and Bathsheba as just one of many examples – show that morality and religion have no necessary connection. (King David saw Bathsheba in her bath, and what he did next, in the way of coveting, adultery and murder, does not bear thinking about, though it makes a very good read.)

Actually, 'honouring parents' has slipped somewhat too; offer this as a divine command to a recalcitrant teenager and count the ways it would be sneered at. It looks as if the original ten have diminished to three, and that perhaps is why some feel that an entire new set is required.

One man who thinks so is Simon Parke, a Church of England vicar who became a supermarket worker, and published a well-intentioned little book called *The Beautiful Life*, offering a new-age list of what to do and not do, which shows strongly un-Anglican influences of Buddhism with a touch of Taoism at the fringes. Out of this eclectic melange he offered a set that is, alas, either hopelessly impractical or hopelessly vague: as follows.

'Be present' is Parke's first commandment, for 'the past is stale, the future does not exist'. This reminds me of Marcus Aurelius's comment that we lose very little when we die, for the past has ceased to exist and the future does not yet exist. Perhaps Parke borrowed the thought from the Stoic emperor. The trouble with the commandment he makes of it is that it enjoins us to live like a cow, which, as Schopenhauer pointed out, is happier than a man because it forgets everything and anticipates nothing, and so lives wholly in the present, indeed wholly in the chewing of the cud that happens to be in its mouth. Parke's mistake is to ignore the fact that we are richly pregnant with our pasts, which makes us what we are, and our moral purpose is directed at the future, which we try to build for the good, not least in thinking of those we love and how best to cherish them – our children, for example. Of course it is important to enjoy the present: but not in bovine fashion, or to the neglect of that much larger thing which is a whole human life.

'Observe yourself' is Parke's second commandment; and yes, that is a good one. 'Be nothing' is his third; and Parke gives us a series of little meditations of Taoist colour to fill it out, for example: 'absence is the cradle in which presence is laid'. If this means it is good to rest and be still sometimes, then yes; but that advice scarcely needs the backing of the Philosophy of the Way to make it good advice. As a general rule it is however not only hard to be nothing, but if one succeeded it would be a decidedly negative state. For let us see what 'being nothing' would involve: do not be a kind person, a caring parent, a seeker for truth, a lover of the good, an enjoyer of beauty, a helpful neighbour – and so on for everything worth being. In short, the injunction is one of those meaningless intellectual gestures of the frothier sort.

Next is 'Flee attachment'. For Parke, 'attachment is unwise' and 'makes us blind'. How emphatically I disagree with this! The essence of life is love and friendship, and the best settings of life are the roots we have in places we love and the loyalties we feel. To live richly is to be committed, not detached; to be entangled with others is to live many more lives than one's own. It has been well said that a full heart has room for everything, an empty heart has room for nothing; and a heart without attachments is empty.

Commandments five and six are 'Transcend suffering' and 'Drop your illusions'. Fine. The next three are further classics of those vague and vaporous adjurations that are the stuff of pop spirituality: 'Prepare for truth', 'Cease separation' (between 'your personality and your essence', Parke helpfully but vacuously explains) and 'Know your soul' ('your soul is everything, mediating between your personality and your essence, and part of both'). This last, as one reads on, turns out to be a dressed-up version of 'Try to understand yourself', which of course is good advice, but it would profit from not being obscured in nonsense.

And the last of Parke's commandments is 'Fear nothing'. The reason rather dimly given by allusion to the mystic Julian of Norwich is that everything will turn out all right in the end, no matter what. Although no deities make an appearance anywhere in these pages, the feeling by now is that all shall be well because tucked away behind the scenes is the author of the now-abandoned original Ten Commandments.

'Fear nothing' is a typically misleading injunction. Fear tigers, I say, and crossing the road in front of a bus, and letting yourself and others down. 'Be courageous' is what Parke should instead have said.

Parke's big mistake is to fail to see that any list of commandments must speak for themselves, without what my teacher A. J. Ayer used to call 'woolly uplift' packed round them in putative explanation. Here is an alternative list of commandments intended to do just that: to be simple, clear, practical and comprehensive. It is: try to (1) do no harm to others, (2) help those in need, (3) love well, (4) seek the good in things, (5) think for yourself, (6) be well informed, (7) take responsibility for yourself, (8) give your best, (9) respect the natural world, (10) be courageous.

If there is any appearance of overlap among the injunctions, it is only an appearance. The duty to be well informed (which, among other things, means educating oneself all one's life long), thinking for oneself (not relying on others' opinions, conventional views and traditional beliefs) and taking responsibility for oneself (paying one's own way in life) are three quite different things, though linked; they constitute autonomy.

The idea behind autonomy is nicely captured in Oscar Wilde's perspicacious observation that 'most people are other people', meaning that most people borrow other people's opinions, attitudes and beliefs, and their lives consequently are imitations of others' lives. But life is short; the average human lifespan is less than a thousand months long; one must make and live a meaningful life for oneself.

I put injunctions about attitudes to others first, because humans are essentially social animals, and our relationships are central to what constitutes the meaning of our lives. It surely goes without saying that the best way of fostering good relationships is kindness and consideration. Both are active things; how can one be happy knowing others are unhappy, often bitterly so, because of the way things are in this unjust world of ours? Note that duties to oneself have to balance duties to others; to 'help others' however one can, sensibly, without derailing one's own life in the process, is plain moral common sense.

Indeed, the whole list has to be prefaced with the words 'Whenever possible – but be honest about this! – try to . . .' Because of course there are occasions when one cannot avoid harming others, in self-defence, in fighting a just war (these are very rare) or when one cannot help others (because one is genuinely not in a position to do so) – and so legitimately on. The moral life is in large part about intention: if one's default position is that one will obey these injunctions whenever it is truly possible to do so, then one has the right ethos, and a strong thread of integrity binds together what one is and does.

And failing to obey the injunctions should not invariably prompt despair. The ancient Greeks did not have a notion of sin; in our dour religious traditions sins are stains that it takes a lot of scrubbing to remove. The Greeks thought of moral failures as *amartiai*, 'bad shots', missing the target. In their sensible and mature outlook, the right reaction is to be determined to take better aim next time. That is how one should apply a modern set of commandments of this kind: constantly trying to hit the target they offer.

Taking Action

Is it wise to 'have a go' against criminals and hooligans? Is it a moral duty to do so?

When you see yobs bullying or beating someone, should you go to the victim's assistance? When news comes of yet another person who has died trying to do just that, the reaction it prompts is mixed. We admire the courage of citizens like that, but their deaths add to the fear that inhibits many people from helping others. And yet the answer to the question has to be an emphatic Yes.

Of course, how one assists depends on the circumstances. If there are twenty brutal thugs, one victim, and you, assistance is best given by calling the police from a safe distance, and if possible taking photographs with a mobile phone. If there are three of you, and you see a couple of men attacking someone else, you can and should physically intervene.

It could be argued that one should intervene even when the odds are against one. It's the principle of the thing: a blow against wrong is never wasted. What no one should ever do is walk on by.

Some years ago a woman friend of mine was attacked by a deranged individual on a crowded subway platform. Her attacker grabbed her by the hair, lifted her off her feet, and swung her round and round. Not a single person did anything to help her, though she screamed and begged them to do so. That was appalling. Put yourself in the situation of a person in danger, under threat, and imagine how you would feel if you saw other people scurrying off because they were too nervous to help you. This thought alone should change the mind of anyone who is determined to keep out of trouble even at the cost of someone else's safety.

Police policy in Britain is that members of the public should intervene when they see yob behaviour. They of course recommend doing it sensibly, but urge members of the public to do it anyway. If everyone was of this view, bystanders would club together and help each other in stopping yobs, profiting from the safety in numbers and their combined strength. Matters might be different in the United States where guns are far more common than in Britain, and the risks of intervening commensurately higher. The worst outcome is for people to start carrying small arms with them for self-protection or to help others in trouble. The more weapons on the streets, the more trouble will ensue.

In the Joseph Rowntree Foundation report on what contemporary society sees as today's social evils, chief among them is said to be a breakdown in the sense of community – which means, among other things, a reduction in people's sense of mutual responsibility and concern as members of society.

This certainly is part of the picture. It is a self-feeding problem, because when fewer people feel that they have a direct responsibility to help others, the more isolated the Good Samaritans among them become; and the more isolated people are as would-be Good Samaritans, the less sure they feel about having a go.

That is not merely a regrettable but in a way a shameful fact. Other considerations would once have weighed with us: questions of honour, of each of us having a responsibility to defend what's right, of being more afraid of cowardice than injury.

No doubt such notions appear quaint now, and we are inclined to think that the person who turns away instead of having a go is not being cowardly but rational. The thugs might have a knife; they might fracture one's skull or rupture one's spleen or kidneys with their boots or baseball bats. A beating is all too likely to be fatal if the stab or the kick lands in the wrong place, and many places in the human body are the wrong place in that regard. And thus it seems common sense not to get involved – one might be thinking of one's own family too.

These are valid points. But the more of us who are persuaded by them to the point of doing nothing to help others, the more alone we each are should we ourselves be the victim. And when danger threatens, none of us should allow others of us to be alone.

Waste

We throw away a remarkable proportion of the food
we buy. As denizens of a troubled planet, should
we not wage war on waste of this kind?

Consider the humble pencil. To use it one must continually shave off the wood surrounding the graphite core, and shave off part of the graphite itself to sharpen it; and every mark made by it, including the ones erased or thrown into the bin on a crumpled sheet of paper, consists of used graphite. Using a pencil, it seems, involves waste. Or is it waste? Is it not rather the necessary accompaniment of use?

It would be hard labour to calculate exactly the right amount of food and drink that the family will consume each week, in order not to leave a crumb over. Shall we carry our unwrapped produce home in our hands, and eat it with the mould on it if it lingers too long in the unrefrigerated (to save energy) cupboard, risking the greater waste of illness?

Not everything that has come to be called waste is waste, but is rather the margin of utility, in which planning to have enough requires having more than is strictly enough, to cover contingencies. And the surplus is not truly wasted anyway;

most of the vegetables that go into the compost or the landfill, instead of through the intestines and into the sewage, will do the work of nature wherever they end up, returning their elements to the world and re-entering its cycles.

Those shoes in the cupboard we never wear, that jacket hanging neglected there: did not someone earn a living for making them nevertheless?

Waste is relative. While people starve elsewhere, the tons of still-edible food we throw away are indeed a scandal: but they are a scandal because of the unfairness, the selfishness, not the fact that the food (whose production, transport, display and sale paid a number of wages) went into a bin instead of a mouth.

One of the more typically dour of Scottish Calvinist sayings is, 'Wilful waste makes woeful want.' This certainly has the taste of last week's porridge about it, all the sourer for missing a great point: that the true waste in life is the waste of life itself: in war, anger, wasted human opportunities through timidity, fear, ignorance, discrimination, unjust social arrangements, economic recession, repressive moralities, distorting belief systems, and all the other mental and social wastages that we impose on ourselves or allow others to impose upon us.

I would like to know who said the following: 'Every day I live I am more convinced that the waste of life lies in the love we have not given, the powers we have not used, the selfish prudence that will risk nothing and which, shirking pain, misses happiness as well.' This is one lesson about waste we should never waste the opportunity to apply.

Change

When is change good, and when is it bad?

For anything to change, something must stay the same. Suppose the universe and everything in it doubled in size every noontide, and halved again at midnight; because we inflate and deflate along with it, we would notice nothing. But if something refused to go along with these fluctuations, and stolidly remained the same size despite them – the family dog, say, or the tree in the garden – we would certainly notice (though it would just seem to us that we were confronted by an inexplicably odd dog or tree).

Thus, change requires a background of relative stability, because change is a matter of comparisons. Intrinsic difference is not enough; we do not notice changes in ourselves until they are reflected back to us by people we have not seen for a while. Of course, we are constantly trying to make changes, in the direction of bigger bank balances and smaller waistlines usually; and constantly aware that the reverse change is the norm with these vexing desiderata. But it is our distraction by these few and in the end marginal changes that blinds us to the thinning hair on our heads, and the grey tinges in what remains, and the parallel but more significant changes within the skull thus clothed, denoting the inevitable progression towards the final stasis to which all change tends.

Confucius remarked that to remain constant either in happiness or wisdom we must perpetually change – because the world changes. Change is life, stasis is its negation. Conservatives do not agree with this, holding instead that some things are valuable enough to preserve just as they are, on the principle that what is not broken should not be fixed, and that anyway a basis of stability is, as already acknowledged, the very condition of change. But as so often happens in sound-bite philosophy, there is only the appearance of contradiction here. To keep something worthwhile in being is itself an act of change against the entropic forces that bring diminishment and decay, because preservation is a constantly changing relationship with what changes around and beyond the thing preserved.

Yet it is equally obvious that to mummify everything, to keep one's eyes fixed on a backward point only, is not an option either. The great secret and perhaps charm of all things human lies in finding the balance between changing changes and preserving changes in order to attain that Confucian equilibrium.

There is another tack into all this. It too often happens, most notably in politics, that everything can be different without anything actually changing. And not only politics, that simple and brutal game governed by just two rules, 'get in first' and 'don't get caught'; for human universals of love and desire, greed and envy, self-interest, pusillanimity and the occasional flashes of courage and grandeur are features of the human condition that one can read about in Aeschylus, Pico della Mirandola, Shakespeare and Dickens, thus proving, in a strangely reassuring way, that change changes little after all.

Happiness

Is happiness the point of life?

Every time the experts look into the question of happiness in the population at large, they find that though people have grown richer than ever, they are no happier as a result; and this fact always prompts renewed discussion about what happiness is, one reason being the hope that public policies can be devised to promote it.

Not only does increasing wealth fail to make us happier, the experts add, but one of the reasons for increased wealth, namely the individualistic and competitive demands of today's predominantly market societies, actually makes us unhappier.

Professor Richard Layard of the London School of Economics is a leading proponent of the idea that public policy can make a real difference to the quantum of happiness in society. On the basis of impressive empirical work in the social sciences he has shown that increased incomes, better housing, possession of cars and television sets, and all the other appurtenances of well-furnished life in the modern West are not what makes people happy, at least once they have risen above a certain material level.

In a lecture at Cambridge University Lord Layard argued that happiness should be taught in schools. More accurately, he argued that schools should raise children's 'emotional intelligence' and thereby help them to understand what makes for happy lives. Again on the basis of empirical research he is able to point to programmes that have reduced depression, bullying and other difficulties in a number of schools, which consequently enjoy a calmer and more collegial atmosphere.

And such an atmosphere, obviously, conduces to higher levels of subjectively perceived happiness among pupils and staff there.

There is no doubt that these ideas have much to recommend them, but they need to be couched in the right terms in order to make maximum sense, and to avoid giving the impression that happiness could be packaged and supplied as if it were some sort of commodity. If matters were that easy, and happiness were just a matter of mild euphoria and indifference to life's vicissitudes, the answer would be to put Prozac in the public water supply just as we put fluoride in it to protect the nation's teeth. But that is not what is at stake here, and nor is that what Lord Layard and other advocates of happiness programmes are saying.

Two points need to be grasped before one can talk seriously about the real question at stake, which is not best phrased as 'how can we increase the amount of happiness in society?' but rather 'how can we equip individuals to live more personally satisfying lives?' Despite seeming to be versions of each other, these are radically different questions. The first misleadingly suggests a view of happiness as a form of welfare that public funding, if suitably directed through education or some other vehicle of social engineering, could subsidise. The second recognises that there are very many ways in which people can use the over-capacious word 'happiness' to describe what they feel when their lives are going well, and that what they mean by it is almost always a very individual thing.

The individual thing in question is typically an enduring mood or mindset arising from the joint operation of a number of factors. The factors include health, the quality of personal relationships, satisfaction in work or other avocations, engagement in creative and pleasurable activities, either financial security or indifference to money, a sense of being valued at work or in the community, and a sufficient degree of independence to be able to make individually important choices and to act on them.

Each of these things in turn requires a degree of understanding and a capacity for self-government which individuals can be helped to acquire both in education and through prevailing social attitudes. For example, health is enhanced by exercise and good diet; that is something that can be taught. Good relationships are based on mature understanding of others, generosity and tolerance, and an ability to express feelings constructively and appropriately; these are more complex matters, and central to 'emotional intelligence', but they likewise can be encouraged and fostered through education and the social debate.

Still, no general prescription is ever going to capture what unique combinations of such factors will suit all individuals. But society can help individuals to acquire the tools they need for the task of building their own uniquely satisfying lives. And indeed, education is the principal such tool. An education that results in an ability to think, to evaluate evidence and arguments, and to know where to find information and to make use of it, is one key; a wide acquaintance with literature and history, and the challenge to respond reflectively to both, is another. Perhaps 'happiness studies' as such will help, but the two keys mentioned are indispensable, and perhaps the only real foundations of a chance for good lives.

There is no guarantee that personally satisfying lives will be built from these materials, but they offer a better chance than education that is too exclusively focused on transmitting employability skills at the expense of personal development. This, I think, is the idea that underlies Lord Layard's argument, and it shows that it is, despite the over-quick formulations that it receives in the media, on the right lines.

But there is a final point that the long philosophical tradition of debate about happiness and the good life shows, and it is this: that the surest way to unhappiness is to try to pursue happiness directly. This is because happiness only ever comes as the outrider to other things that are in themselves independently fulfilling and rewarding. Happiness is like the dot of light in a very dark room which you can only see out of the corner of your eye, but which vanishes when you look directly at it.

Instead of looking for happiness, therefore, one should look for achievement in a worthwhile field, or service to a noble cause, or the good of one's family or community, or the personal pleasure that comes from creative endeavour. As surely as night follows day, happiness will attend effort in any of these arenas. Learning the value of these things is what constitutes an education in happiness; applying the lessons thus learned is what offers the best chance of finding it.

Sport

What is so wrong about cheating in sport? Sport is just sport, after all, and why not use every means to win?

There is scarcely a sport anywhere in the world that seems to be immune from cheating in one form or another, from the taking of performance-enhancing drugs to rule-breaking on the playing field or athletics track. The general impression is that sport is no longer very sporting, but has been hijacked by people careless about breaking rules in their eagerness to win – an eagerness all the more acute in professional sport, where the rewards of success are great, and not always just for the sportsmen and women themselves.

To cheat is to take unfair advantage over competitors, invariably in secret so that the competitors cannot respond with counter-measures. The suspicion that one's competitors are universally trying to get an edge by foul rather than fair means is a major inducement to break the rules oneself. But the biggest reason for cheating is that the stakes – in money terms – are now so high that the risk seems worth it. It is not just professionalisation of sports that has made them a grimmer enterprise, but also the fact that top sporting personalities can expect a boost to their earning power through advertising and post-retirement sports-related jobs; which makes winning far more than a matter of pride and personal fulfilment: it is quite literally an investment in the future.

The fundamental assumption of sport is that one person's or one team's natural endowments and efforts are pitted against those of others, to determine who is swiftest, strongest or best in some respect. In team sports both individual talents and their combination constitute what is measured against opposition. The first formalisers of games whose practices we know about in any detail, the ancient Greeks, crowned sporting success with poetry; in celebrating famous victors in the Games, Pindar's odes conferred something greater than today's monetary rewards, namely, literary immortality.

Not that cheating was unknown to the Greeks; far from it. The myth of Atalanta veritably enshrines it. Atalanta was a maiden who ran so fast that she vanquished all the suitors who, in order to marry her, had to beat her in a foot race. (The penalty for losing against her was death.) By means of a ruse, one Hippomenes succeeded where the rest had failed; he rolled a golden apple off to one side of the track every time Atalanta drew ahead of him. She, being (of course) a mere girl and therefore attracted by the glitter, chased after the apples, thus enabling him to win.

Ancient or modern, cheating in sport is a direct breach of faith with the assumption that competition is either or both of two things: that it consists of unembellished nature pitted against unembellished nature, and that the spirit of the game really matters. That is why cheating is so bad: it undermines true contest, so that one does not really know who the real winner should be; and so it turns every result into a lie.

There are two kinds of cheating. One sits in the shadow of a grey area in sport, and partly shares its nature – namely, that it is legitimate to enhance performance by training, coaching, diet and psychological technique. The step is small from these careful regimes to the use of substances and methods which are proscribed. Consider: sportspeople from a rich country with excellent facilities, medical monitoring and expert attention compete against sportspeople from Third World countries with scarcely a training shoe between them. How fair is that? What is the difference between this and the unequal contest between a competitor who takes a performance-enhancing substance such as nandrolone and one who does not?

The other kind of cheating – once the only or at least principal kind – involves breaking a game's rules for advantage, in the hope that the referee or umpire will not notice. Tampering with the seam of a cricket ball, or surreptitiously using one's hands in a rugby scrum, are examples. Even here there are gradations. Ball-tampering in cricket is regarded as heinous, but handling in the scrum is all right if a player can get away with it. The difference is one of ethos. Cricket was once, in a greener age, the archetypal sporting game, in which a batsman left the field if he knew he was out, and in all other ways played the gentleman in his concern for scrupulous behaviour. In rugby a rough-house principle prevails of everything being fair (which includes the unfair) in love and war. Because of the tacit consent to this by both sides, it becomes a point of honour to get away with breaking the rules if one can; which makes it scarcely cheating after all. But tampering with a cricket ball is definitely cheating, and the opposition will never like it, not even now when sporting standards are for sale in the hard-nosed market-place sports have become.

The prevalence of cheating has, in consequence, made sport a domain of suspicion. Regulatory bodies have to test sportsmen and women for drugs, and sportsmen and women are under intense pressure to perform: the race these days seems to be more between regulators and possible cheats than between athletes on the field. And that is a great pity.

Philosophy

Does philosophy progress?

Remember first that ever since its self-conscious origin in classical antiquity, 'philosophy' in essence has meant 'enquiry'; and second, that its central concern is enquiry into the two most fundamental questions facing mankind: what is the nature of the world, and which of the things that exist in it and happen in it really matter?

Each question comprises a set of sub-questions. The first asks what exists, and what does it consist of – and how can we know either, truly and accurately? The second asks what is valuable, both ethically and aesthetically, and how do we decide? All the law and the prophets – to coin a phrase – are summed up here.

And from this one can see that philosophy does indeed make progress. In classical antiquity itself it was a giant step forward for humanity to begin thinking systematically about the organisation of society and forms of political authority, and to examine the premises and assumptions of ideas about moral conduct. In the process the ancient philosophers articulated the first canons of logic and the first theories of knowledge, and advanced the first tentative scientific theories about the structure and properties of matter, the nature of the universe and human psychology, and offered the first rational critiques of superstition.

The philosophical quest was all but suspended in Europe for more than a thousand years of religious hegemony over thought which began when Christianity became the official religion of the Roman empire. It revived in the Renaissance, one of whose corollaries, the Reformation, broke the hold of ecclesiastical authority over what could count as permissible enquiry. Until lately the world has not looked back.

In the sixteenth and seventeenth centuries philosophy gave birth to the natural sciences by finding fruitful ways of asking questions about the nature of the world, and answering them quantitatively. In the eighteenth century philosophy gave birth to psychology, in the nineteenth century to sociology and empirical linguistics, and in the twentieth, along with earlier offshoots in mathematical logic and psychology, to artificial intelligence and cognitive science.

At the same time, every generation has to re-examine the questions of how to organise itself politically and comport itself morally. The duty to reflect, to examine assumptions and challenge them afresh, to remain vigilant against the forces that always seek to erode the gains mankind manages to make in the direction of liberty and rights, is perennial. The questions remain insistent for the obvious reason that change happens, new conditions arise, new possibilities and new forms of old difficulties appear, and the analogue of the entropic force that ceaselessly works to make things fall apart in nature even more deeply infects human arrangements.

One of the most progressive things about philosophy, therefore, in addition to the progress it has generated in the above-mentioned ways, is its effort to defend the progress it makes in the face of the tireless endeavour of power and superstition to drag mankind back to a pre-philosophical infantilism, in which people are commanded not to think for themselves, but to believe and behave as instructed.

Enlightenment

What is meant by the term 'the Enlightenment'?

Any discussion of the Enlightenment has to begin with the definition that one of the greatest Enlightenment figures, the philosopher Immanuel Kant, himself gave. 'Enlightenment,' he wrote, 'is man's emergence from his self-imposed immaturity. Immaturity is the inability to use one's understanding without guidance from another. This immaturity is self-imposed when its cause lies not in lack of understanding, but in lack of resolve and courage to use it without guidance from another. *Sapere Aude!* (Dare to know.) Have courage to use your own understanding! That is the motto of enlightenment.'

This passage is from Kant's 1784 essay *What Is Enlightenment?* It was not intended to herald the arrival of an enlightened age, as Kant himself was keen to make clear, but only the beginnings of a process that might lead to one. Progressive thought in the eighteenth century was far in advance of the social and political realities of the time, but the thinkers who were in its vanguard were sure they were witnessing a new dawn in human affairs. The revolutions in America and France, together with much that has happened in Western history since then, have proved them right, even though fierce counter-Enlightenment movements have contested its principles at every step.

It is important to distinguish between 'The Enlightenment' as a complex historical phenomenon mainly of the eighteenth century, and more general talk of 'Enlightenment' or 'Enlightenment values' which are still asserted and defended today, these being rationality, liberty, democracy, pluralism, human rights, the rule of law and the centrality of science to a proper understanding of the world. Today's Enlightenment values are direct descendants of those put forward by eighteenth-century thinkers, but with the modifications one would expect from changed historical circumstances.

For example, in the eighteenth century atheism was regarded with special abhorrence; therefore to announce publicly that one was an atheist was impossible unless one was prepared to accept pariah status in society. Consequently almost all agnostics and atheists described themselves as 'deists' – that is, as claiming to believe that the world was created by a deity who has since taken no further interest in it – and they limited their criticism of religion to criticism of the Church.

As an historical phenomenon 'The Enlightenment' is the eighteenth-century movement of thought that emphasised reliance on reason, sought to take a scientific approach to social and political questions, was a champion of science itself, and opposed the clergy, the Church and all forms of superstition as obstacles to human progress. Enlightenment thinkers promoted the idea of the rights of man and correlatively opposed the tyranny of absolute monarchy and all unjust social systems associated with it.

It is to some extent arbitrary to confine the Enlightenment just to the eighteenth century, because all the developments in science and philosophy since the Reformation of the sixteenth century were essential components of it, and because most of Western history since is fundamentally shaped by it, especially by the growth of democracy, human rights and the ubiquitous application of science. But there are definite events and personalities at the heart of the Enlightenment phenomenon, and they help to define it.

The flagship project of the historical Enlightenment was the compiling of a great encyclopaedia, the *Encyclopédie ou Dictionnaire raisonné des sciences, des arts et des métiers* edited by the philosopher Denis Diderot and the mathematician Jean le Rond d'Alembert. It was published in multiple volumes between 1751 and 1772, and sought to bring together all the best that had been discovered and thought in the natural and social sciences, in technology, in the arts and crafts, and in philosophy. It was an ambitious project, and its influence was as much a product of its ambition as of the content of its various volumes – a lot of which, because of the relentless march of research and discovery, was soon enough out of date anyway.

The project began with a proposal to translate into French the English-language *Chambers' Encyclopaedia*. Progressive thinkers in France were under the spell of John Locke and Isaac Newton, and wished to import the enlightened thinking of the former and the discoveries of the latter into their own country. But Diderot and his collaborators found the *Chambers' Encyclopaedia* unsatisfactory, and resolved to produce their own instead.

The compilers of the *Encyclopédie* were conscious that their effort to summarise the fruits of science and technology, and to encourage the application of scientific styles of thought to politics and society, would meet with opposition from traditionalist quarters. This would not least be so because they wished the new knowledge and ways of thinking to create a new social order, and even a new and freer kind of human being, characterised by the ability to think for himself and the courage to act upon his thought. In his *Supplement to Bougainville's Voyage* Diderot has Nature say to Mankind, 'In vain, oh slave of superstition, have you sought your happiness beyond the limits of the world I gave you. Have courage to free yourself from the yoke of religion . . . Examine the history of all peoples in all times and you will see that we humans have always been subject to one of three codes: that of nature, that of society, and that of religion – and that we have been obliged to transgress all three in succession, because they could never be in harmony.'

Because Enlightenment ideas challenged the vested interests of Church and state, and because they continue to threaten those who, for wrong reasons or right, fear that scientific rationality will undermine their cherished beliefs, there have always been vigorous counter-Enlightenment movements. These critics blame the Englightenment for all the worst excesses of recent history, from the Terror of the French Revolution to Nazism and Stalinism in the twentieth century, and blame it likewise for demoting beauty, morality and faith from the pedestals they once stood upon, whence they civilised humanity in the way that scientific rationality (so the critics say) never can.

The first counter-Enlightenment activists were of two broad kinds: reactionaries who defended the traditional powers of Church and monarchy, and Romantics for whom nature, emotion and imagination were far more important sources of authority over life than reason, which they saw as reductive and desiccating.

Reactionaries blamed Robespierre's excesses on the Enlightenment, choosing not to see that the Terror was the opposite of an event promoting pluralism and individual liberty. Their chief spokesman, Edmund Burke, vigorously repudiated the Enlightenment thinker's claim that ultimate political authority lies with the people. For Burke, 'the people' were nothing but an anarchic mob, and democracy was nothing but mob rule.

The Romantics thought that the Enlightenment's scientific emphasis was not only reductive but mechanistic and even deterministic. They recoiled from it therefore, and elevated feeling over reason, extolled the passions as routes to truth, and applauded spontaneity and chance as superior to rigorous enquiry. No one would wish to deny the importance of feeling;

but out of Romanticism also grew nationalism, theories about the spirit of a people or race, and a new impetus for religious enthusiasm.

After the atrocities of Nazism and Stalinism in the twentieth century new criticisms of the Enlightenment were advanced, notably by members of the Frankfurt School of sociology. They argued that the Enlightenment's rationalism had soured into repressive notions of bureaucratic efficiency and control, individuals had become enslaved to economic forces, and science had bred scientism, a salvation myth falsely promising scientific solutions to all problems, replacing religion as a deceitful and malignant force.

This analysis is odd, for at least the reason that it chooses to ignore a key feature of Enlightenment thought, namely that it specifically opposed the monolithic hegemonies of Church, state and ideology, arguing for pluralism and individual freedom in their place. Monolithic hegemonies demand that everyone must believe the same thing, and must conform and obey; the tyrannies of Nazism and Stalinism were precisely monolithic hegemonies in this sense, and therefore were as far from being descendants of the Enlightenment as they could be. Rather, Nazism's roots lay in Romantic notions of race and its purity as the highest good to which all must be subservient. And Stalinism was the same kind of juggernaut, using much the same kind of methods – terror, oppression, show trials, execution – as the Inquisition in fifteenth-century Europe.

When people talk about 'Enlightenment values' today they generally mean a modernised and admittedly somewhat idealised version of what the eighteenth-century Enlightenment thinkers proposed. Today's Enlightenment values take the form of a set of commitments to individual autonomy, democracy, the rule of law, science, rationality, secularism, pluralism, a humanistic ethics, the importance of education, and the promotion of human rights. These are not empty or abstract ideas merely, because their realisation in individual lives makes a vast difference. If one thinks of what it was like to live as an ordinary person in, say, the sixteenth or seventeenth century, and compares it to the kind of life we can enjoy now, the impact of the Enlightenment on the structure and practice of society can be fully appreciated – and, one is bound to say, admired.

Evil

Does the concept of evil apply outside a religion-based ethics?

For wrongs that are very great, and at the same time have a conscious malice in their perpetration, the word 'evil' readily comes to mind. It is a word derived from a Germanic root meaning 'beyond the bounds' or 'outside the boundary', but which gradually came to have a stronger, indeed far stronger, sense to denote what is beyond the bounds of any moral exculpation. It denotes what is wicked, vicious and profoundly wrong to an exceptional degree.

For some, evil relates to the idea in religious ethics of 'sin', and of especially serious sin. Sin means disobedience to the deity (the first sin in Judaeo-Christian eyes was the disobedience of Adam and Eve in the putative Garden of Eden). Because the greatest religious sins are pride and rejection of the deity – these are the same thing – and refusal to accept the message of salvation, and because this means eternal damnation and torment, sin sufficient to be described as evil was and is sin of a peculiarly horrible degree. Extension to all perversely vicious, wicked, depraved and shocking moral crime thereby gives rise to the chief content of the concept of evil.

The industrial murder of European Jews by the Nazis during the Second World War is an example of evil; the crimes of Stalin against the kulaks, of Pol Pot in Cambodia, of the genocide, mass rape and other crimes against humanity perpetrated in the Congo, are examples of evil. Alas, examples are legion.

Consider an individual example, in recent public memory, of something appropriately definable as evil: the horrifying years-long imprisonment and sustained incestuous rape perpetrated by the Austrian Josef Fritzl against his own daughter. There is a different order of moral pathology in crimes that take as much organisation and effort as this, and it opens a window onto the point of using the term 'pathology' in connection with the worst forms of moral crime.

Contemplating what had to pass in Fritzl's mind as, first, he planned the details of a dungeon to imprison his eighteen-year-old daughter Elisabeth in, then built it, then imprisoned her there and ignored the agonies of her first months and years as his prisoner and victim, then dealt with the births of seven children, inventing stories for those he brought into the light and raised in his seemingly normal upstairs life – all this threatens to overwhelm one's imagination, not least because the hideousness of it involves such a calculating and conscious disjunction between the outer and inner nature of that man's life.

In trying to describe this case, the word that springs most readily to mind is indeed 'evil'. But evil is perhaps an insufficient notion, even a distraction from thinking properly about what Fritzl did, if it stops one thinking further. It might be more instructive to try making sense of Fritzl's crime in terms of what might be described as 'moral insanity', where the adjective 'moral' does double duty: in addition to its standard sense, it flags the fact that the insanity in question is not cognitive. That is, it is not that Fritzl's reasoning ability or ordinary thinking processes were deranged or dysfunctional – very far from it: keep in mind the meticulous planning and twenty-five-year-long execution of the plan – but that his conscious moral choice was deliberately, by choice, contrary to every claim of rightness.

To repeat, because the point is central: by 'insanity' I do not mean insanity in the standard sense of psychosis, severe neurosis, episodes of mania or delusion, and the like. Fritzl was no madman. He was not a madman because the deeply rational and carefully planned nature of his actions, and their successful continuance over a quarter of a century, bespeak intelligence and capability of a high order. Rather, I mean that the decision to do something utterly contrary to the most basic moral guidelines of behaviour has the mark of perversion in a disgustingly conscious, deliberate, chosen way. If Fritzl was not aware that what he was doing was wrong, he would not have taken such elaborate steps to conceal it. He knew it was wrong, yet chose to do it; he might even have revelled in how clever his plan was and how well he carried it out. This is the mark of moral pathology, electively distorting the premise of how one human being should treat another at the simplest and most obvious level.

From Auschwitz to the Congo, proof of moral insanity runs through humanity like a stain. Another word used to describe its work is 'enormity'. But sometimes even enormity is multiplied. An individual soldier who, out of his own temporary dehumanisation during a conflict, rapes and murders a woman, acts with a savagery that is at least explicable though emphatically not excusable by the circumstances. Rape as a weapon in conflicts, deliberately encouraged, is many notches higher again in degree of culpability. Twenty-five years of sexual slavery in a basement, inflicted by a man on his own daughter, is on a scale that vanishes beyond all bounds. It is moral insanity of the same kind that planned and perpetrated the Holocaust and other systematic, conscious, chosen violations of morality.

If there is a crumb of comfort anywhere in the case of Josef Fritzl as a contemporary embodiment of individual evil, it is that the world is appalled by what he did, and that is a change from just a few centuries ago, when something not very different was regarded as normal and acceptable on the part of slave-owners, conquerors, and the like. The degree of outrage Fritzl prompted is a measure of how far some parts of humanity have come in attitudes to moral insanity as a blemish in human nature: it suggests that we no longer wish to accept that it is ineradicable.

Prudery

Is there any place for prudery in modern morals?

There is a Tibetan Buddhist temple in Beijing, China, housing an array of erotic statuettes depicting the opportunities and possibilities that an athletic prince might explore, if he so chose, with his wives and concubines. This traditionally was where the sons of the emperors had their sex education. Today it is open to tourists, but with a particularly characteristic post-1949 Chinese twist: which is that the intriguing statuettes have all the operative parts of themselves obscured by torn-off sheets of the *People's Daily* newspaper.

It is an odd fact that Chinese Communism is vastly more prudish and moralistic about matters sexual than its imperial forerunners. The enthusiasts of the new order closed Shanghai's most famous brothel, the Great World, directly they captured Shanghai, and all the pensioned prostitutes went to live in the same street in the Bubbling Wells Road district, there to regale passing Party tourists with stories of their oppression under capitalism.

It is as if China was modernising into Victorianism, the age in which the blushes of British ladies were saved by curators chipping off the embarrassing bits of classical nude Greek statues and secreting them in museum cupboards. There was an irony in this: those muscular athletes typically had disproportionately modest appendages, proving that size matters in an unexpected direction, for smallness signified moral continence (think of the rampant contrast presented by statues of Priapus); so the curators were removing symbols of restraint – and vandalising works of art in the process.

The ethical applications of the *People's Daily* newspaper in China extend beyond the Lama Temple in Beijing. Go to the Takla Makan Desert near the ghostly ruined cities of Gaocheng and Jiaohe, with the Flaming Mountains undulating in the heat as if indeed on fire on the northern horizon, and there you will find the underground tombs of Xinjiang's ancient inhabitants. There the corpses lie, preserved by desiccation in the desert air, husband and wife on a shelf, a servant or two dried into pemmican underneath; mirthlessly grinning the grin of mummified death, all naked except for strategically placed scraps of the *People's Daily* newspaper.

The Great World figures in Josef von Sternberg's memories of making *Shanghai Express* with Marlene Dietrich. He wrote that the cheongsams of the girls on the ground floor were split to the thigh, on the first floor to the hip, and on the top floor to the armpit. Something of this luxurious decadence belonged to Marlene Dietrich herself, and shimmers in von Sternberg's movie as if each frame of film stock is a silver-gelatin print. There was no prudery in him, her, or the film; it appeared just as Hollywood was losing its nerve in the face of the Catholic-led moralising crusade that threatened to neuter it (though in the event the Production Code called forth much wit and intelligence in response).

Only prudery could make Catholicism and Chinese Communism thus get into bed together. The moral speaks for itself.

Inarticulacy

'If one must speak, one must speak clearly':
is that a genuine principle?

William James (brother of the more famous Henry) defined the task of philosophy as 'the dogged struggle to achieve clarity'. Philosophy itself is no more or less than enquiry – into everything, about everything. When its questions become clear and methods of answering them are found, philosophy becomes science, or psychology, and so on for the other special disciplines. The achievement of understanding ourselves and the world is therefore the product of that remarkable dogged struggle: to achieve clarity.

Leaving things unsaid, or only half-said, can sometimes be useful or helpful, but quite often it is not. Humans make themselves eloquent in lots of ways – art and music, theatre and dance included; but different eloquences are required for different subject matters. For example, one cannot teach engineering through ballet. The great dispute in the sixteenth century over the nature of religious truth was whether, if it is for the salvation of souls, it has to be perspicuous enough for an unlettered peasant to understand, or whether it could only be half-glimpsed through the last refinements of metaphysical abstraction. The answer is suggested by a parallel thought about ethics, where clarity about the good is necessary if one is to be able to live it: that all the deepest and most beautiful truths of morality, in all the greatest traditions of thought, are simple – and utterly clear.

Unclarity, obfuscation, mysticism passed off as deep insight: there is a sharp contrast between this and the simple truths of the profoundest morality. On the day these words were written I went to the funeral of a three-week-old baby. It was hard to imagine the suffering of his mother at this loss. But she had chosen a remark of the Buddha (a philosopher, not a priest or a god): 'The pine tree lives a thousand years, the mayfly lives one day: each fulfils its destiny.' All the things one can be prompted to think by this remark in such circumstances are worth all the volumes of philosophy one could read, seeking what substance they might contain. I cannot think of a single such volume capable of doing the human heart as much good as this insight does, even though the idea of destiny is figurative, and destinies are for people to make: so the lost child had none, but was an element in that of others.

The physicist who, seeking deeper levels of explanation for the nature of quarks and leptons in quantum theory, hypothesising superstrings or 'branes' or multiverses, is not inarticulate: note that he does not leap to a dogma or an ancient text to get closure for uncertainty, but keeps on articulating possibilities and hypotheses and keeps on seeking how to test them.

Some people wish to take seriously the idea of the ineffable, the admissibility of pure feeling, absolute subjectivity, as justification for believing and doing. What would one say if a serial murderer or a Nazi tried to justify what he did by saying he just felt like it; that it seemed as if he had a calling, but that there was no more to be said than that: inarticulacy makes up for the absence of justification. Would that do? Alas, that is the kind of thing religious devotees say.

If we take seriously the injunction to love our fellow human beings and seek their good it is because they are our own, and we can know something by sympathy and fellow-feeling of how things are for them. Scarcely anyone, whatever his or her beliefs, could see someone fall and hurt themselves, and walk by: we are Good Samaritans by nature. That's the real hope for humankind. And that is a point that can be stated, clarified, defended by argument: it is not a point that is made by muteness, unless the different eloquence of action makes it instead.

The Case of Ashley X

*How far are we ethically justified in making drastic decisions
on behalf of those unable to take them for themselves?*

A ll the hardest moral dilemmas are those where the
opposing considerations are each powerful, and each aim
at a genuine good. Such a dilemma is exemplified in the case
of Ashley X, a severely disabled girl with a mental age of three,
who cannot talk, eat or sit up unaided, and whose parents and
doctors acted to keep her not only small in size by growth-
inhibiting treatment, but an infant by surgical and hormonal
treatment designed to keep her physiologically immature in
perpetuity.

In a blog written after details of Ashley X's case became
public, her father explained the reasoning that had led to her
being given the treatment just described. It was done, he said,
to ensure that Ashley can be looked after better. It was done so
that she could be carried more easily, and therefore have more
chance of social interactions and opportunities to go outdoors
and on trips, than she would as a wholly helpless adult. In the
latter case she could be condemned to bed all day staring at a
television, at risk of the diseases of inactivity.

And it therefore further means that she can be cared for
at home by her family instead of being institutionalised,
which would happen if her family could no longer physically
manage her. And in the latter case – that is, if she had to be
institutionalised – her being permanently prepubescent would
reduce the risk of sexual assault.

When Ashley X was aged six her uterus and breast glands
were removed to prevent pubescence, and she was put on

oestrogen treatment to inhibit growth. Critics of what was done to her – and some of the criticism was ferocious – say that she has been forcibly sterilised and stunted solely for her parents' convenience, that she is a Frankenstein's monster created by cold logic, and that her rights and dignity as a human individual, whether or not disabled, have been violated.

One thing missing from the reactions has been a sense of the terrible predicament of the caring family. As a severely disabled individual grows into an adult, every difficulty of care is magnified. Middle-aged or elderly parents having to heft the dead-weight of an adult any number of times a day, to prevent bedsores and lung congestion, to change his nappies and wash him, to help him eat and drink, is an almost unimaginable burden – and this is apart from getting him into a wheelchair for an outing every day. That is why so many victims of severe disability have to go to institutions eventually. What looks like an invasion of human integrity in Ashley X's case might be the best way of helping her to a far better life because it can be manageably lived with her family.

The critical reaction is understandable, but as these thoughts suggest, misplaced. It is understandable because a flock of associations gather as soon as one hears that Ashley X's parents and doctors decided to sterilise her by surgery and medicate her to inhibit growth. In India and Africa parents have sometimes been known to lame their children deliberately to make them more effective beggars. Nazi doctors forcibly sterilised gypsies and other 'undesirables'. Visions abound of a future in which human beings are genetically engineered or pharmacologically manipulated to make some of them tall and beautiful and to turn others into uncomplaining workers. The emotional revulsion against these things lies behind some of the reactions in the Ashley X case too.

The phenomenon is one of moral squeamishness. The term 'squeamishness' is appropriate and not flippantly intended. As an illustration of how squeamish attitudes can make matters worse when we should be bold enough to make them better, here is an example that is extremely minor in comparison to the difficult and tragic case of Ashley X, but in its own very small way educative. My children once had a pet hamster which one night suffered an awful accident. The vet advised, on the telephone, that we end her sufferings by breaking her neck with a twist of the hands. I could not bring myself to do it. The vet then advised putting her in a plastic bag, placing the bag under the wheel of the car, and driving over her. I could not bring myself to do that either. The result was that she died slowly and agonisingly through the course of a long night. Afterwards I was appalled at the unkindness my squeamishness produced; for the truth is that it masked moral cowardice.

Many of our squeamish moral attitudes increase suffering in the world in this way. In the case of our fellow human beings, who are our primary concern and who rightly demand the tenderest respect and most careful thought, our inability to agree on euthanasia for people who desperately want it, our objections to stem-cell work, medical cloning, and other scientific research aimed at curing or palliating human suffering, is sincerely motivated by a desire to put human life at the forefront of moral concern, but often stands in the way of doing just that.

Sometimes we do not even make ourselves ask the question 'What is truly in this person's best interests?', and instead only consider what we can bear to do and not to do – in short, what is in our own emotional interests. No person of ordinary sensibility could tolerate the idea of doing to a normal child what Ashley X's parents have done to her, and they export that perfectly understandable sentiment to her case. But she is not a normal child, and her carers are trying to make her future better by logical and practical means. It cannot be in her best interests to become increasingly difficult to move and carry, to have to leave her family home perhaps, and in that case to be a sexually mature woman lying helplessly in bed in an institution. If someone said, 'Surely everything should be done to make it possible for Ashley X to stay with those who love her most and will care for her best', everyone would agree. It is the means that divide opinion.

Some critics say that real help for Ashley X would consist in providing the help and equipment that would give her the quality of life her parents want for her without surgery and growth-inhibition. That is certainly an option where possible: a very costly one. If society would really help carers bear that cost, it would make the dilemma over Ashley X unnecessary. As it is, what Ashley X's carers have done is to try to care for her best.

Contrarianism

Is deliberate contrarianism helpful to public debate?

There is a rich and flourishing tradition of public debate in Britain, but one thing that perennially threatens to undermine it is contrarianism. By this is meant the deliberate adoption of oppositional points of view in order to generate controversy, mainly in order to sell more newspapers or to attract more viewers to television programmes. Opposing someone's point of view not because of genuine disagreement, but purely to get an argument going, can have deleterious consequences for the national discussion, because it distorts the true state of opinion, and stands in the way of sensible conclusions.

Contrarianism, as disputation for the sake of disputation, is the bastard offspring of something that is worthwhile and appropriate, namely the process of testing views, theories, policies, or whatever else is offered for public consumption in the way of ideas, by challenge and debate. The idea that truth, or at least sensible conclusions, can be reached by these means is what underlies the traditional adversarial methods of Parliament and courts of law. Debates in the former, together with questions to ministers and the work of select committees, serve the same function as the presentation of cases for the prosecution and defence in court. Claims are subjected to scrutiny and evaluation by the forensic technique of cross-examination, which is central to eliciting clarification and, in the ideal, truth.

The principle underlying the legitimate parent of contrarianism is what Plato called 'dialectic', the process of debate that reaches sound conclusions through the co-operation of the parties, who ask seriously intentioned probing questions, and answer them truthfully and constructively. Adversarial challenge for the sole purpose of defeating an opponent, or merely rousing controversy, is a different thing, which Plato called 'eristic', a word with unedifying connotations of 'wrangling' and 'strife'.

Eristic is what contrarianism is all about. Although the main reason for its prevalence in contemporary public debate is that controversies, quarrels, exposés and attacks sell newspapers and get people switching on their television sets, there is another reason besides. This is that the public media think they are engaging in dialectic on whatever happens to be the hot topic of the day, when despite their good intentions they are in fact promoting eristic.

A good example is the BBC's scrupulous endeavour to achieve balance in discussions on the airwaves. This admirable aim very often results in distortions, because it gives the impression that the world divides fifty-fifty on every topic, whereas often the proponents of opposing views represent very different actual weightings of opinion – the whole scientific community against one maverick, for example. And whereas the maverick might be right and the whole scientific community wrong on the particular question at issue, it is somewhat more usual that matters are otherwise. The maverick might even be pushing an irresponsible line – for example, over childhood vaccinations – and by being made to appear 50 per cent of the expert opinion on the subject, might so influence the public that the result is harmful for efforts to control childhood diseases.

I have often been a member of panels discussing some question about the place of religion in public life. Typically such panels have five members: a Protestant Christian, a Catholic Christian, a Muslim, a Jewish person, and myself as the token atheist-cum-humanist-cum-secularist. Between them my four fellow panellists (who are four because they disagree with each other theologically) represent an active constituency of at most 8 per cent of the population, meaning by 'active' that proportion of the population which attends a religious service at least once a week. Whereas a majority of the population might have various beliefs of a feng-shui, astrology, deistic or vaguely Christian kind, it is practically certain that they do not wish to have their lives run by a religious organisation intent on imposing a uniformity of belief and behaviour on them. Accordingly I represent, at least partially, some aspect of functional secularism in the majority of the population; yet in debates on the subject I sit as one out of five (and sometimes more) on the panel.

The desire to have all viewpoints represented is the worthy cause of this distortion, but the downside of it is that it feeds the contrarian nature of public debate. Contrast the case of having disinterested (not, note, uninterested) experts discussing the question rather than an assemblage of partisan representatives with agendas and a stake in seeing their own preferred outcomes prevail. Invocation of disinterested expertise was once a frequent option in debates about matters of public concern, but it suddenly became much less so in the early 1970s (and has remained so since) as a result of a rapidly influential view that no such thing as disinterested expert opinion is possible. All viewpoints are partisan, said the new voice of suspicion, and sonorous expertise is just a disguise for the Establishment view, or anyway some hidden tendentious position.

And so indeed it can be; the suspicion is not without grounds. Moreover the ideal of allowing all voices, especially minority ones, to have their say, and to advance all gradations of opinion into the light, is not just an application of one of the most precious of all liberties, namely freedom of speech, but an intrinsic good. For all society to hear the opinions of the various constituencies it contains, and to be exposed to contrasting suggestions about how things should be, is healthy and positive.

How is this latter desirable state of affairs to be protected from collapsing into mere eristic and contrarianism? One suggestion might be to take a hint from the way courts of law conduct themselves. In criminal proceedings a jury considers the case presented to it by the prosecution, and listens to considerations adduced by the defence in order to cast doubts on that case, and then debates what it has heard and seen before telling the judge what it concludes. During the proceedings jury members are likely to hear the accused being questioned by both sides, the prosecution examining his testimony and the defence eliciting his explanation of why the alleged facts in the case appear as they do. Other witnesses might be called, having things to report that bear relevantly on the matter in hand.

The essential characteristic of the parts played by counsel, defendant and witnesses in court is that they are genuinely relevant to the case, and the judge ensures that the contributions they all make to the process are appropriate and pertinent. If public debate in general were conducted according to similar principles, there would be much less likelihood of the process being trumped-up for the mere purpose of having an argument.

But who or what is to play the role of judge, ensuring that the process is fair and that the participants behave appropriately? One answer might be: the public. But this is an optimistic suggestion. Cynics will point out that Rome's emperors well knew what they were about in providing spectacles in the Colosseum – gladiator fights, martyrs fed to lions, even sea battles enacted with half-size ships in a flooded arena (and with real fighting leading to death and dismemberment in Rome's usual and deplorable way). In short, the public appetite is for a fight, say the cynics, with blood as at least a figurative preferred outcome. The niceties of courteous debate with everyone observing canons of fairness is not half so much fun.

Even without going the whole length of this cynical view, it is obvious enough that the reason why so many newspapers and television programmes offer eristic rather than dialectic is because eristic attracts the punters. To that extent it really is over-optimistic to expect editors always to choose debate modelled on subdued courtroom niceties.

Of course it is not true that judicious and constructive debate is wholly absent either from print media or the airwaves; serious magazines and late-night programmes achieve exactly the kind of collegial dialectic that Plato would applaud. But they serve small minorities, and the cynics were not thinking of them when they pointed to the Colosseum as the model for today's contrarianism.

The worst feature of contrarianism is that it paralyses proper debate about a range of serious and important public issues. Take, for example, the questions of drugs and prostitution. The criminalisation of certain drugs, some of them less harmful than tobacco and alcohol, creates rather than solves problems by promoting a flourishing and dangerous criminal industry (which in turn soaks up huge amounts of police time and effort), by forcing the supply and use of drugs underground, by obliging many users to become criminals to feed their habits, by putting them at risk of impure or variable quality supplies, and by discouraging them from seeking medical help.

Likewise the laws governing prostitution force sex workers onto the street and into the arms of pimps, encourage human trafficking, link prostitution to the drug industry, and leave sex workers to the doubtful mercies of criminals and inclement weather, while most of these problems would be at least diminished by legalising brothels. In view of the fact that prostitution is nigh impossible to get rid of, a more humane and sensible policy towards it should prevail.

But neither of these matters can be discussed sensibly in the prevailing climate of contrarianism in public debate. Imagine a senior politician proposing the legalisation of drugs and brothels. The tabloid headlines and the amplification for eristic purposes of the voice of Outraged of Tunbridge Wells would not merely warp the debate into an exchange of hysterical one-liners, but would end the career of the politician who started it. For this reason the profoundly unsatisfactory state of the law with regard to personal morality continues to create difficulties which in human terms (and far less importantly, but hugely, in money terms too) represent a dramatically heavy cost.

In the absence of the kind of public seriousness and maturity that would make all debate about such questions take the form of Platonic dialectic rather than eristic, the remedy has to lie in the hands firstly of those who are invited to take part in contrarianly contrived debate, and secondly in the good sense of those for whom it is staged. Another experience commonly had in this connection by 'content providers' (as the media call them, meaning the people invited to comment or contribute) is being telephoned by a television programme, radio station or newspaper, seeking someone who will propose or contest a view for which they have the opposite party already lined up. It might be a topic in which the 'content provider' has an interest or some expertise; but if he or she agrees with the other 'content provider' already waiting, the broadcaster or newspaper will keep looking until they have found someone to disagree.

Sometimes this is a function of the desire to have a view tested by disagreement; sometimes it is mere contrarianism at full throttle. The desirable state of affairs is for the public to become good at distinguishing which is which, to the point where the media find it less easy to get away with stirring up arguments for the mere sake of their pulling power, indifferent to whether the debate will produce truth or a worthwhile conclusion.

That is the key to what is wrong with contrarianism: its indifference to worthwhile conclusions. The aim of eristic is nothing other than itself – it exists just for the sake of the wrangle and the strife. Given that the aim of dialectic is truth or better understanding, it is at best a scandal and at worst a tragedy that the former is so often substituted for the latter. But that is how it is, and will doubtless remain so until better days dawn.

Authority

What, if anything, justifies one person or
body having authority over others?

In the state of nature as envisaged by Hobbes, it is easy to imagine how the competence, experience, superior skill or strength of certain individuals would make them obvious candidates for leadership roles that others might be pleased (or wise) to accept. This remains true, in a local way, in all human groups; 'natural leaders' emerge, and familiar aspects of social dynamics prompt others to submit to their authority in particular respects.

But in the state of nature, or situations very like it, authority tends to be arrogated by the strong, and then protections and remedies against its abuse prove hard to come by, making justice unlikely because contingent on the whim or personality of those in charge. This does not make for desirable forms of civil society, as history very painfully shows. But rather than reject the idea of authority altogether, as an anarchist might recommend, the solution is to constitute it properly, so that its benefits can accrue, the chief of them being co-ordination of social effort, peace, justice and protection of the weak.

Civil society is premised on the rule of law; laws have to be made when required, so a person or body has to be invested with power to devise them, and there has to be an expectation that they will be observed. This in turn requires enforcement and sanctions where necessary, which in turn again requires the existence of suitably empowered agencies such as a police force and courts.

To secure these desiderata there has to be an agreement to accord authority to law-making and law-enforcing agencies, subject (so the democratic principle insists) to the possibility of revocation by those on whose behalf it is exercised. If I am party to, and beneficiary of, a standing decision to have a police force, then if I am stopped for exceeding a speed limit, and required by policemen to produce my driving licence, this is an acceptable subjection to their authority. And the example can be generalised: the existence of legitimately constituted authority is fundamental to the functioning of a good society.

But, obviously, authority has to be constrained and revocable to be acceptable, and there has to be proper remedy against its abuse, which is why the bearers of delegated authority have themselves to be subject to bodies that can hold them to account – in Western liberal democracies, an electorate and an independent judiciary.

Justified authority is what exists when arrangements of these kinds are in place, and work. By analogy and derivation, the authority of school teachers, team captains and other archons in more local hierarchies has the same kind of ground.

Eccentricity

Do mavericks and eccentrics have a use?

An unkind legend once circulated about the tribes who live along the shores of Lake Malawi in Africa's Great Rift Valley. It was that their witch-doctors traditionally killed large-headed babies in order to use their skulls for medicine pots, with the result that the tribes became progressively less intelligent and more conformist.

Apart from the fact that intelligence and skull size are not correlated in this simplistic way (women have smaller heads than men on average, but are infinitely smarter), it is unclear whether it was ever true that Lake Malawi witch-doctors engaged in this impeachable practice. But it relates interestingly to the thought that innovation and originality are so valuable that anything likely to militate against them – such as decapitating big-headed babies – seems doubly bad, once for the crime itself and once for depriving the community of a chance for progress.

Some invention and novelty doubtless owe themselves to grey-suited men in committees, but the pressures that generate conformism and conservatism in today's intricately complex societies are very great, not least because intricate complexity is so easily disrupted. That places a premium on keeping the boat steady, on maintaining the status quo, on sticking to precedent.

In consequence, new ideas and practices, new things generally, tend to come from sources other than grey-suited committees – from highly individual sources, from mavericks and eccentrics. And that is why originality so often has a battle to be taken seriously; it has to break through conservative barriers, overcome timidity, snobbery, uncertainty, and in most cases get itself a hearing and a backer in a grey-suited committee before it can get what it needs – funding, usually – to fly.

Etymologically both 'maverick' and 'eccentric' have interesting pasts. One of Samuel Augustus Maverick's successful ventures in nineteenth-century Texas was ranching, and he used not to bother to brand his cattle. They acquired the label 'mavericks' as a result, and the term by extension denoted anything (usually, anyone) stubborn, wilful and determinedly independent.

'Eccentric' has an even more exotic derivation. In the model of the heavens devised by the second-century CE astronomer Claudius Ptolemy, the five visible planets ('planet' meaning 'wanderer' because of the irregularity of planetary paths traced across the fixed background of stars) were thought to move in circles ('deferents') around the earth, with two ingenious qualifications: that each also moved in a little circle ('epicycle') around a point on its big orbital circle, thus explaining their irregularities of motion, and the big circle's centre was not the earth itself, but a point somewhat off to one side (the 'equant'), thus making the circle 'eccentric'.

Both etymologies explain the great usefulness of these terms to describe human sources of novelty in things.

Religion

What is the solution to quarrels over religion?

There is an increasingly noisy and bad-tempered quarrel between religious people and non-religious people in contemporary society. It has flared up in the last few years, and has quickly taken a bitter turn. Why is this so? As one of those participating in it – and, confessedly, contributing to its acerbity – my answer might seem partisan. But both sides of the current dispute agree that the current quarrel over religion raises important questions about the place of religious belief in modern society.

Until a few years ago people tended not to fall out with one another if they discovered that they held different views about religion. There were three main reasons for this. Most believers did not brandish their faith publicly, society had become increasingly secular in most major respects, and memories of the past's murderous religious factionalisms had bequeathed a reluctance to revive the problem. The final point's lingering consequences in Northern Ireland anyway served as a distasteful warning.

But in recent years all the major religions have again become more assertive, more vocal, more demanding and therefore more salient in the public domain. Followers of Islam were the first to push forward; protests against Salman Rushdie's *Satanic Verses* were an early indication of what has since become an insistent Islamic presence in the public square. Not willing to be left behind, other faiths have followed suit. Sikhs closed a play in Birmingham, Hindus complained about Christmas cards Christianising an Indian theme, evangelical Christians protested against *Jerry Springer – the Opera*.

But it has not all been about protests. In Britain public funding has gone to Church of England and Roman Catholic schools for a long time; now Muslims, Sikhs and Jews ask for public money for their own faith-based schools, and receive it. The licence-fee-funded daily religious broadcasting on BBC Radio has steadily increased the air time available to religions other than the established one. Requests for extra protections in law, and alternatively for exemptions from the law, to cater for religious sensitivities soon followed these developments: criminalising offensive remarks about religion, and allowing faith-based organisations to be exempt from legislation outlawing discriminatory practices, are the main examples.

Government in Britain has been as concessive and inclusive as it can be to all the religious groups that now exist in Britain. This is well intentioned but misguided, as the single example of faith-based schooling shows. The example of Northern Ireland teaches that if children are ghettoised by religion from an early age, the result is disastrous. In the last decade exactly such segregation has been given a publicly funded boost in the rest of the United Kingdom, at just the time that religion-inspired tensions and divisions in society are increasing. The remedy for the latter should be to ensure that schooling is as mixed and secular as possible; instead, tax money has gone to deepen the problem because the government thinks that by giving sectarianism its head they will appease it. Yet history teaches that appeasement never satisfies appetites, it only feeds them.

In the face of the growing volume and assertiveness of different religious bodies asking for preferential treatment in the ways described, secular opinion has hardened. The non-religious response has come largely from individuals who happen to have a platform or the talent to speak; and they speak for themselves, not for an organisation. This is because non-religious people do not generally go in for organising themselves into the equivalent of churches or mosques; they think for themselves and therefore tend to be independent and unaffiliated.

Consider the situation in the United States, where according to some estimates the 'Religious Right' numbers about sixty million. In comparison, as recent polls show, about thirty million Americans define themselves as having no religious commitment. But whereas the 'Religious Right' is a formidable body whose constituent churches and movements have salaried administrators, vast funds, television and radio outlets and paid Washington lobbyists, America's non-religious folk are simply unconnected individuals. It is no surprise that the 'Religious Right' has political clout, and can make a loud noise in the American public square, whereas the non-religious voice is muted. One result is that it is impossible for anyone to run for public office without at least claiming to be a church-goer.

There are two main reasons for the hardening of responses by non-religious folk. One is that any increase in the influence of religious bodies in society threatens the de facto secular arrangement that allows all views and none to co-exist. History painfully shows that in societies where one religious outlook becomes dominant, an uneasy situation ensues for other outlooks. At the extreme, religious control of society can degenerate into Taliban-like rule, as has happened too often in history.

Look, for example, at the period in which liberty of conscience was at last secured in Christian Europe – the sixteenth and seventeenth centuries. It was an exceptionally bloody epoch: millions died as a result of a single church's reluctance to give up its control over what people can be allowed to think and believe. The famous Treaty of Westphalia in 1648 accepted religious differences as the only way of preventing religion from being an endless source of war. Religious peace did not come straight away, but eventually it did, and most of Europe for most of the years since 1700 has been free of religiously motivated strife.

But this is under threat in the new climate of religious assertiveness. Faith organisations are currently making common cause to achieve their mutual ends; but once they have achieved them, what is to stop them remembering that their faiths are mutually exclusive and indeed mutually blaspheming, and that the history of their relationship is one of bloodshed?

The second reason why secular attitudes are hardening relates to the reflective non-religious person's attitude to religion itself. From the non-religious point of view, religious belief of all kinds shares the same intellectual respectability, evidential base and rationality as belief in the existence of fairies. This remark outrages the sensibilities of those who have deep religious convictions and attachments, and they regard it as insulting. But the truth is that everyone takes this attitude about all but one (or a very few) of the gods that have ever been claimed to exist. No reasonably orthodox Christian believes in Aphrodite or the rest of the Olympian deities, or in Ganesh the Elephant God or the rest of the Hindu pantheon, or in the Japanese emperor, and so endlessly on – and officially (as a matter of Christian orthodoxy) he must say that anyone who sincerely believes in such deities is deluded and blasphemously in pursuit of 'false gods'. The atheist adds just one more deity to the list of those not believed in; namely, the one remaining on the Christian's or Jew's or Muslim's list. And he does so for the same reason as any of these do not believe in Ganesh or Aphrodite.

Religious belief is mankind's earliest science. Judaism, Christianity and Islam are young religions in historical terms, and came into existence after kings and emperors had more magnificently taken the place of tribal chiefs. The new religions therefore modelled their respective deities on kings with absolute powers. But for tens of thousands of years beforehand people were fundamentally animistic, explaining the natural world by imputing agency to things – spirits or gods in the wind, in the thunder, in the rivers and sea. As knowledge replaced these naiveties, so deities became more invisible, receding to mountain tops and then to the sky or the earth's depths. One can easily see how it was in the interests of priesthoods, most of which were hereditary, to keep these myths alive.

With such a view of religion – as ancient superstition, as a primitive form of explanation of the world sophisticated into mythology – it is hard for non-religious folk to take it seriously, and equally hard for them to accept the claim of religious folk to a disproportionate say in running society. This is the more so as in contemporary Britain the active constituency of all believers – those who go to church, mosque, temple or synagogue every week – is about 8 per cent of the population. A majority of the population might have vague beliefs and occasionally go to church, but even they do not want their lives dictated to by so small and narrow a self-selected minority.

The disproportion is a staring one. Regular C of E church-goers make up 3 per cent of the population, yet have twenty-six bishops in the House of Lords. There is something fantastical in this anachronism, which has been allowed to slumber while religious folk kept their views more or less private, but which is not tolerable now that religion is bustling onto centre-stage asking for everyone's taxes to pay for faith-schools and exemptions.

And all this, it must be remembered, is happening against the background of atrocities committed by religious fanatics, whose beliefs are not very different from the majority of others in their faith. The absolute certainty, the unreflective credence given to ancient texts that relate to historically remote conditions, the zealotry and bigotry that flow from their certainty, are profoundly dangerous: at their extreme they result in mass murder, but long before then they issue in censorship, coercion to conform, the control of women, the closing of hearts and minds.

Thus there is a continuum from the suicide bomber driven by religious zeal to the moral crusader who wishes to stop everyone else from seeing or reading what he himself finds offensive. This fact makes people of a secular disposition no longer prepared to be silent and concessive. Religion has lost respectability as a result of the atrocities committed in its name, and because of its clamouring for an undue slice of the pie, and for its efforts to impose its views on others. Where politeness once restrained non-religious folk from expressing their true feelings about religion, both politeness and restraint have been banished by the face that faith now turns to the modern world, contradictorily using the computers and aeroplanes of modern science to assert its ancient utter certainties.

This is why there is an acerbic quarrel going on between religion and non-religion today, and it does not look as if it will end soon.

Existence

Why is there something rather than nothing?

Some philosophers think this question is genuinely puzzling on the grounds that nothingness is vastly simpler than somethingness, and might rationally be supposed the more natural state in view of the presumably infinite effort required for anything to emerge from nothing. And yet there is something: so, they wish to know why.

Others ask why there is something rather than nothing because they expect, or at least desire, an answer incorporating the claim that the universe exists for a purpose, which the answer accordingly identifies.

The vacuous hypothesis that there is something because it was created by a supernatural agency can be dismissed immediately. The hypothesis in effect says that the reason why there is anything at all is because something else made it, which is either question-begging or invites an explanatorily null regress. It is one of the most persistently lingering human fatuities that the universe's origins (or indeed anything else) can be explained by arbitrarily invoking an entity equally arbitrarily defined as fully equipped to be the explanation of what is to be explained.

As reflection will show, dismissal of a theistic pseudo-answer terminates hopes of an answer couched in terms of purpose also.

A second and better way with the question is to point out that it is unanswerable. This is not the same as saying that it is pointless – though it is, given the brute fact that there is indeed something, and that the really interesting questions relate to what exactly that something is, and what – if anything – in it is valuable from the perspective of conscious experience. Nor is it unanswerable because we are not the kind of creature capable of finding or understanding the answer, as some (defeatists, surely) also claim about the puzzle of consciousness.

Rather, it is unanswerable because it is radically unlike questions which, like 'why do elephants have trunks?', validly prompt an expectation of informative answers. 'Why does anything exist?' does not do so because it is like 'what colour are ideas?' – it makes a category mistake. For 'nothing' denotes privation or absence relative to something, not a state or condition existentially on a par with somethingness. When all the chocolates are eaten there is nothing in the box because there was something there before; you cannot introduce nothing ('nothingness'?) to a box other than by not putting something in it, or by taking everything out. So the primitive condition is that there is something, and we only understand 'nothing' relatively and locally by its absence.

It is quite something to say that there is nothing more to the problem than something like that: but nothing, I submit, is a better answer.

Self-Deception

Are human beings especially prone to self-deception?

If proof were needed that humanity is a self-deceiving species, it is offered by the belief that people are either optimists/idealists or pessimists/realists. In fact this is a double proof of human self-deception: for not only is the real division here not between optimists/idealists and pessimists/realists, but between people who are overt optimists/idealists and those who are covert optimists/idealists, these latter being the ones who masquerade as pessimists/realists.

And yet: all of these folk, whether overt or covert optimists/idealists, at some deeper level than consciousness can penetrate more than three or four times in a lifetime, secretly know that if there were indeed any actual pessimists/realists, they would be right.

Confused yet? You are being led here through a labyrinth of important distinctions which will make no difference to your life, except that you will have had another of those passing glimpses of truth which, every now and then, will prick your memory with a vague feeling of unease – and give you further motivation for the optimism/idealism without which you could not possibly ever get out of bed.

I have been turning the pages of a favourite author – Arthur Schopenhauer – who alone of all philosophers, indeed almost alone among mankind, was able to stare the truth about the human condition in the face. This, to be brief, is: you get older, and sicker, and then you die. In the process you lose everything of value: first, the broad range of possibilities that were open to you when young; then the love you so passionately felt, also when young; then your slender waistline; then your sense of humour.

Life is like a false spring. The sun shines, it is warm, crocuses and daffodils bloom. Then suddenly it gets freezing and wet again, and that foolish burst of delight at the thought that grey winter has passed is shown for what it was. And yet: it is a rare individual, taking the figures in their due proportion, who refuses to get out of bed in the morning (or does worse even than that) because of these disappointments. The reason is: hope.

Ah, Hope! She was the last of the creatures to flutter from Pandora's Box, preceded by all the evils that afflict mankind. Was her presence there an act of kindness on the part of whoever filled that box, or an act of additional malevolence? Either way, it is the eternal springing of hope, the crazy, fact-denying, sustaining, deceiving, motivating impulse of hope, that keeps 95 per cent of the world's population believing that something better might yet happen, despite the slimmest of evidence that it will.

Dr Johnson called second marriages 'triumphs of hope over experience'. This, as we see, applies to life itself. For my part, speaking as an optimist/idealist of the first water, I am glad that it is so. For out of it come the music, literature, art and moments of ecstasy that make life worth living after all.

The Meaning of Life

What is it?

If there is a single question taken to be the ultimate philosophical question, it is: what is the meaning of life? The answer is: the meaning of your life is the meaning you give it; it consists in what you create through the identification and pursuit of endeavours that your talents fit you for and your interests draw you to, together with the relationships you form in the process. First and foremost, good relationships give meaning to life; so does the pursuit of worthwhile goals; so do pleasure and enjoyment; so do respect and friendship, both given and received in the course of endeavour. Life can thus be very rich in meaning, and not uncommonly is so.

This answer, though unquestionably right, is much more complicated than its breezy certainty and simplicity make it look.

First, there is not one thing, a one-size-fits-all thing, that is 'the meaning of life'. People are various, life is various, circumstances differ; there are many ways that life can be good, flourishing and meaningful, just as there are many causes of misery and failure, despair and tragedy. Luck, and things beyond any individual's control, most certainly have their place in determining the character of a life, and all lives encounter difficulties of some kind. But meaning is something that incorporates these things too, and the way they are faced and borne.

Those who think there is a single thing that is everyone's meaning of life – they are usually the purveyors of some ideology or religion that claims to know what this one-size-fits-all thing is – naturally wish to force everyone into the same mould, no matter what their individual starting shape might be. Of course many people like others to do their thinking for them, and accordingly want others to tell them what is valuable and how they should live. Bertrand Russell remarked, 'Most people would rather die than think, and most people do.' They wish to go to the supermarket of ideas and take out a frozen pre-cooked packet of beliefs, effort-free and ready to apply. So long as they continue not to think, this might do; though it is not uncommon for people to become uneasy after a while, and to have to expend energy on shutting their minds to doubts.

There can obviously be lives that feel meaningful to those living them which are not, by any reasonable criteria, good lives. A sadist in the SS might take great satisfaction in committing horrors, but the fact that all moral thinking must lie under the government of the Harm Principle – which states that it is never right to harm others in their own endeavour to make meaningful lives for themselves – condemns such people, and denies that their lives are good. So a necessary condition of a life that is good from the wider point of view of ethics, and not just from the point of view of an individual preference, is that it is not one whose meaning requires that other lives be deprived of meaning.

A few seemingly fortunate individuals might have all the good things in the world handed to them on a plate, and might be so constituted that they do not mind being the passive and merely lucky recipients of them, their own merits or activity having no part in the case; and they might accordingly be happy about, or even just comfortably indifferent to, this latter fact. Is theirs a meaningful life? At least one thing it is natural to think is that an individually meaningful life is a product of activity and choice; that it is the agent's own work.

Albert Camus dramatically states in his essay *The Myth of Sisyphus* that the great philosophical question is: Should I or should I not commit suicide? For if the answer is No, this is because there is something one wishes to live for, something that makes life worthwhile; and this thing is the meaning of one's life. It is an interesting conceit, but although it sharply reminds one of the role of hope and desire, it does not guarantee to identify the pieces of the particular jigsaw that constitutes the meaning of this or that individual's existence for him.

One thing is for sure: telling people that the meaning of life is what they make of it is always going to seem, at first, unhelpful. 'Ah what dusty answer gets the soul,' wrote George Meredith, 'when hot for certainties in this our life!'; and we are hot to know what is really good, really worthwhile, really meaningful. To say that meaning is made, not given, and that it is as various as the individuals willing to make it, presents meaning as hard work, not least because the business of thinking seriously about what is good, what is valuable, what one's own talents for the good are and what one should do with them, is exactly what people did not want to engage in: they want the sages, the poets or the priests to tell them. And when they are told that it is love, or work, or having worthwhile goals, these generalities seem as vague as the formula 'meaning is what you make it', and no less unsatisfying. But – they are also no less true.

Note, though, the interesting nuances that enter when one finally accepts the challenge to think for oneself about what would make one's own life meaningful. For example, is it achievement in some field, or is it the sincere effort to achieve? Will life be meaningless if one strove to do or to make something worthwhile, but did not realise that aim, or only partially realised it? Well: consider what you think of your friends. Do you honour them for what they would like to succeed at, or only for their actual successes? There you have your answer. There are plenty of clichés that will do the work of this insight: 'it is not the arrival but the journey that matters', and so on.

The proper question, in sum, is not 'what is the meaning of life?', but 'what is the meaning that, out of my relationships, my goals, my efforts, my talents, my various doings and interests, my hopes and my desires, I am or should be creating for my life?' Trying to answer it is itself part of life's meaning.

Index

A NOTE ON THE TYPE

The text of this book is set in Adobe Garamond. It is one of several versions of Garamond based on the designs of Claude Garamond. It is thought that Garamond based his font on Bembo, cut in 1495 by Francesco Griffo in collaboration with the Italian printer Aldus Manutius. Garamond types were first used in books printed in Paris around 1532. Many of the present-day versions of this type are based on the Typi Academiae of Jean Jannon, cut in Sedan in 1615.

Claude Garamond was born in Paris in 1480. He learned how to cut type from his father and by the age of fifteen he was able to fashion steel punches the size of a pica with great precision. At the age of sixty he was commissioned by King Francis I to design a Greek alphabet; for this he was given the honourable title of royal type-founder. He died in 1561.

ALSO AVAILABLE BY A. C. GRAYLING

THE GOOD BOOK
A SECULAR BIBLE

The Good Book is a book of insight, inspiration, wisdom, solace and commentary on the human condition drawn from the great humanist traditions of thought and literature of the world. Its principal concern is how life – the good life – should be lived. Stimulating, thoughtful, rational and rewarding, it makes essential reading.

The Good Book is an alternative, non-religious Bible and has been made just the same way as the Judaeo-Christian Bible was made: by redaction, editing, paraphrasing, interpolation, arrangement and rewriting of texts from the last three thousand years of the great secular traditions. For a secular age in which many find that religion no longer speaks to them, this is a book of life and practice, focusing the light of great minds onto the perennial challenge of being human.

'There is an immense display of human wisdom on display here, and five minutes with any passage will have you contemplating all day'
INDEPENDENT ON SUNDAY

'Truly it was a good book, full of sage counsel, wise advice and comfort for the sorrowing'
OBSERVER